IMAGES
of America

AROUND GREAT MOOSE LAKE

On the cover: Please see page 9. (Courtesy of Lonna and Bill Trauth of Castle Harmony.)

IMAGES
of America

AROUND GREAT MOOSE LAKE

Brenda Seekins

ARCADIA
PUBLISHING

ISBN 978-0-7385-4503-5

Published by Arcadia Publishing
Charleston, South Carolina

Printed in the United States of America

Library of Congress Catalog Card Number: 2006923204

For all general information contact Arcadia Publishing at:
Telephone 843-853-2070
Fax 843-853-0044
E-mail sales@arcadiapublishing.com
For customer service and orders:
Toll-Free 1-888-313-2665

Visit us on the Internet at www.arcadiapublishing.com

Contents

Acknowledgments

Compiling this book, *Around Great Moose Lake*, was not an idea that was ever brewing as a great tale. It was a plan that evolved from available data and photographs that needed a means to be a story.

It would not have been possible without the assistance of so many people in the four towns, including the respective historical societies in Hartland, Harmony, Athens, and St. Albans.

A special thank-you is extended to Lorna Trauth and her son, Bill Trauth, for their appreciation of the rich piece of local history that they own at Castle Harmony, and for caring for the photographs and records of the original owners in order to tell their story. The Trauths also are part of the lake history with their many years operating Wild Goose for Boys at the site of the original Wild Goose Club.

Other individuals who contributed photographs, assistance, or information include: Lois S. Braley, Virginia S. Agostinelli, and Ed and Polly Nichols of Pittsfield; Hilda E. Nutter, Myrtle L. Marble, B. J. Childs Frosch, Laura Crummett, Ken and Helene Stickney, Beverly Martin, Frank Nichols, and Louise Nomani of Hartland; Mary Ellen Bossom of Scarborough; Dale Perkins of Monmouth; Paul Herrick of Harmony; Guy Anton of Athens; Sally and Ronald Hughes of St. Albans; Janice McAllister of Abbot; and Paul Neal of Inverness, Florida.

My personal interest in history was fostered long ago by elderly relatives who shared their experiences of 19th- and early-20th-century lifestyles with me, allowing me to understand that the "modern" conveniences I enjoyed in the 1950s and 1960s were miracles beyond their own childhoods. I was fortunate to know and treasure these people with active minds and experiences they were so willing to share with an inquisitive, if not nosy, child. My curiosity continued to grow with the help of two high school history teachers who always knew the stories behind the stories in the driest of textbooks. Working nearly 30 years as a news reporter, freelance writer, and now personal historian has only enhanced my interest in local and family history.

No acknowledgment would be complete without a sincere thank-you to my family members for their patience, assistance, and most of all for indulging me in continuing interest in everyone's stories of earlier times.

INTRODUCTION

It was not until after the Revolutionary War that organized settlements appeared in the area that would one day become Hartland, St. Albans, Harmony, and Athens. Reading the early history of those towns, Great Moose Lake is a sentence here or there where early settlers crossed a stream or the lake itself or they harnessed the power of the streams or rivers. In the early days of development, the lake was incidental to the primary objective of creating a new life in new communities.

As the four towns were still building and growing, adventurers from the urban areas to the south were already looking for a playground away from their busy lives. They came north.

This book attempts to tell something of two different lifestyles, and in some ways how one helped the other. The settlers came to build a life. The sportsmen, or "sports," from Massachusetts came to benefit from the life they or their families had already built. Locals found employment with the sports and the sports demonstrated a different lifestyle and pleasure in the lake.

By the time the sports arrived to enjoy the lake, the settlements were more than 50 years old. The visual history of the four towns and their lake does not begin until the late 1800s, some of the earliest photographs date back to 1888, captured by the adventurous sports from away.

The settlers arrived around 1800 and incorporated their towns within the next decade or two. They came east and northeast, overland and not up the streams and river, often clearing their own roads and paths as they came. Some optimistic adventurers purchased land in Athens and Harmony, sight unseen, when large tracts became available as schools and towns of early Massachusetts sold their state land grants in the wilderness of Maine to raise cash. Some settlers scouted the area first, leaving to return a year or two later to bring their families to the new settlements.

In 1792, Ephraim Ballard and Samuel Weston were the first surveyors of record in the region, labeling some of the area as ranges in Waldo Patent and north of the Plymouth Claims. It would still be another 28 years before the land would be part of a state known as Maine. Much of Maine's population at that time lived along the coast or on the lower reaches of the major rivers. Interior Maine had only attracted adventurers and squatters to that point.

Dr. John Warren of Revolutionary War fame was one of the earliest landowners, owning all of Hartland and St. Albans in addition to neighboring Corinna and Palmyra. His land was a grant for his services during the war. In Athens, David Copp of Jackson, New Hampshire, and six other men became land developers. Copp purchased the land from Berwick Academy, while Charles Vaughn purchased Harmony lands from Hallowell Academy. All the communities were originally land grants to communities, schools, and individuals by the Massachusetts state government.

Telling the story *Around Great Moose Lake* is not a comprehensive history of the lake, but merely a collection of stories, facts, and photographs that begin to tell some history of the lake and the towns that border it.

—Brenda Seekins, 2006

One

HARTLAND
AT THE LAKE

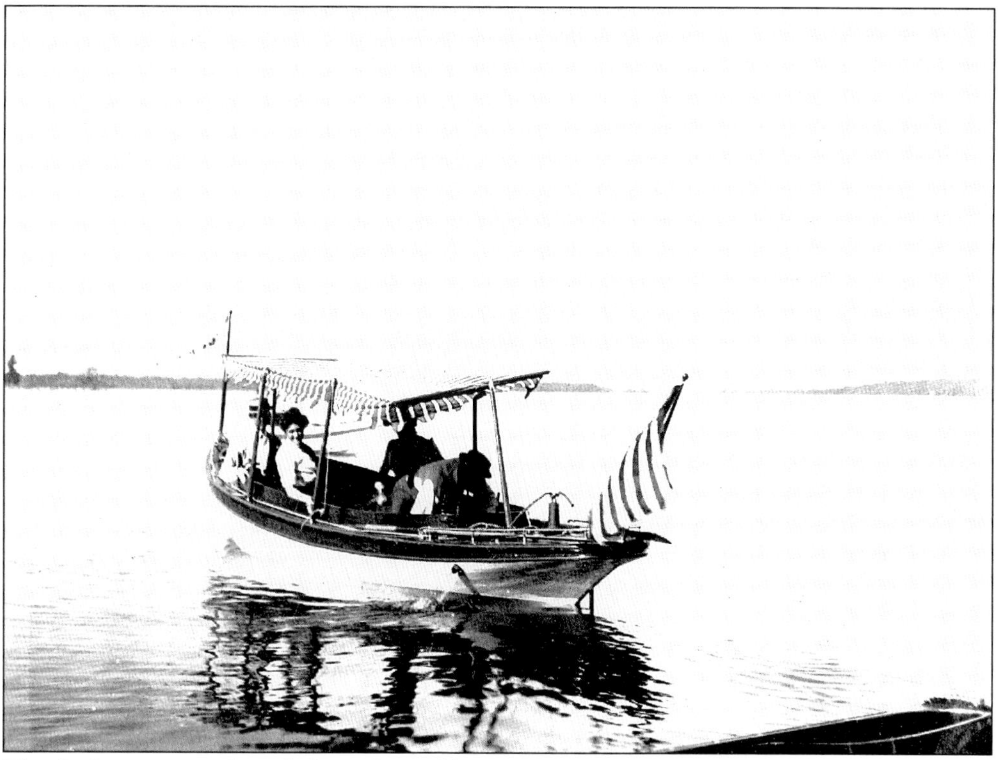

The *Gosling*, a motor launch from the Wild Goose Club, was a common sight on Great Moose Lake in the late 1800s and early in the 1900s. The motor launch and others like it allowed members of the hunting and fishing club to travel between the main lodge at Castle Harmony, on the northern shore at the outlet of Main Stream, and the Commodore Club, a lodge built by a second generation of club members, on the southwest shore of the upper lake.

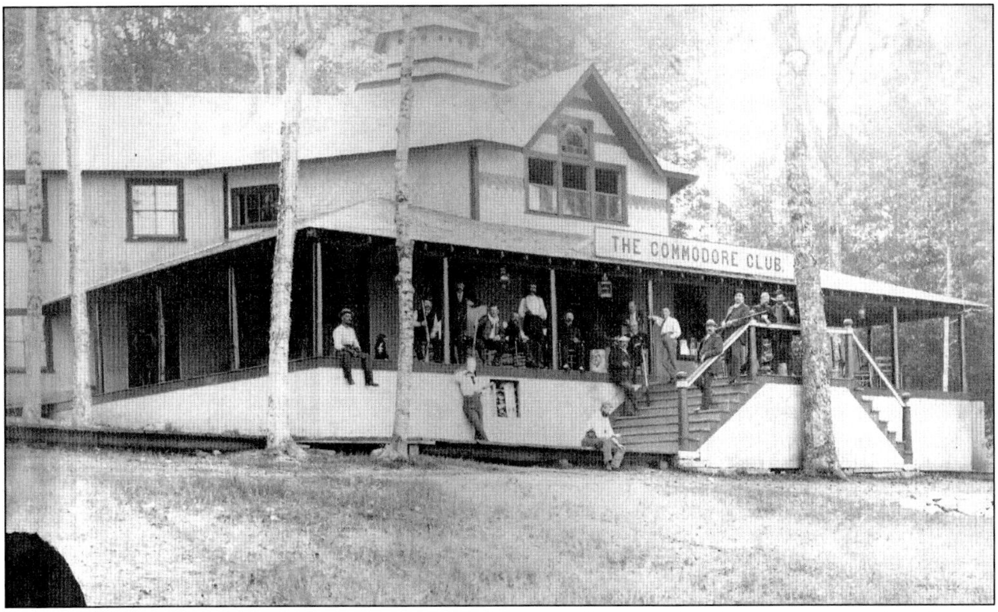

Originally built in 1888, the Commodore Club was still a popular destination nearly 30 years later in 1917 and already had a new addition to provide adequate space for its members and families. The Wild Goose Club and its Hartland and Harmony lodges hosted sportsmen and their families, primarily from Massachusetts, for more than 60 years.

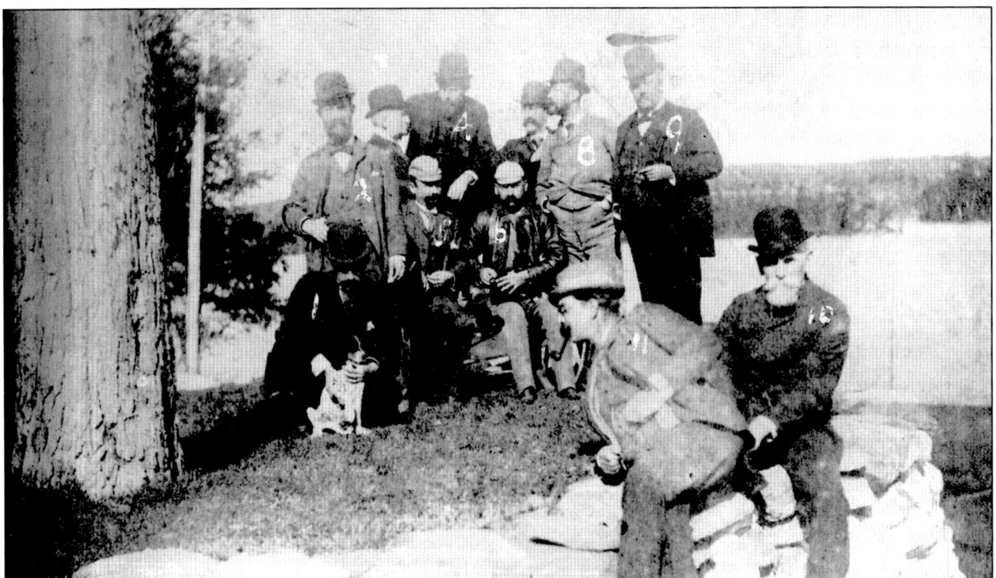

The sportsmen of 1917 were a polished, but rugged bunch. Jackets, white shirts, ties, and often knickers were the general attire whether the men were hunting, fishing, or simply enjoying their woods and water surroundings. Members are posed here in front of the Commodore Club. Most of the photographs generously left behind by club members were identified and numbered. This early group includes (1) E. A. Adams, (2) William V. Kellen, (3) Rufus Brown, (4) J. J. Enneking, (5) George W. Hastings, (6) B. T. Stephenson, (7) F. S. Sherburne, (8) C. L. James, (9) William Lawrence, (10) Henry Stephenson, and (11) ? Hawley.

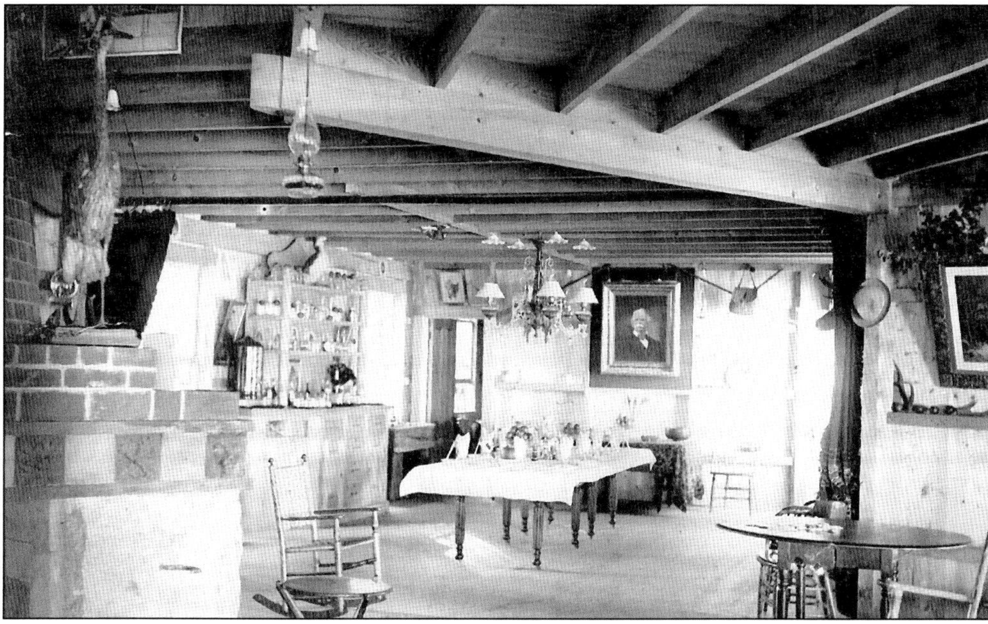

The original dining room of the Commodore Club remains mostly unchanged from its original 19th-century construction. Lights, lanterns, chairs and tables, and a massive central fireplace welcomed the club members back to Great Moose Lake for more than 40 years. Pictured in 1898, it shows the club owners' interest in fine dining always including china, crystal, and linens, whether they dined on duck, deer, or fish, and all were plentiful in the early days of both clubs.

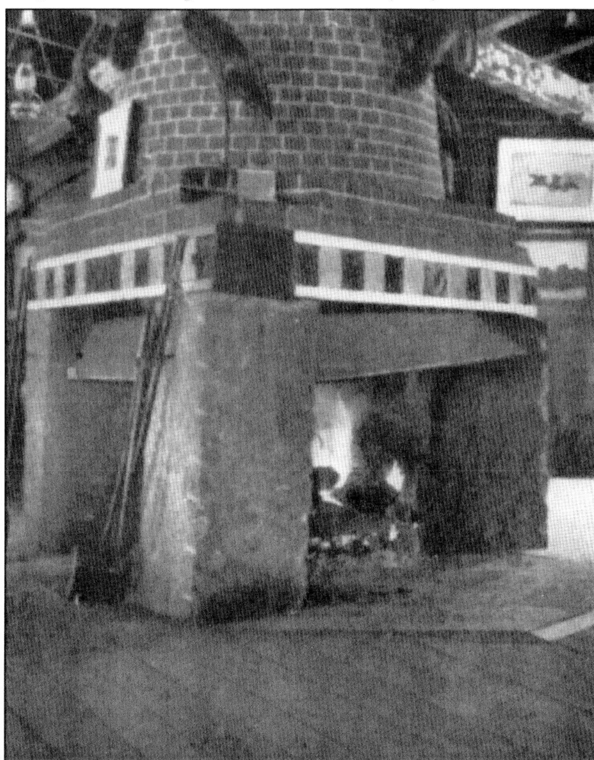

The club's massive fireplace was such a showpiece when it was built along with the building in 1888, it apparently earned the attention of the postcard photographers so prevalent around 1900. The fireplace with its three granite blocks was open on all sides as a copy of a similar one that the club's Commo. George Hastings saw in a Scottish hunting lodge.

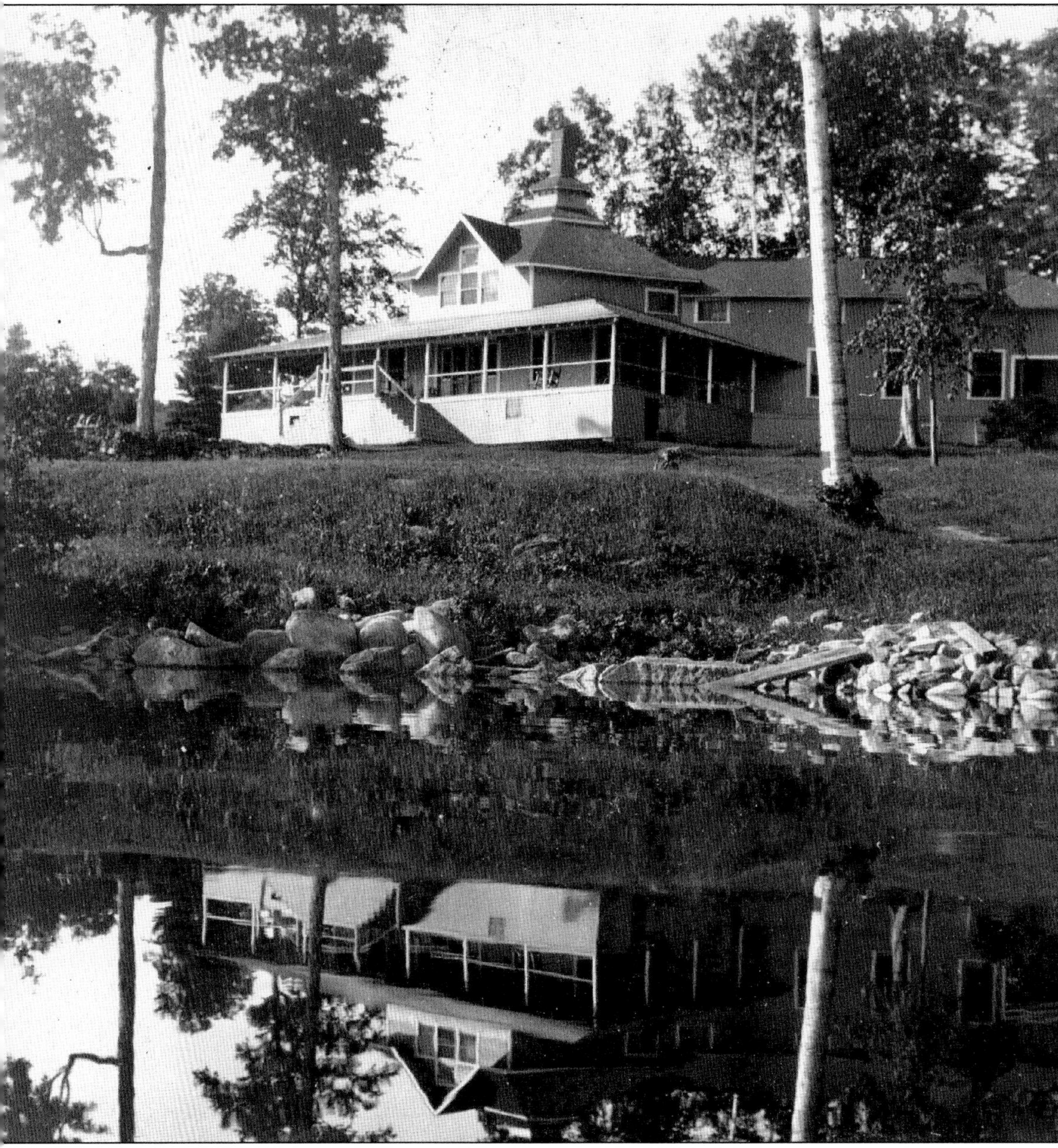

By the 1920s, the Commodore Club was taking on a more manicured look. Another addition appears to have been added to the west end. The lawns have been groomed and the shoreline readied for boats and the motor launch the *Gosling* was likely still making regular trips between the club and the castle on the eastern shore. After the Wild Goose group lost its interest in the Hartland lodge, either figuratively or financially, the Commodore Club was operated as a commercial lodge and dining facility well into the mid-1900s. Owned as a private family property today, it still carries the name of the original facility.

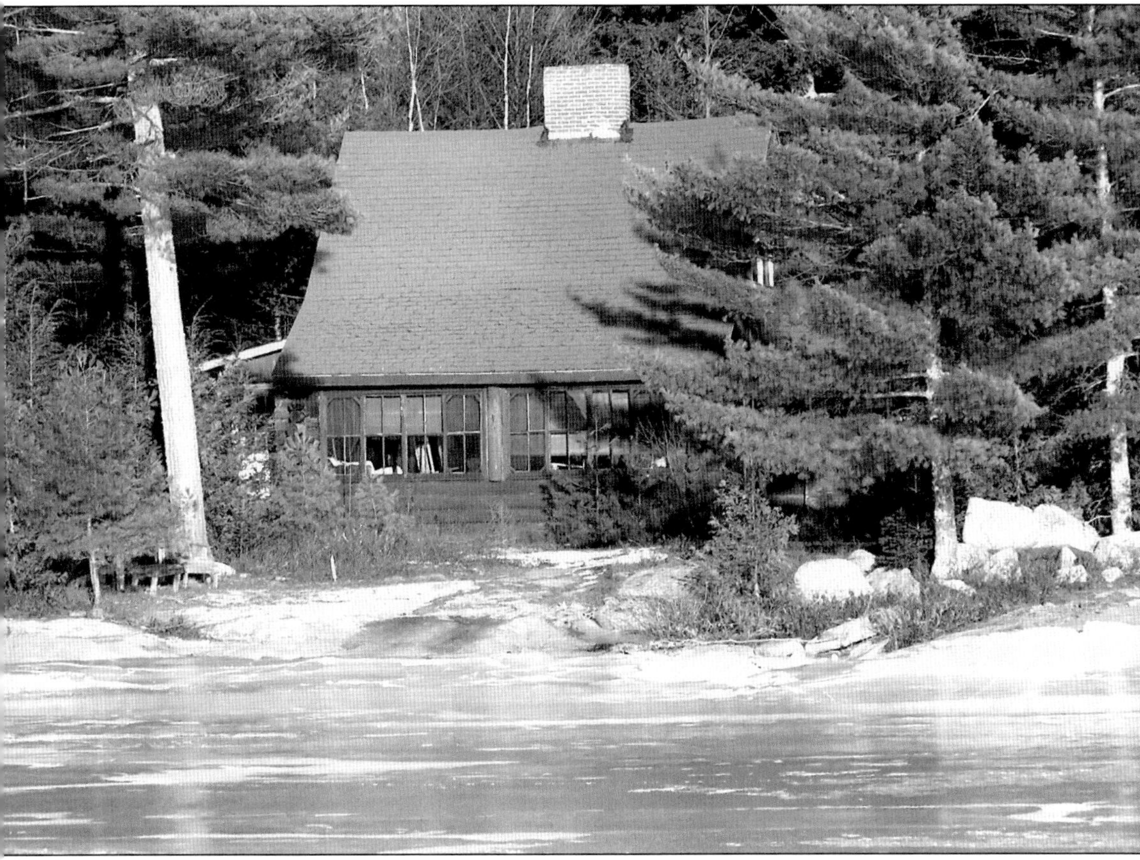

A well-known landmark on Great Moose Lake is the log cabin at Bernard's Point. Dr. Albert J. Bernard, a Skowhegan practitioner, first brought his family to "camp" around 1945, following his service aboard a destroyer in World War II. Bernard's daughter Louise Nomani, who currently owns the property, first came to camp atop her father's shoulders as he picked his way along a wooded path. Her memories of the early camp include the additions of the log cabin front to an older structure, a fireplace, slate hearth and granite wall to take 4-foot logs, a slate sink, and gas fixtures for light. "The camp upstairs was a dark and dreary place with small windows that served only to frame the black pine fingers that waved at us at night. The sound of waves and loons was better than a music box though and mesmerized us until we slept warm with blankets and feather pillows," Louise wrote in a memoir of her early days on the lake.

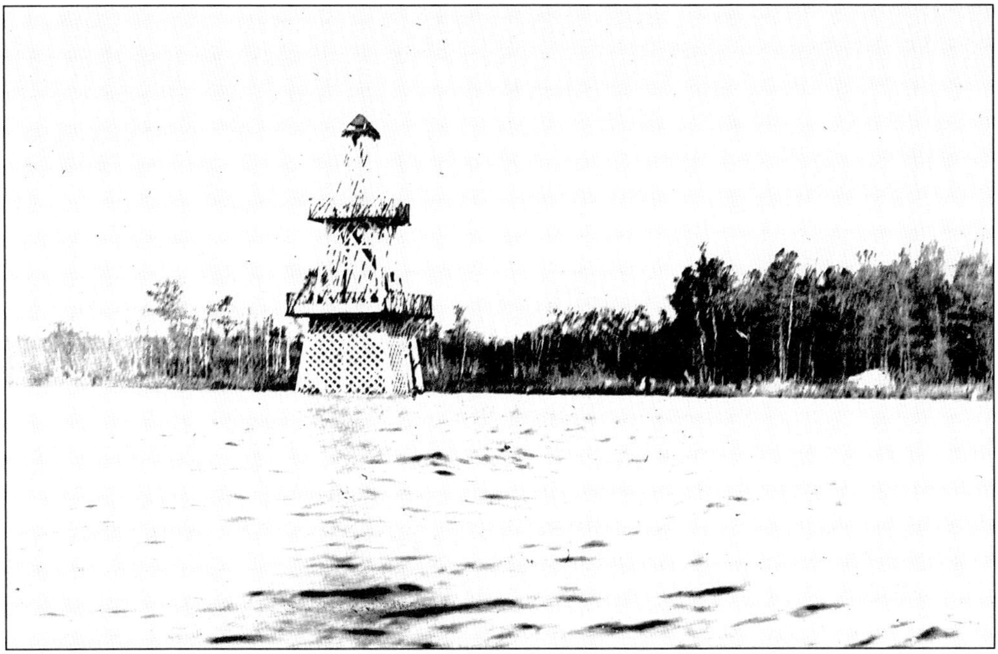

A lighthouse marked the entrance to the Bay of Galashiels, or Main Stream, from the early days of Castle Harmony and the Wild Goose Club. Lanterns were hung at the top of the tower when club members were expected at the lodge, enabling them to arrive late by train from Massachusetts and make their way by boat the length of the lake and find the easily hidden entrance to the stream. The Scottish heritage of some of the members is the reason behind the bay's name and the naming of the wooden lodge as a castle, as many country estates in Scotland were once called. The original lighthouse also held a ladies' changing room in its base for the ladies to use once they had walked out to the point for swimming.

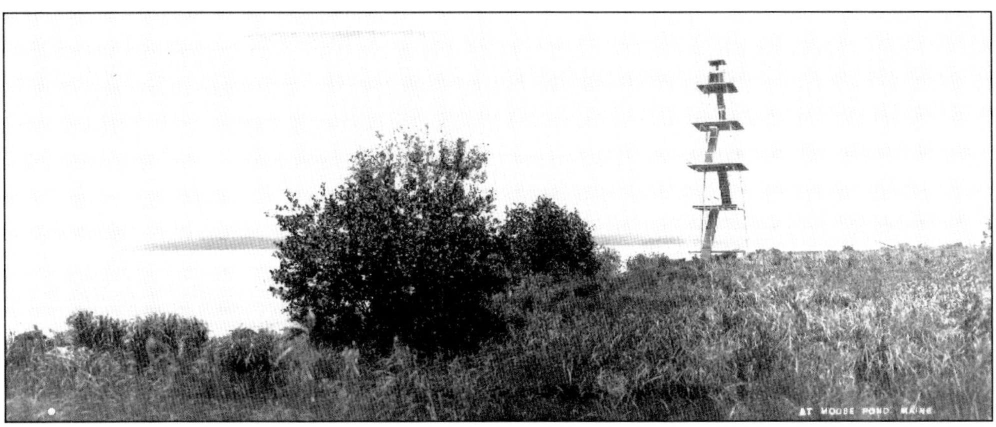

The original wooden lighthouse blew down in a storm in 1911 and an iron tower was built in its place in 1912. The framework of the later tower still stands today, hidden among the trees and shrubs on the northwest side of the stream entrance.

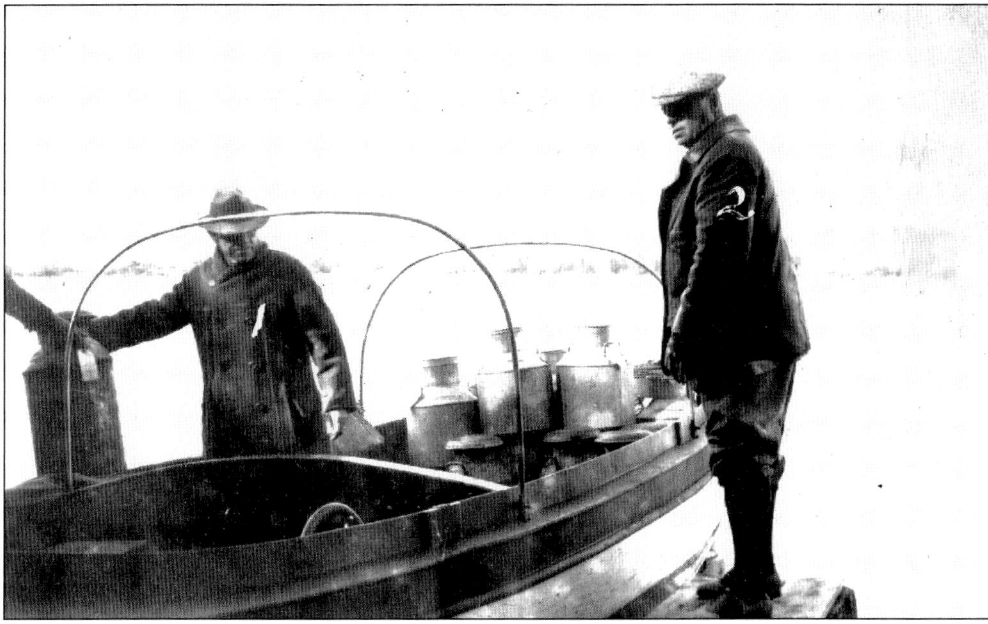

Deliveries to the hunting lodges on the lake began at the club's boat wharf above the upper dam in Hartland. For many years, locals provided a variety of services and goods to the two lodges, as well as other seasonal residents on the lake, using rowboats and motor launches. In October 1922, Wild Goose Club members snapped this image of G. M. Lancey (left) and T. A. Appollonio (right) as they readied a delivery for one of the lodges.

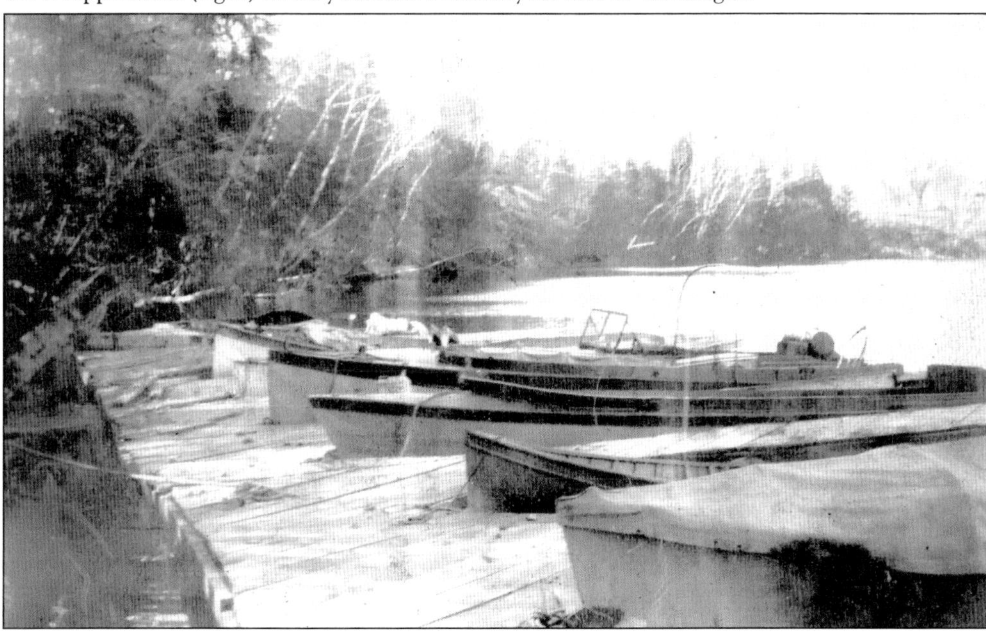

The boat wharf on the Sebasticook River at Hartland was built to hold the bow of the boats tight to the sides. The wooden docks on the west shore of the river were accessed by sets of steep stairs down the embankment somewhere behind the Ireland Cemetery on Pleasant Street. Older residents recall seeing well-dressed couples using the docks in the 1920s to reach the motor launches taking them upriver and up the lake for social gatherings at various lodges.

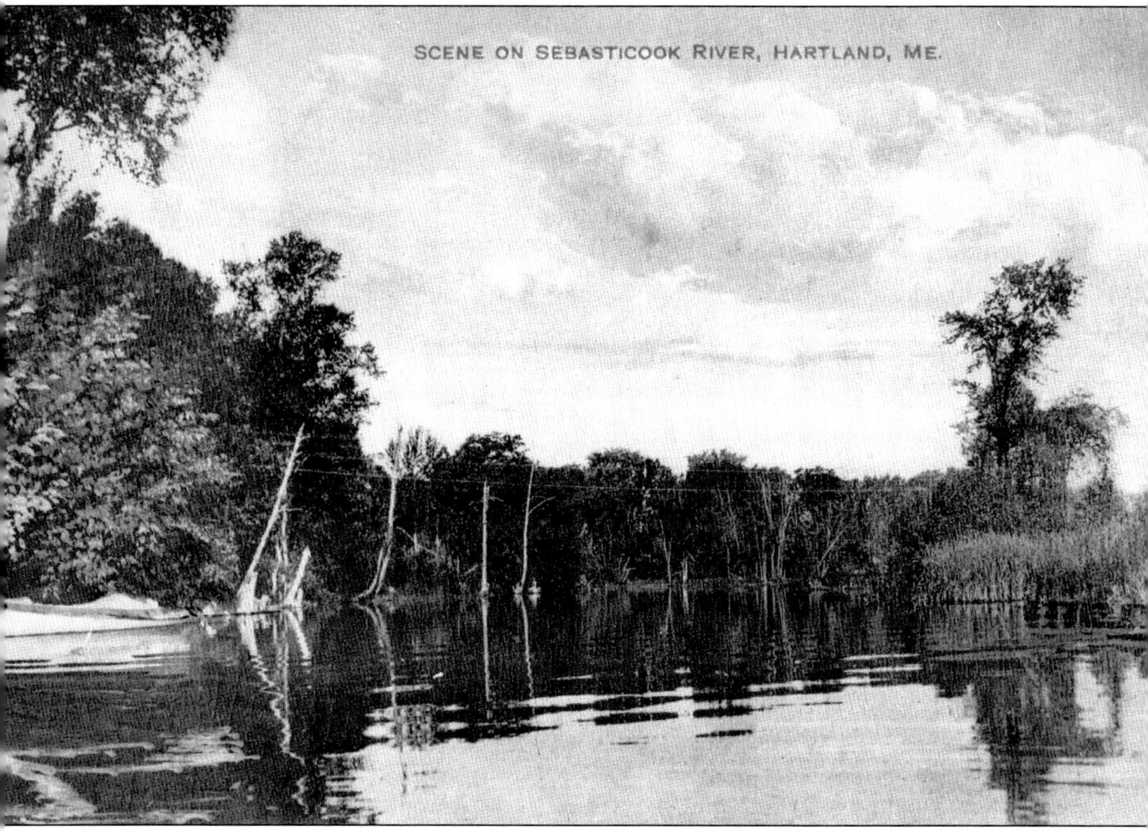

Traveling upriver from Hartland around 1900 was a wilderness experience of its own, with little development on the winding stretch until the development of Great Moose Drive along the west shore brought more year-round homes to the lake and river.

Two

Hartland
In the Village

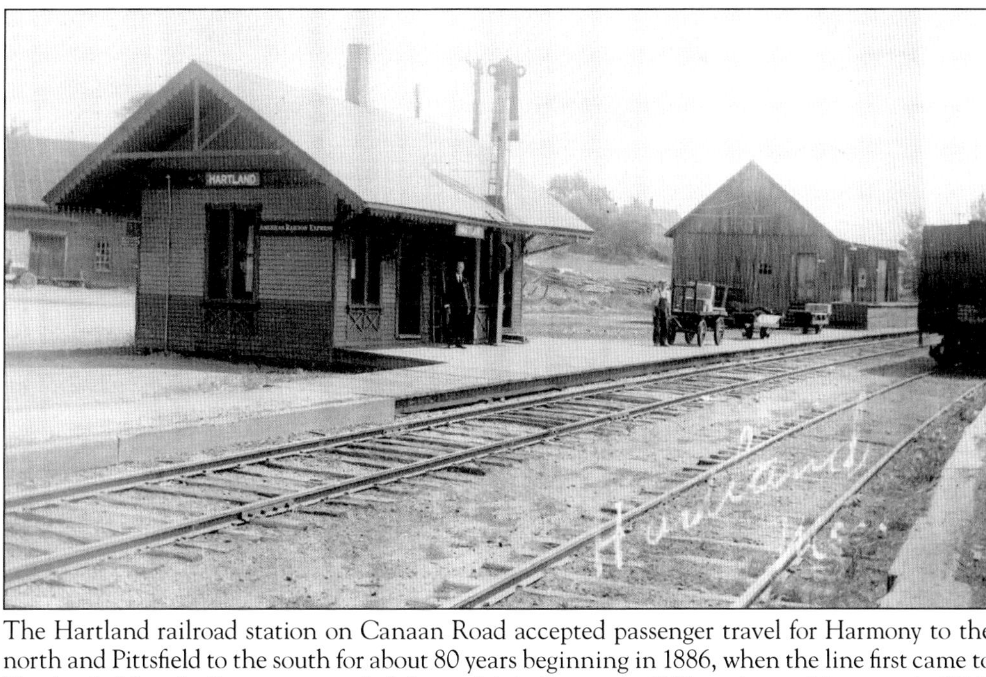

The Hartland railroad station on Canaan Road accepted passenger travel for Harmony to the north and Pittsfield to the south for about 80 years beginning in 1886, when the line first came to Hartland. After the line was extended, first to Main Stream in 1901, and on to Harmony in 1912, the train brought summer residents to camp, took them to town for shopping, and allowed the breadwinners in the family to make weekly commutes to the family's summer quarters. The train routinely stopped for passengers when flagged down on the tracks along the lake. The train was a daily presence along the shores of the lake until the Harmony line was discontinued in 1966 and the trestle and tracks disappeared soon after. The train from Hartland to Pittsfield continued for several more years, ultimately ending with the removal of the tracks and a transformation to a trail system for off-road vehicles in all seasons.

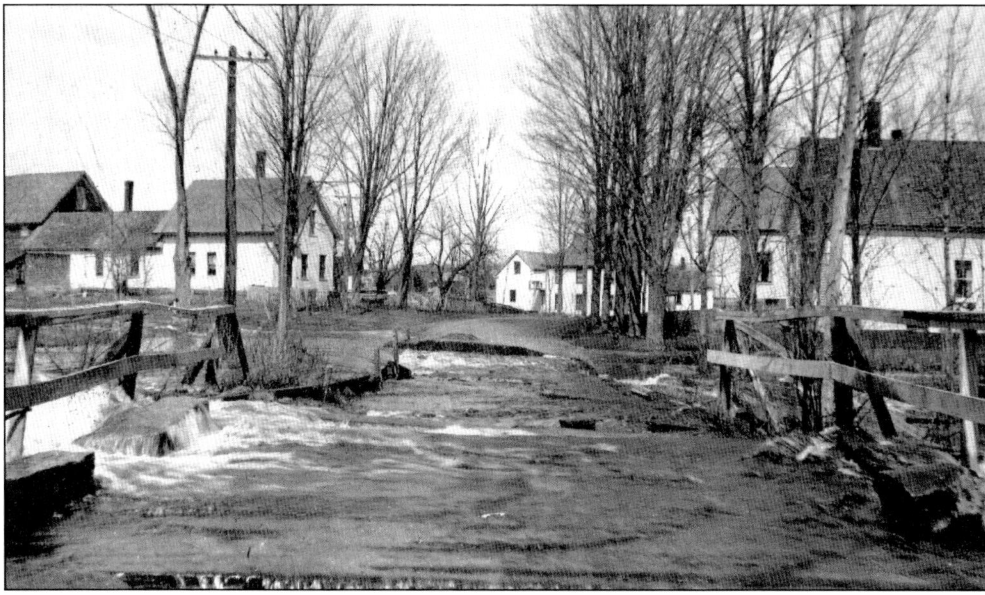

In 1923, the waters of Great Moose Lake and the Sebasticook River rose to record levels, engulfing much of the residential neighborhood that included North Street as well as Mill Street and Water Street to the south and the area known then as Upper and Lower Georgetown.

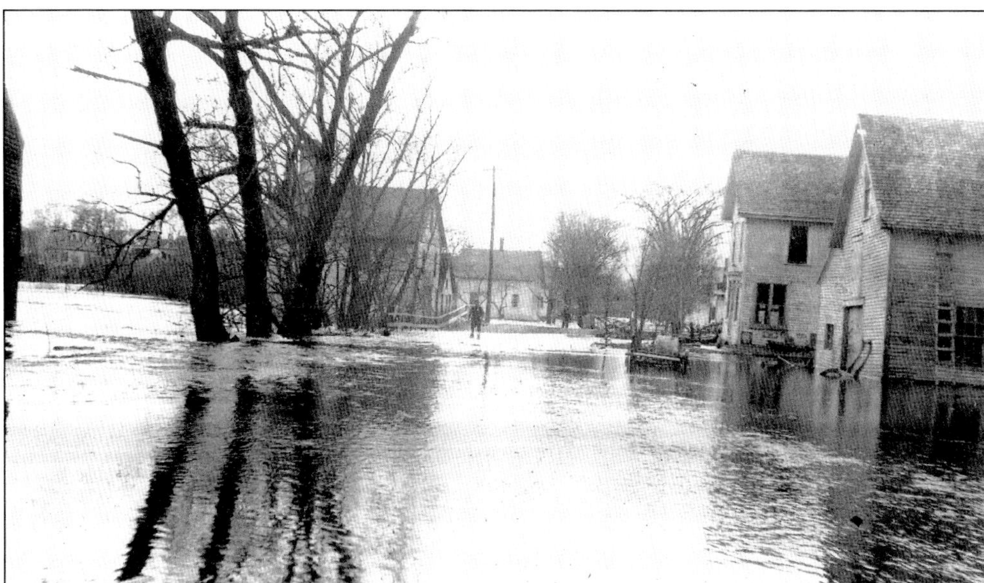

The flood covered the road and surrounding houses on Water Street, forcing several families to move to the second floor or leave until the floodwaters subsided.

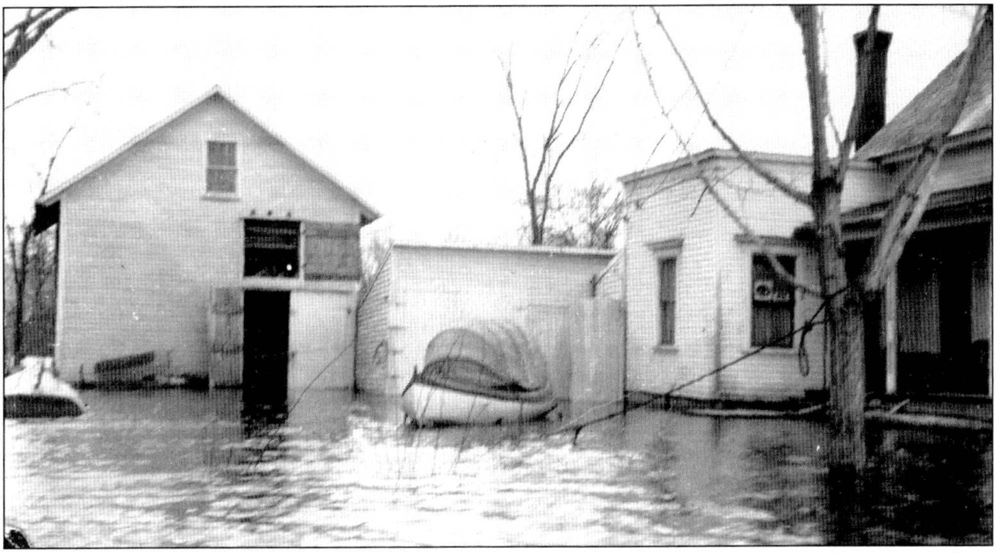

At least one homeowner on Water Street appeared ready for the rising water with a boat tied up by the back door.

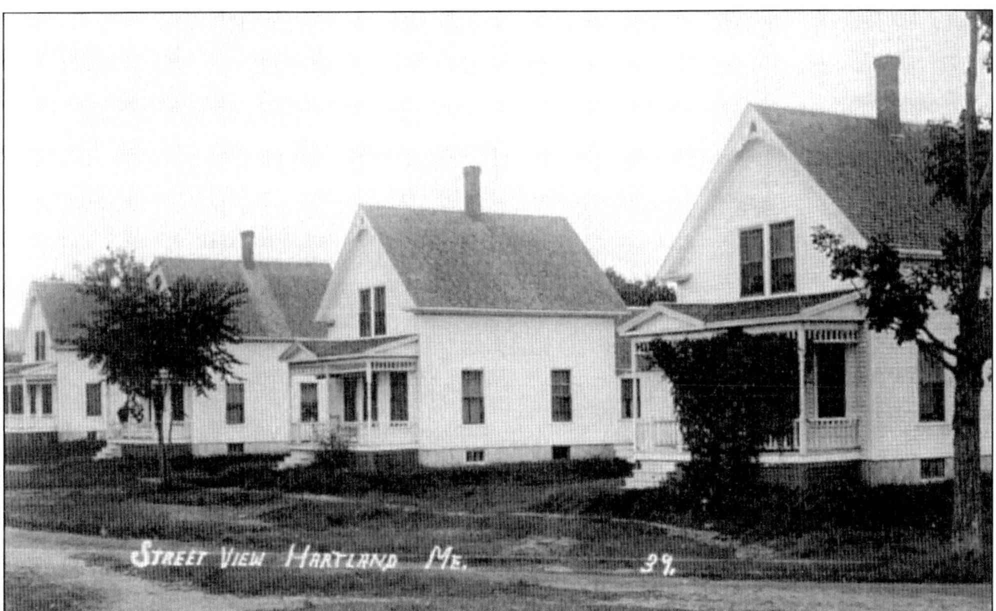

Mill housing was part of Mill Street in the early 1900s and remains today, although the homes were developed to be more individualized as private homes.

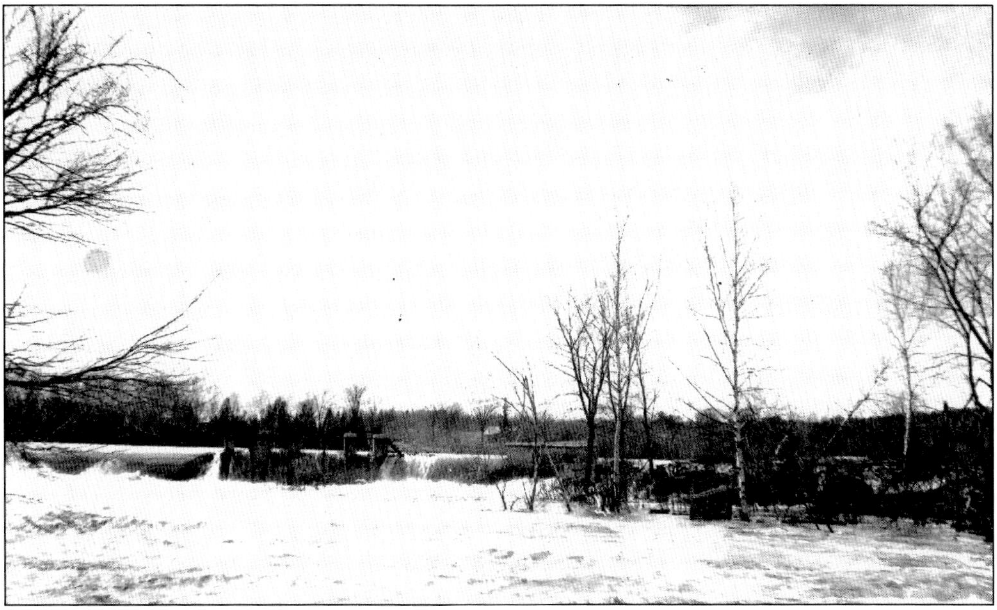

The upper dam on the Sebasticook River in Hartland appears to have been built and rebuilt several times. This earliest view is reportedly from around 1910, when floodwaters took out an early wooden structure. The dam was reconstructed of logs and apparently stood until 1923, when it again succumbed to a flood. It was eventually reconstructed of concrete and stood several decades until a four-foot high section broke off the top of the dam in 1987, flooding areas of Hartland and the valley as far south as Pittsfield. Federal money helped rebuild the dam to the modern structure it is today.

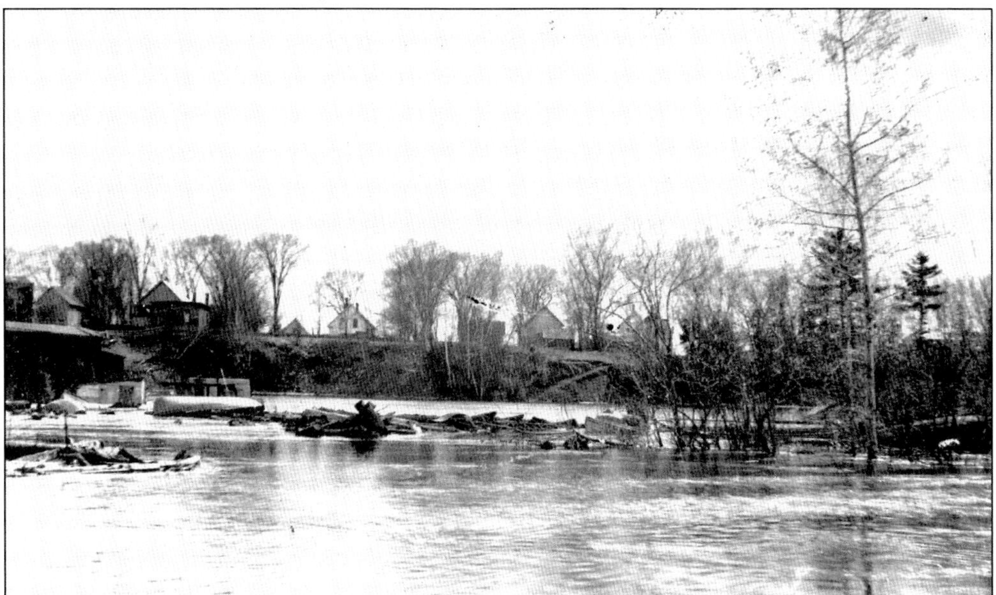

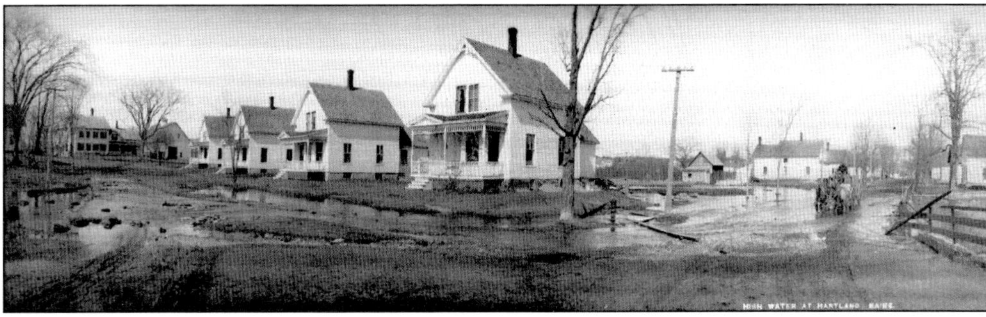

Floodwaters along Mill Street in 1923 swamped the bridge, closing Mill and Water Streets. Automobiles, still relatively new to Hartland, found themselves stranded, and local residents were more than happy to rely on horse-drawn transportation until floodwaters and the resulting damage subsided.

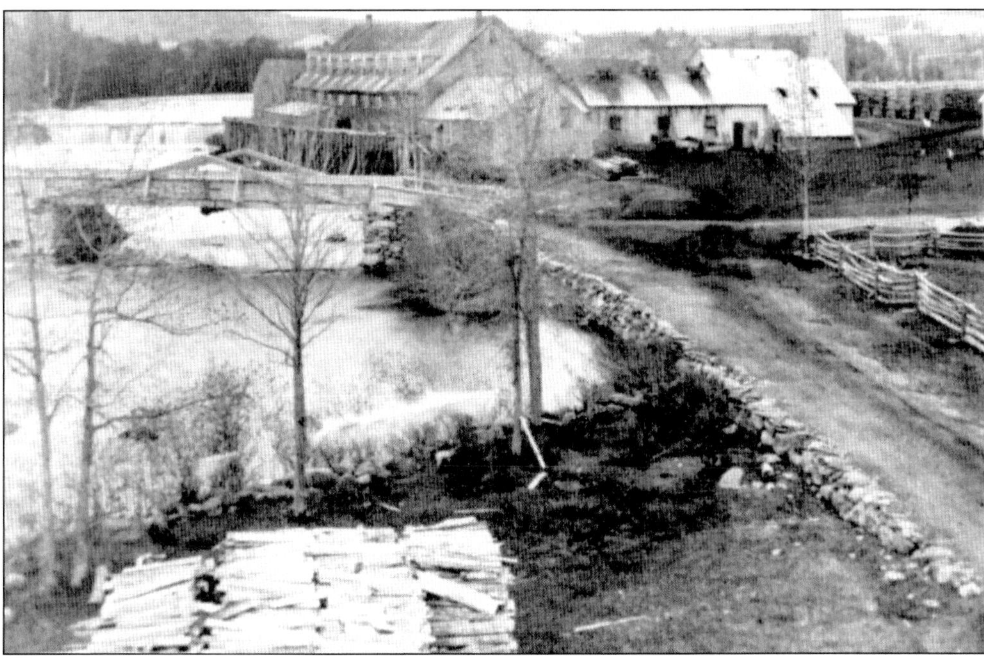

A sawmill and lumberyard at the upper dam initially controlled the water level for the river and the lake above it. The water level on the lake was much lower than it is today when many camp owners initially built their cottages in the first part of the 1900s and into the 1950s. The mill stood at the end of what was initially known as Billings Street, named after one of the mill owners.

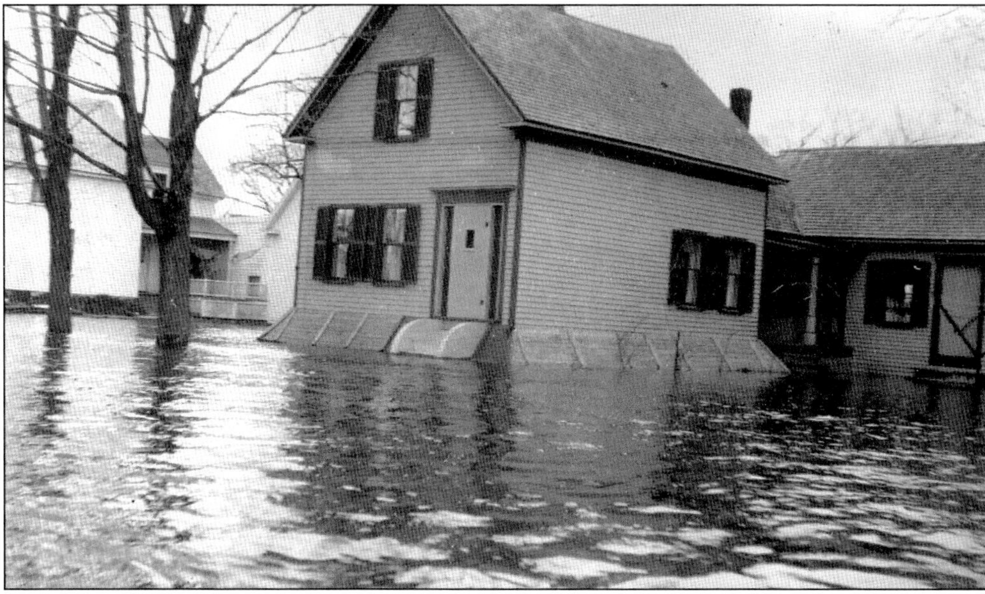

Although the flood of 1923 was late in the spring, around May, some homes had not yet given up on winter with the standard banking boards still around the outside and appearing to provide some protection from the high water.

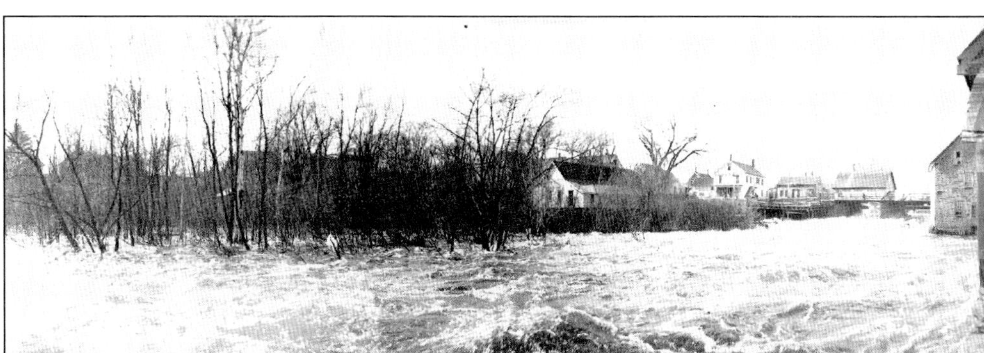

Below Main Street, or lower dam, and the bridge, flood waters rolled on much as they do today during high water. A flood protection wall, built by the Army Corps of Engineers, protects the local industry, Irving Tanning, from the rising and rolling water today.

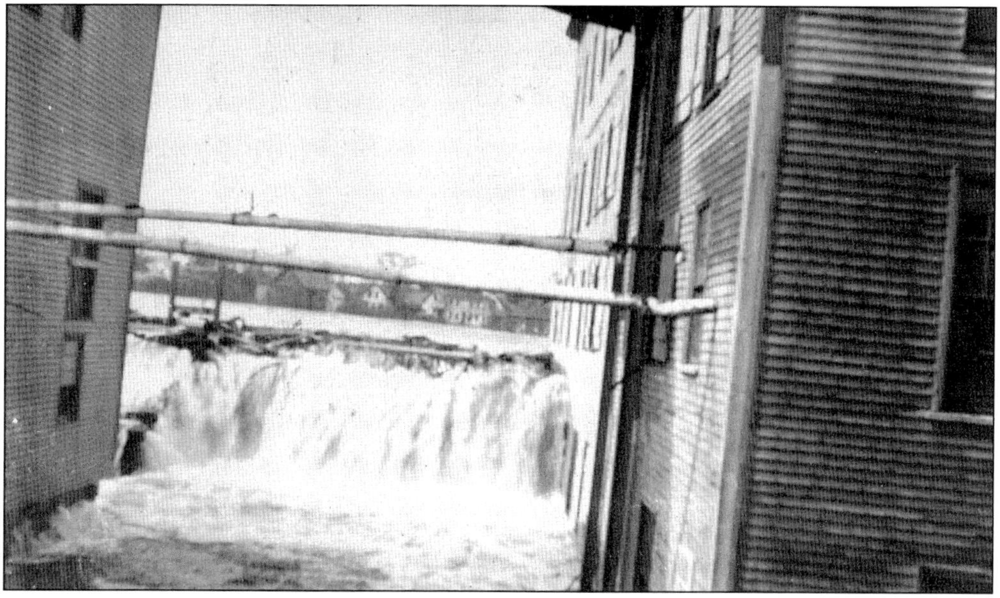

The flood of 1923 threatened buildings at American Woolen Mill much as the flood of 1987 threatened the Hartland Tannery, now known as Irving Tanning.

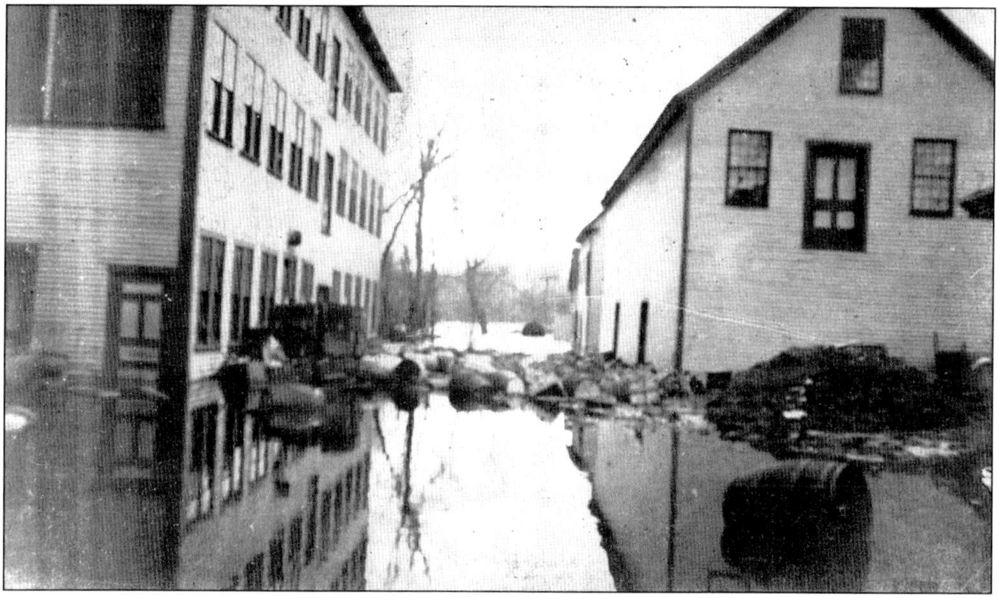

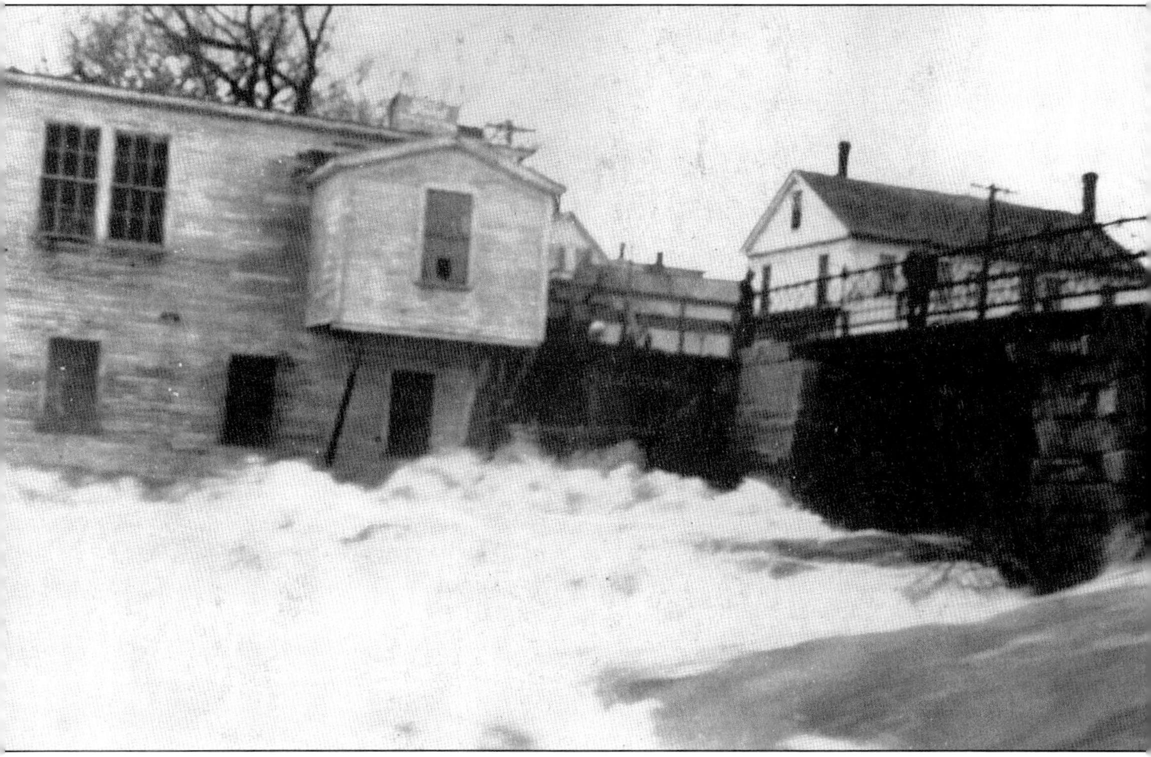

Flood waters boiled south of the Main Street bridge in 1923, but failed to damage the bridge as later floods did.

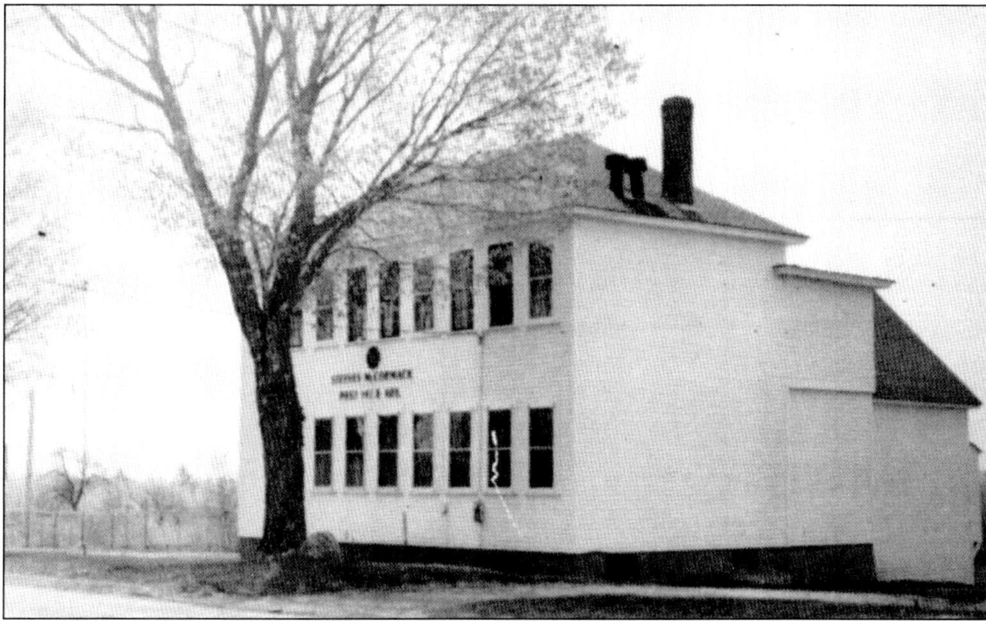

The Ireland or "little" School on Pleasant Street disappeared in recent years. Increasing deterioration forced the recent occupants, the Steeves-McCormack Post American Legion, to demolish the property in hopes of having a newer structure some day. The school educated a large number of Hartland residents in the primary grades.

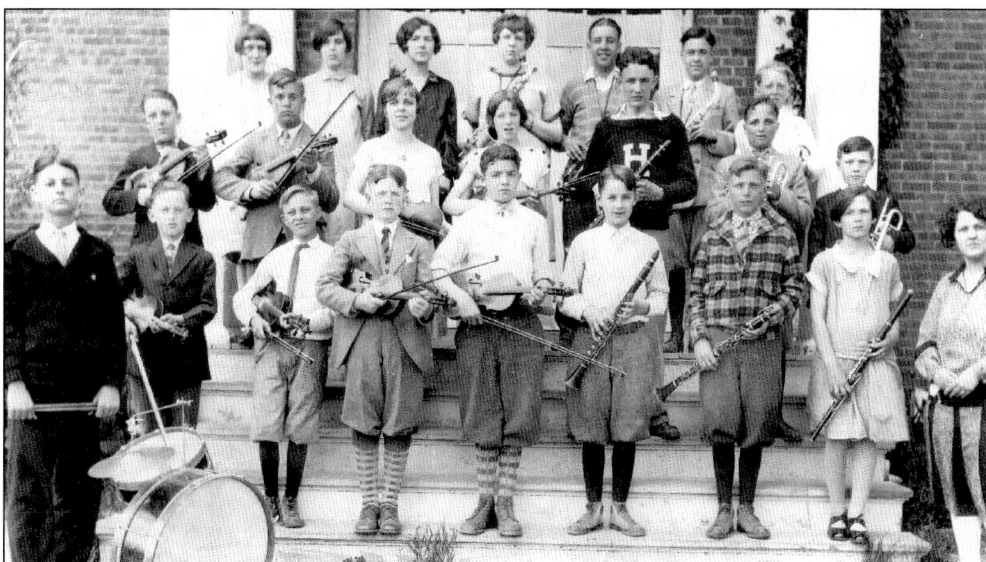

Education at Hartland Academy included music education during much of its long tenure. The Hartland Academy orchestra, seen here around 1928, included, from left to right, (first row) Howard Gray, Raymond Waltham, Howie Jamison, Clarence Genthner, Francis Coston, Edson Goodrich, Ted Griffith, Florice Steeves, and music teacher Doris Harlow; (second row) first two boys Earl Hart and unidentified, Fanny Griffith, Mary Hart, Jimmy Fuller, Roger Baker, and Don Randlett; (third row) Angilee Fuller, Bernice Harding, Eileen Seekins, Geneva Merrill, Frankie Mathews, Darrell Currie, and Philip Nelson.

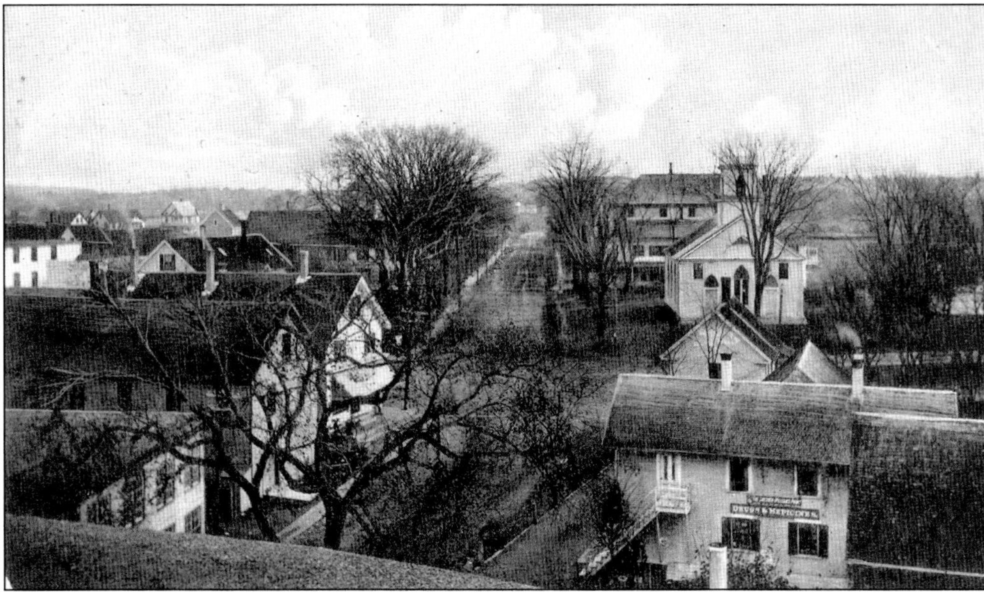

Hartland village looking east on Academy Street shows a tree-lined community still growing around 1900, or shortly before. Miller's drug store is in the foreground. The Baptist Church is at the center of the village, and the St. Albans town line is on the horizon to the east.

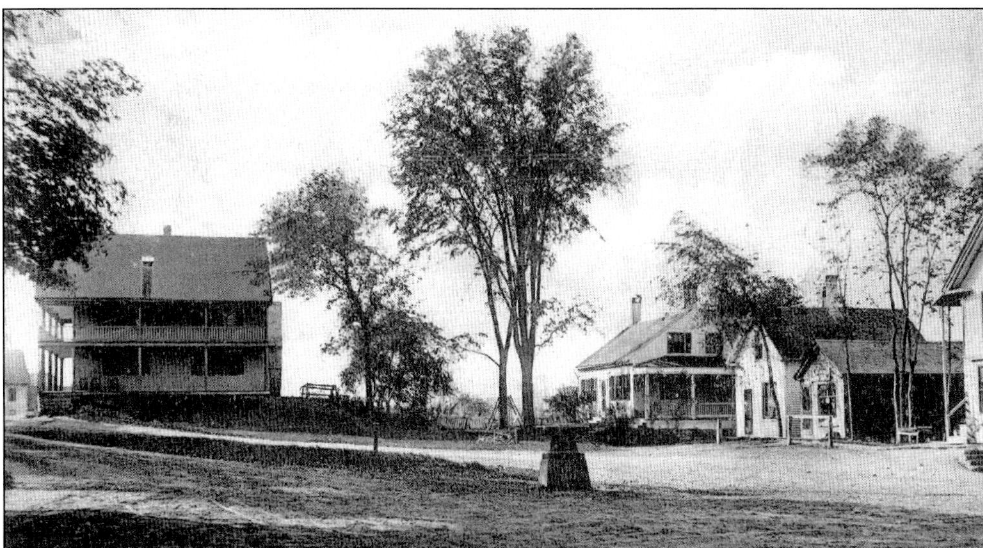

Warren Square was truly an open square with a water trough to accommodate horses in the early 1900s. The town bandstand appeared in later photographs. The Hartland House stood on the corner of the square where it meets Elm Street, and a busy business block bordered the square on the west. Over the years, the block included small stores, restaurants, law offices, and the last occupant was V&R Variety before it was destroyed by fire. Vicky and Rocky Rice relocated the store to a new structure at the corner of Main and Mill Streets where it stands today.

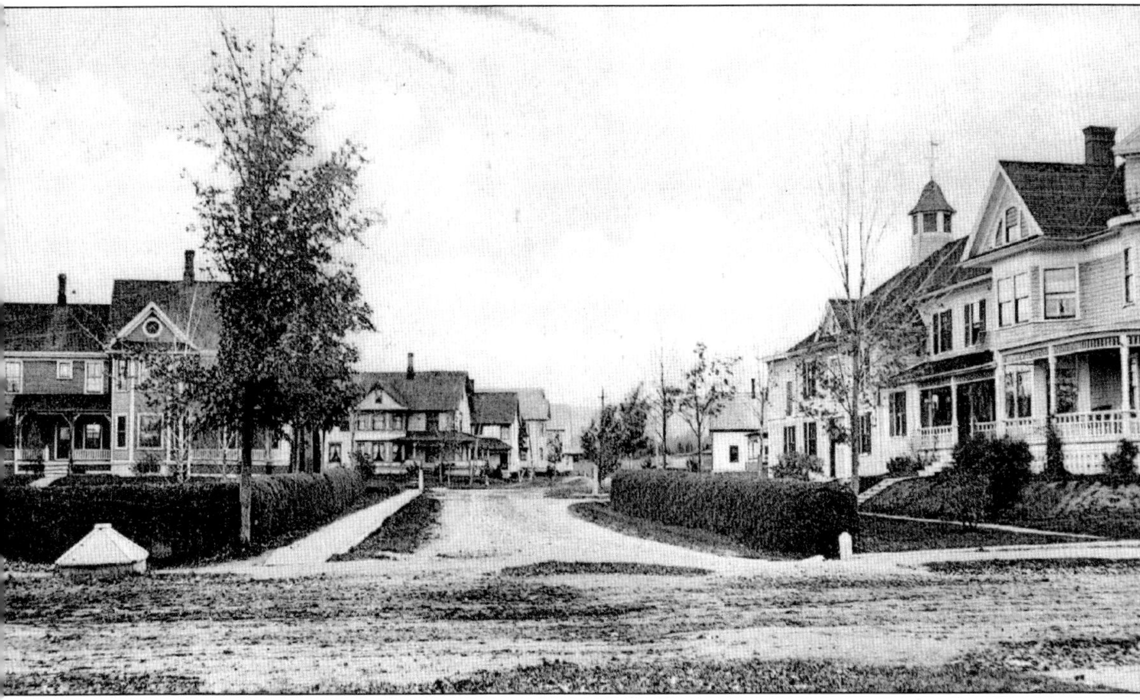

Blake Street has changed very little in 100 years with the exception that it is now the entrance or access road to Hartland's new Somerset Valley Middle School that houses fifth through eighth grades for the west side of School Administrative District 48. The home on the left was a doctor's home for most of the 1900s, Dr. Blanchard being the first occupant and followed closely by Dr. Paul Briggs. The home on the right operated as Crestwood Nursing Home for many years.

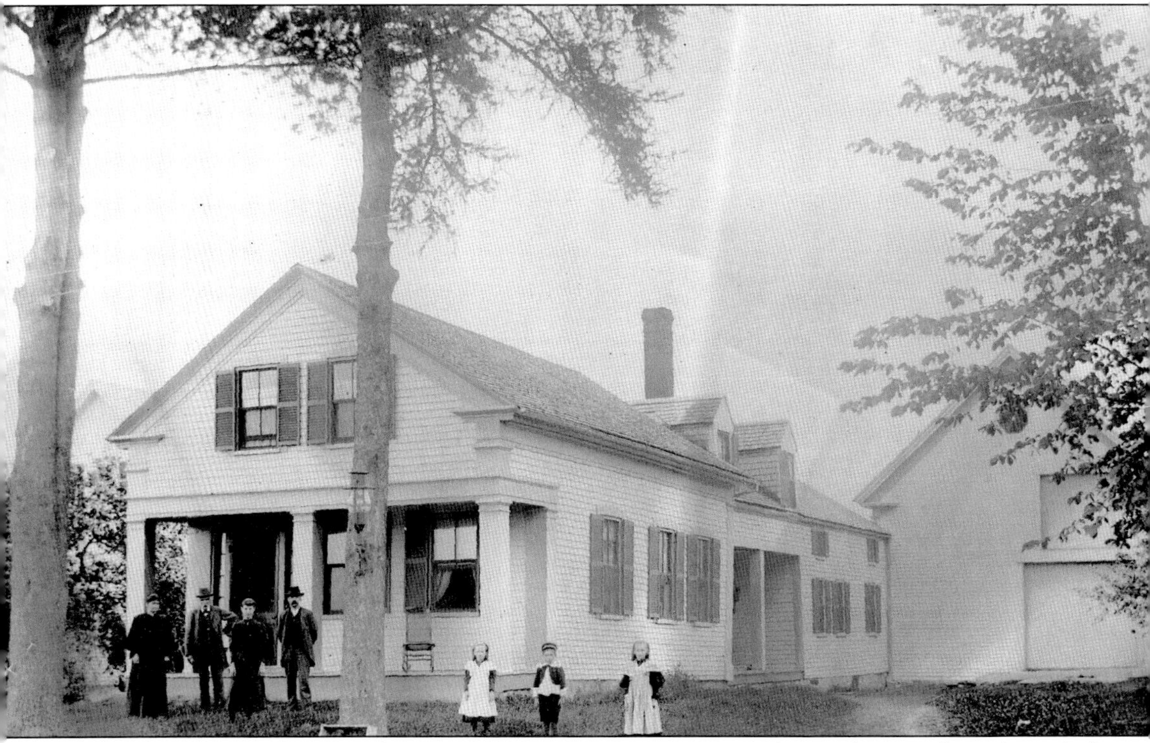

The Pennell home on Academy Street was an attractive structure close to the opera house/town hall. Its latest use was an attempt to start a pizza shop that burned shortly after it opened around 2000.

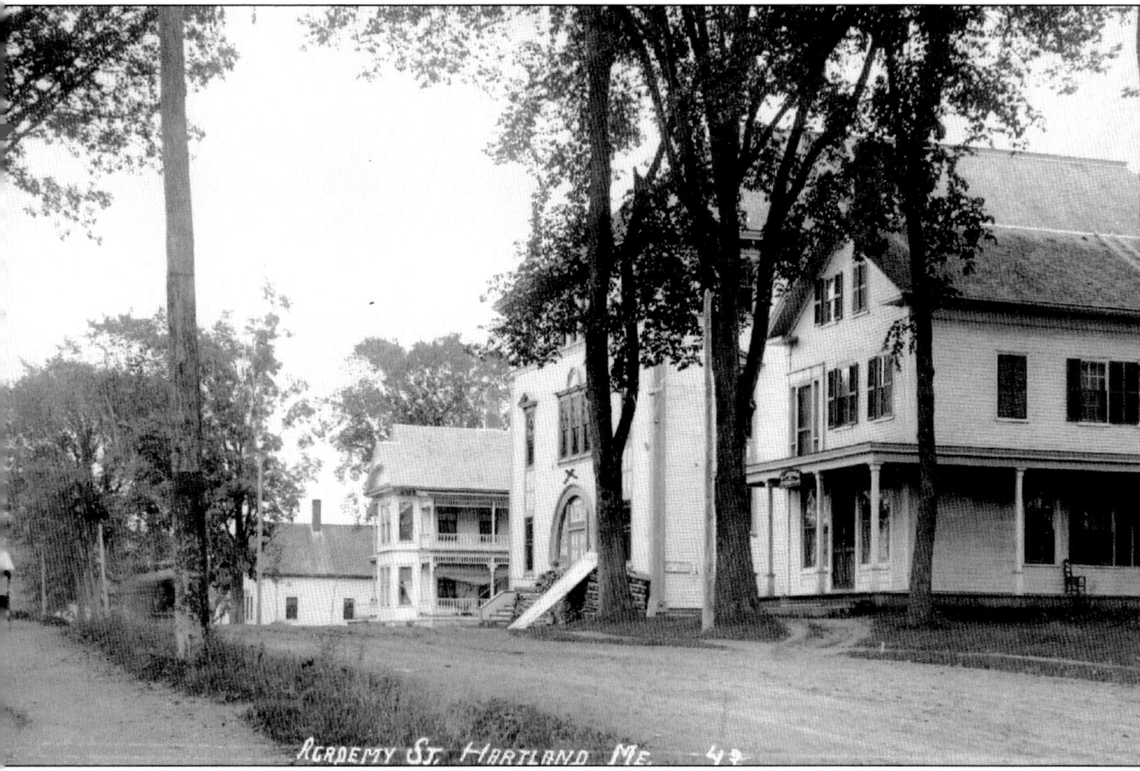

On Academy Street, the opera house/town hall that still stands today was built shortly after being destroyed by fire in 1895. The new construction cost about the same as the first, $6,000. The home on the right of this photograph still stands today, while the one to the right of the building has been replaced. The home to the east of the opera house also burned in a fire in 1895.

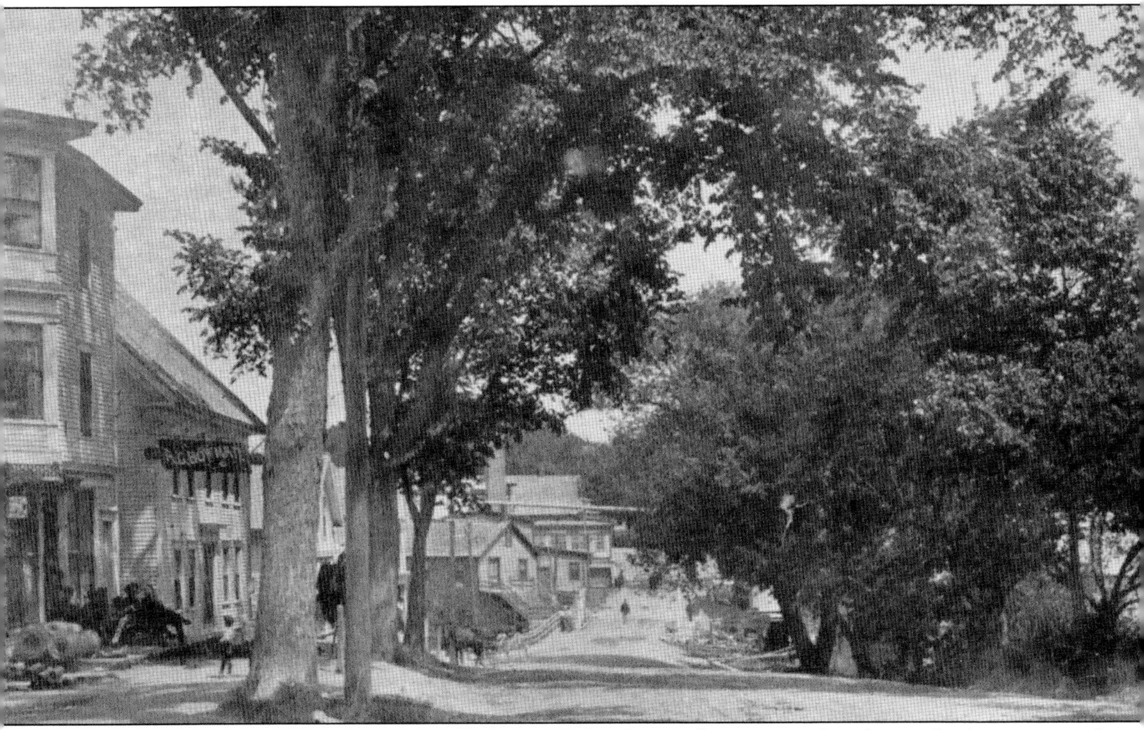

Looking east on Main Street, the American Woolen Mill was in its heyday at the beginning of the 1900s. Main Street was tree-lined and shaded at that time. Roads were still unpaved and occupied by horse and wagon. A. G. Bowman operated a store, the second building on the left, now occupied by Michael Wiers Law Office.

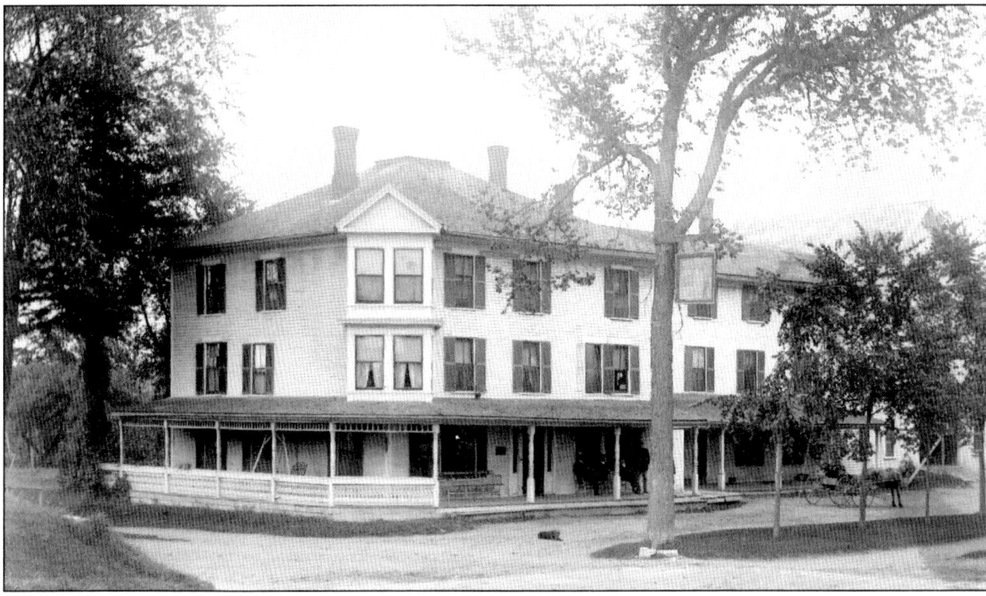

The Park House, at the corner of Mill and Main Streets, was a well-known and well-used inn in the early 1900s. The lore of the inn includes a murder involving a staff member. Today the location is home to V&R Variety's Shurfine, also known as Moose Lake Market.

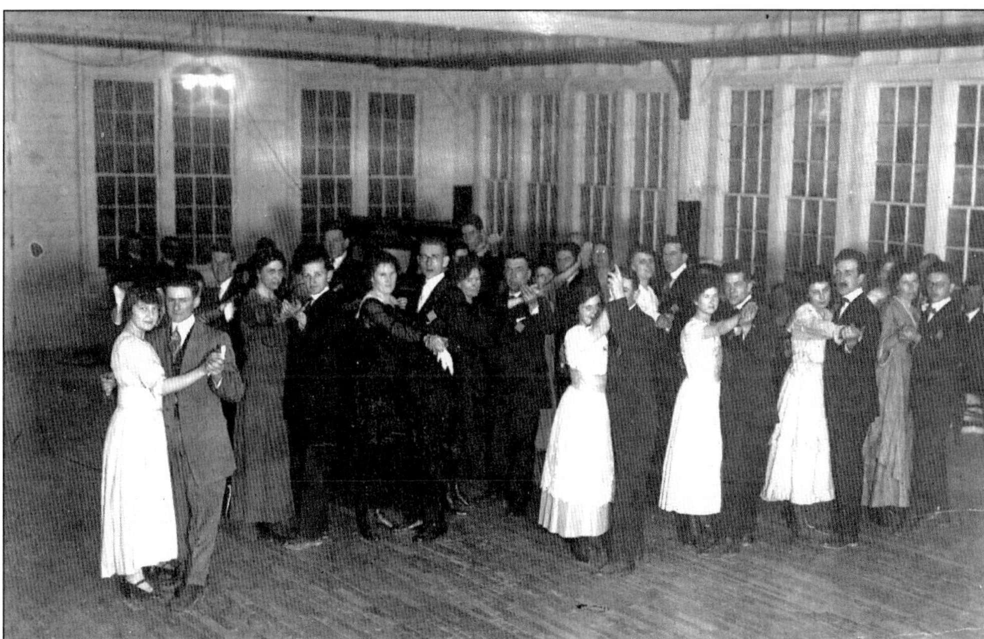

Early in the 1900s, the H&Y skirt shop on Mill Street hosted a company dance to dedicate a new building. About 80 couples attended including Burge and Pearl Emery. Pearl Emery is in the dark dress with white collar. Dancers used the second floor of the building where the pressmen would normally operate. In later years, the building became the Blue Moon Roller Rink.

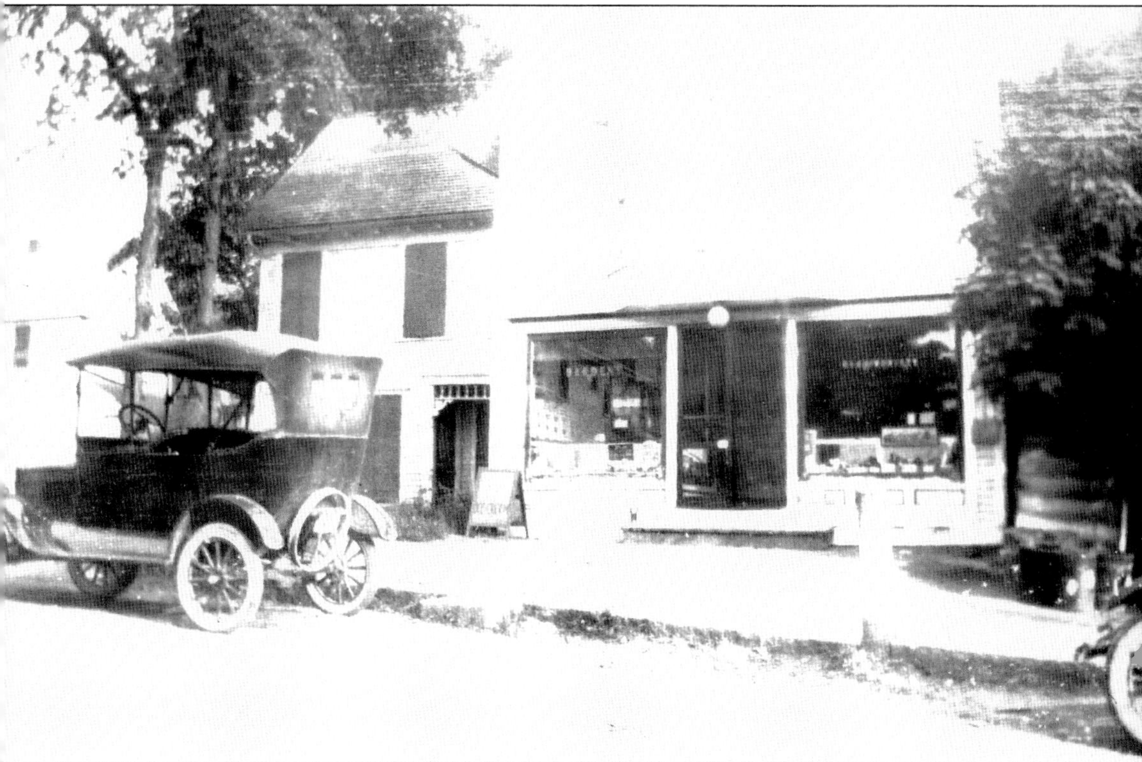

Lewis and Eda Barden used the Miller building on Main Street for their first general store in the 1920s.

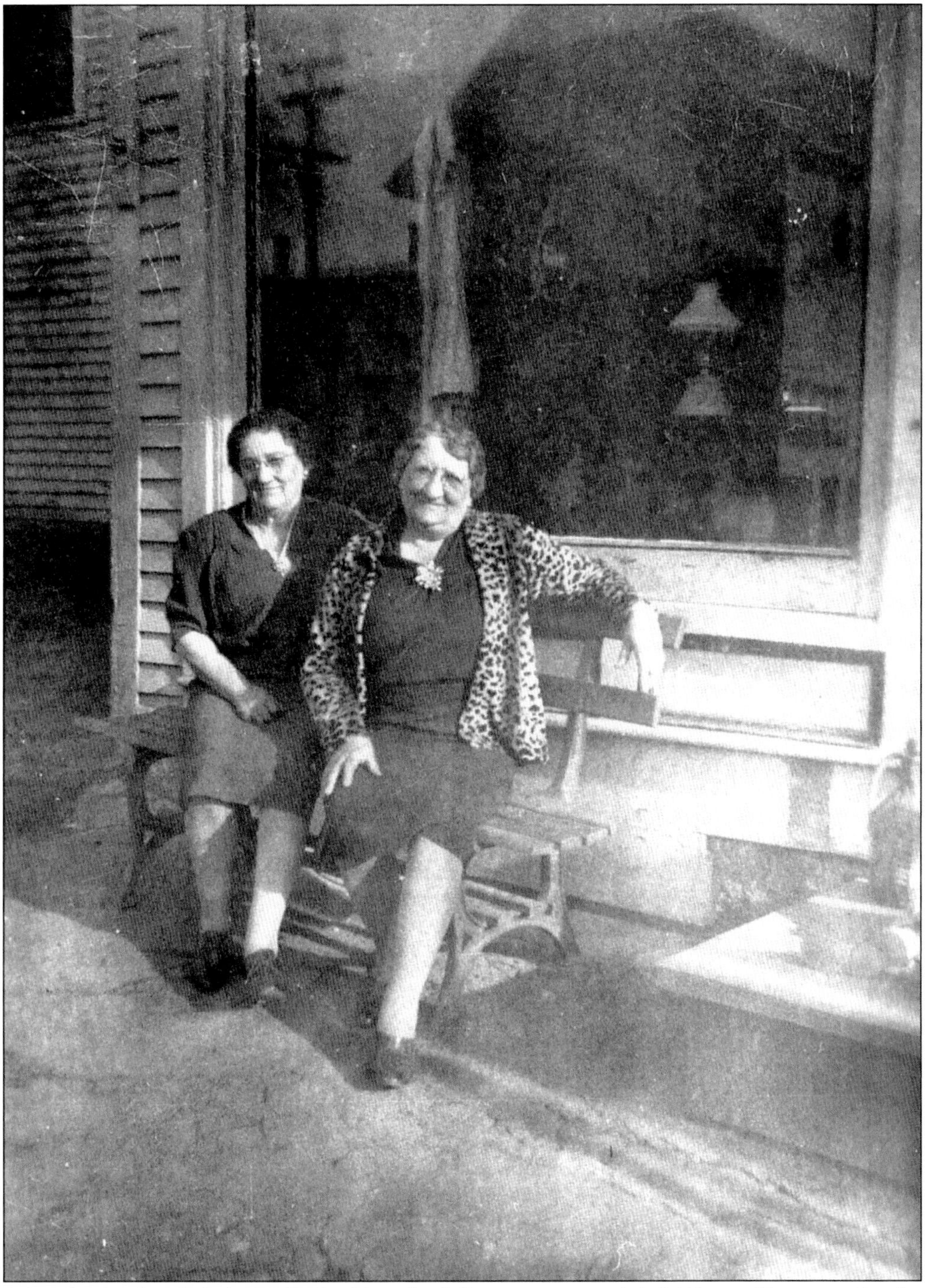

After the Bardens left the Miller building for different quarters, Ada Miller and her sister Bertha Davis operated a secondhand shop in the building.

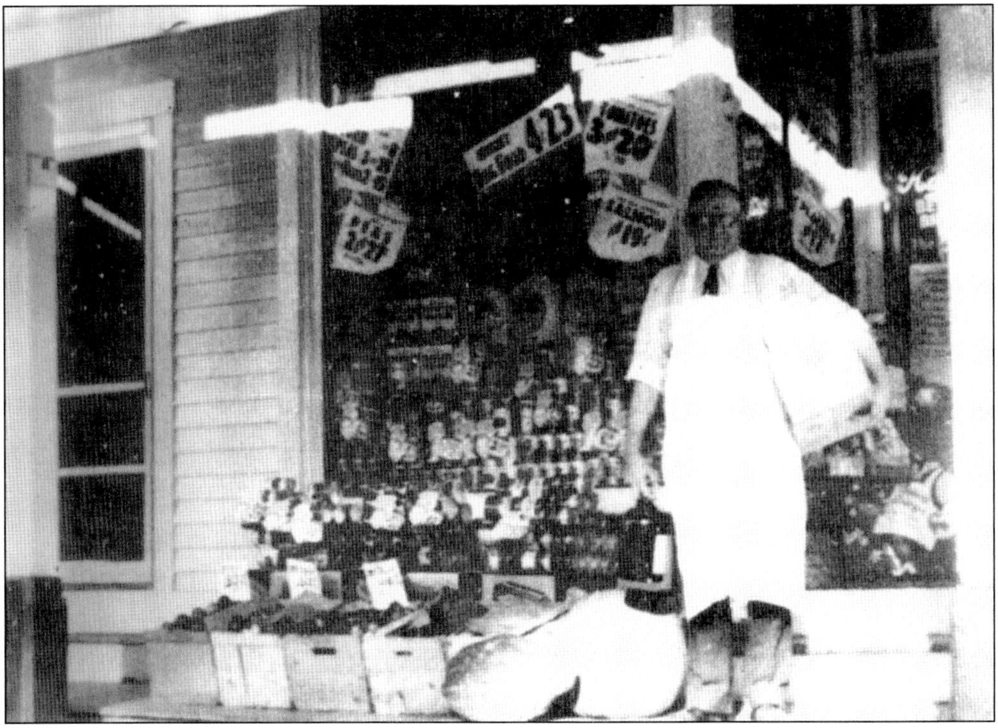

On Commercial Street, Lewis Barden operated an IGA with fresh produce, canned goods, and fresh meat and fish. It was a time when salmon cost 19¢ a pound, dog food was four cans for 23¢, and tomatoes were three for 20¢.

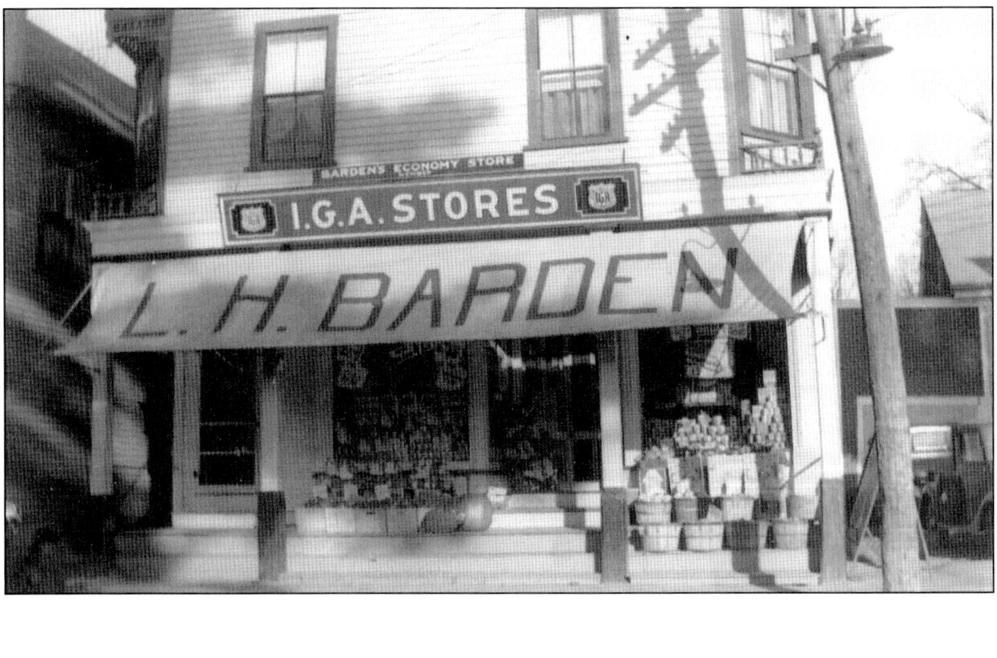

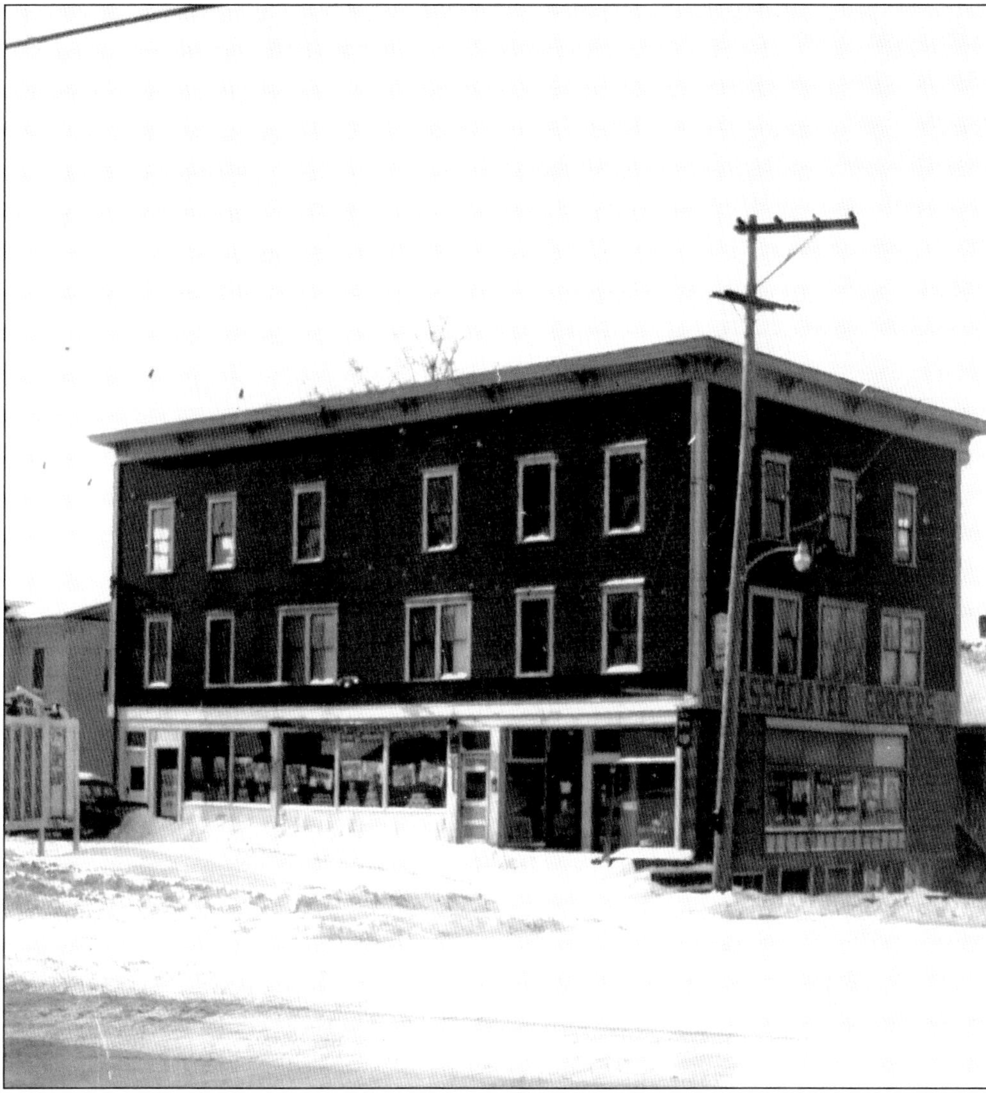

The Bardens eventually moved the business block on Warren Square where it was the center business in a three-business building. The property included a competing grocery and a barbershop. Bardens also sold dry goods and shoes. The Barden's business was sold in the early 1950s after the owners lost their son Lewis Jr., who had helped with the store for many years. Their daughter Laura Barden Crummett recalls working in the store as a teenager. The building stood until late in the 1990s, when it burned taking with it a grocery store and hair salon that later relocated to a new building on Main Street.

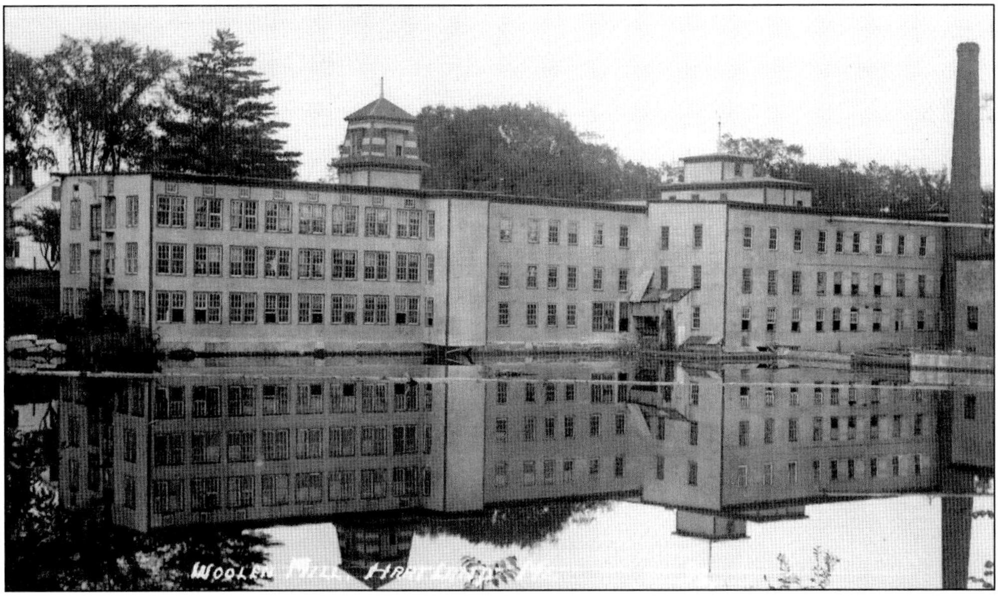

The center of the village has been dominated by a mill for much of its history, a woolen mill and later a tannery. The original Linn Woolen Mill began in 1860, owned by local benefactor Archibold Linn. It was sold to American Woolen in 1915, a company that lasted until shortly after the stock market crash of 1929, eventually closing in 1932. Meyer Kirstein opened the facility in 1936 as Hartland Tanning Company. It is the same operation that is Irving Tanning today.

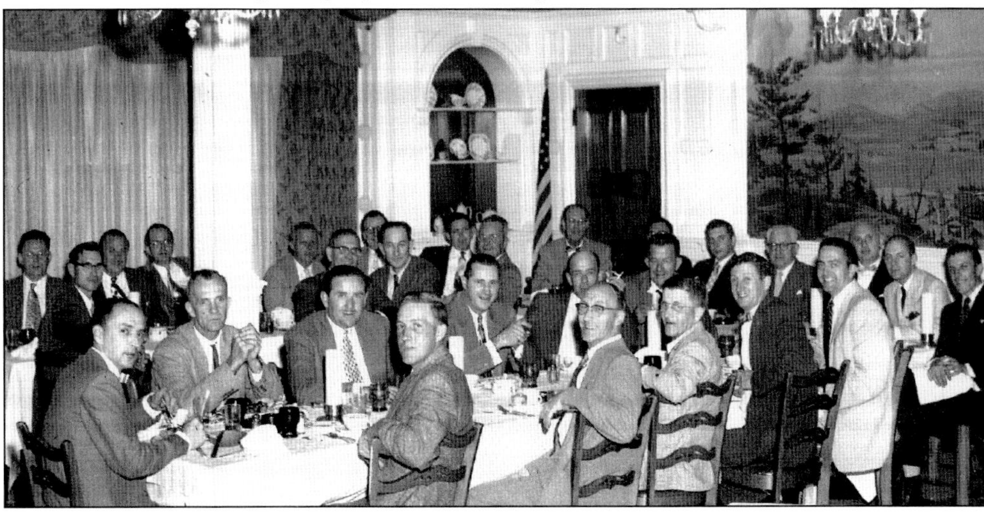

In 1936, a group of Hartland developers as Hartland Citizens Incorporated, sold the former mill property to Meyer Kirstein, and the Hartland Tanning Company was born. Kirstein is remembered for his dedication to the employees, often maintaining production despite a lack of orders, and enabling his crew to continue working. This image, taken at Pittsfield's famed Lancey House in 1957, captures a gathering of tannery employees including, from left to right in the back row, Don Pelkie, Elwood Allen, Tom Kelso, Earl Buker, Jim Krupsky, Rudolph Snow (?), Walter Sauer, Fred Libby, Ralph Hoyt, Dan Pelkie, Dan Connelly, Isadore Lerner, H. Kaplan, Meyer Kirstein, Emery Hunas, Joel Stacey, and Lindy Bradstreet; around the table, clockwise from left, Dick Webber, Arnie Cummings, Arthur Firestone, Jake Reifschneider, Don Randlett, Vaughn Chadbourne, Gabe Hikel, Don Hollister, Joseph Spencer, William Brawn, and Linwood Wheeler.

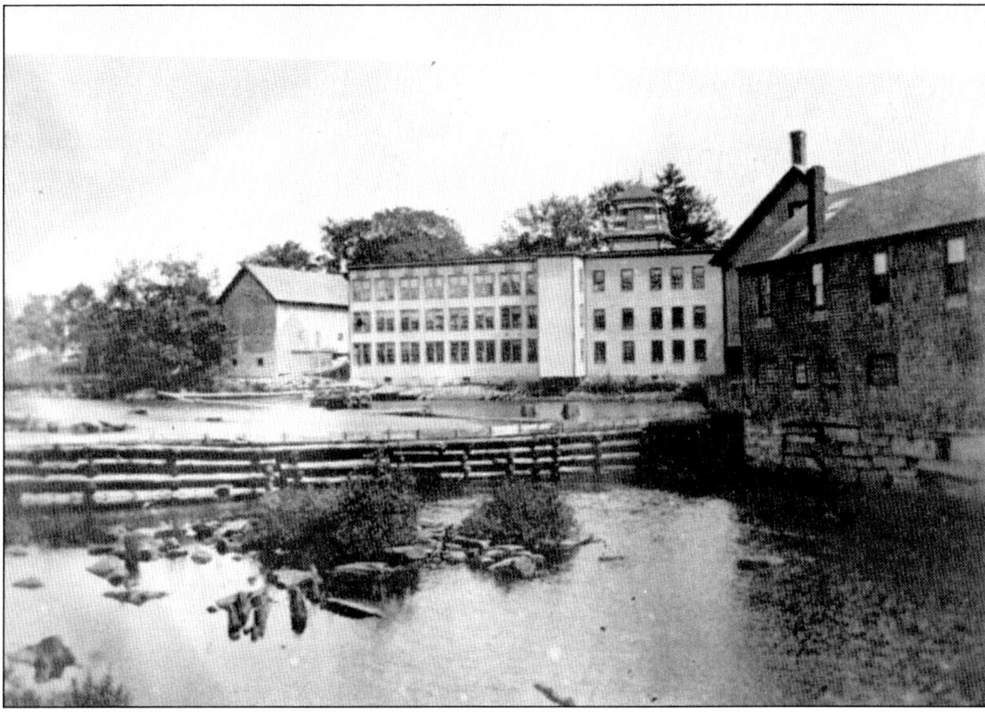

From the Main Street bridge, a wooden dam is visible as well as the expansive mill property upriver, seen here in the 1920s.

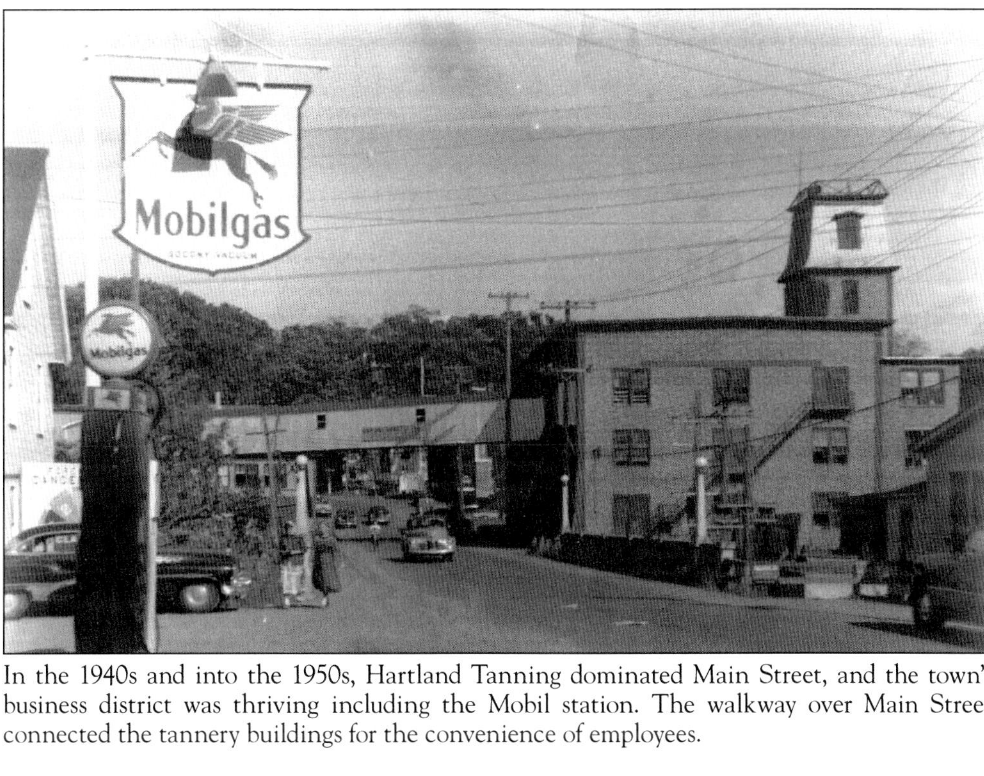

In the 1940s and into the 1950s, Hartland Tanning dominated Main Street, and the town's business district was thriving including the Mobil station. The walkway over Main Street connected the tannery buildings for the convenience of employees.

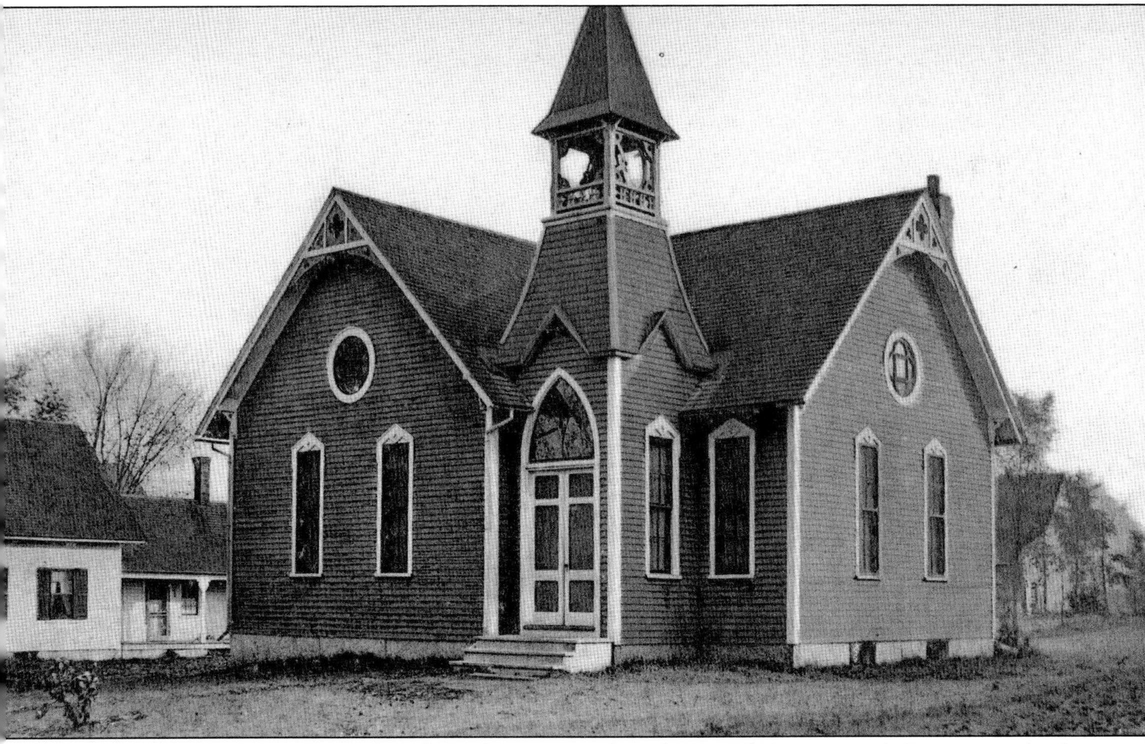

Grace Linn Methodist Church at the corner of Seekins and Commercial Streets was built in 1884 and dedicated to Grace Linn. Popular lore reports the only time she was present in the building was for her funeral.

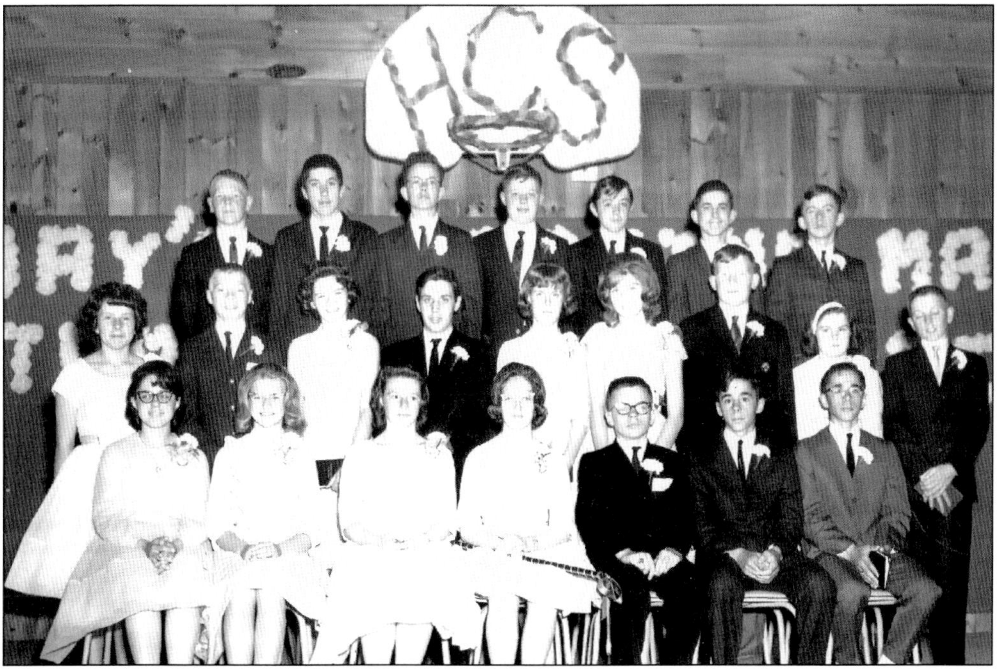

The eighth-grade graduating class at the Hartland Consolidated School in 1965 poses for a picture in the gymnasium. The room has since been turned into a cafeteria. Students from left to right are (first row) Mary Turcotte, Sharon Stedman, Jayne Lary, Linda Curtis, Gerald Morgan, Davis Gervais, and Donald Gervais; (second row) Wanda Lindsey, Bruce Taylor, Corinne Waldron, Dana Smith, Margaret Johnson, Erlene Mitchell, Scott Nutter, Carrie Ann Nichols, and Philip Ripton; (third row) Robert Merrow, Wayne Hewins, Dennis Stafford, Danny Gilbert, Timothy Munn, Michael Sherburne, and Ryan McDougal.

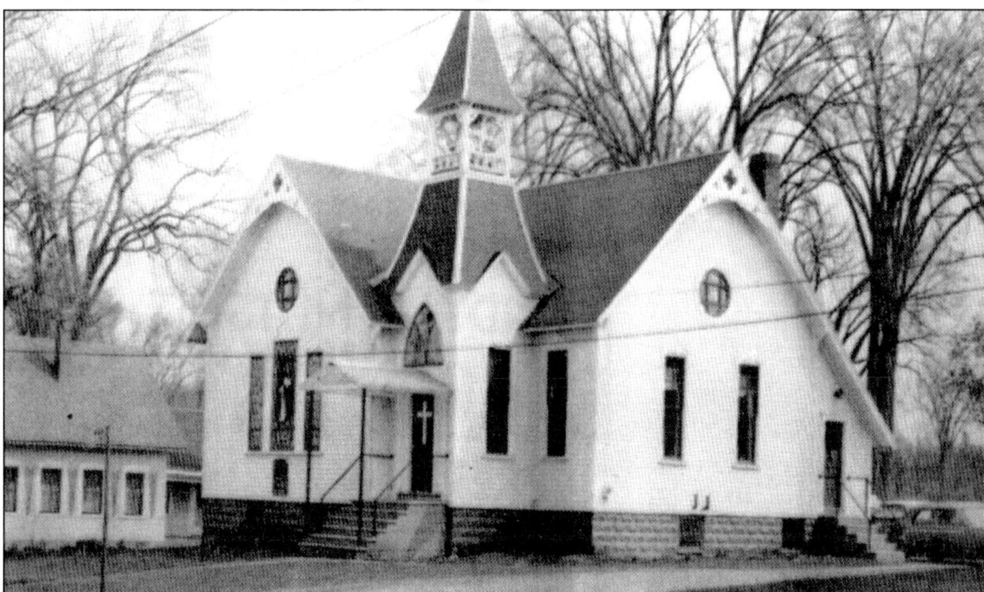

The Grace Linn Methodist Church at the corner of Commercial and Seekins Streets has been renovated and enlarged many times since its first construction in 1884.

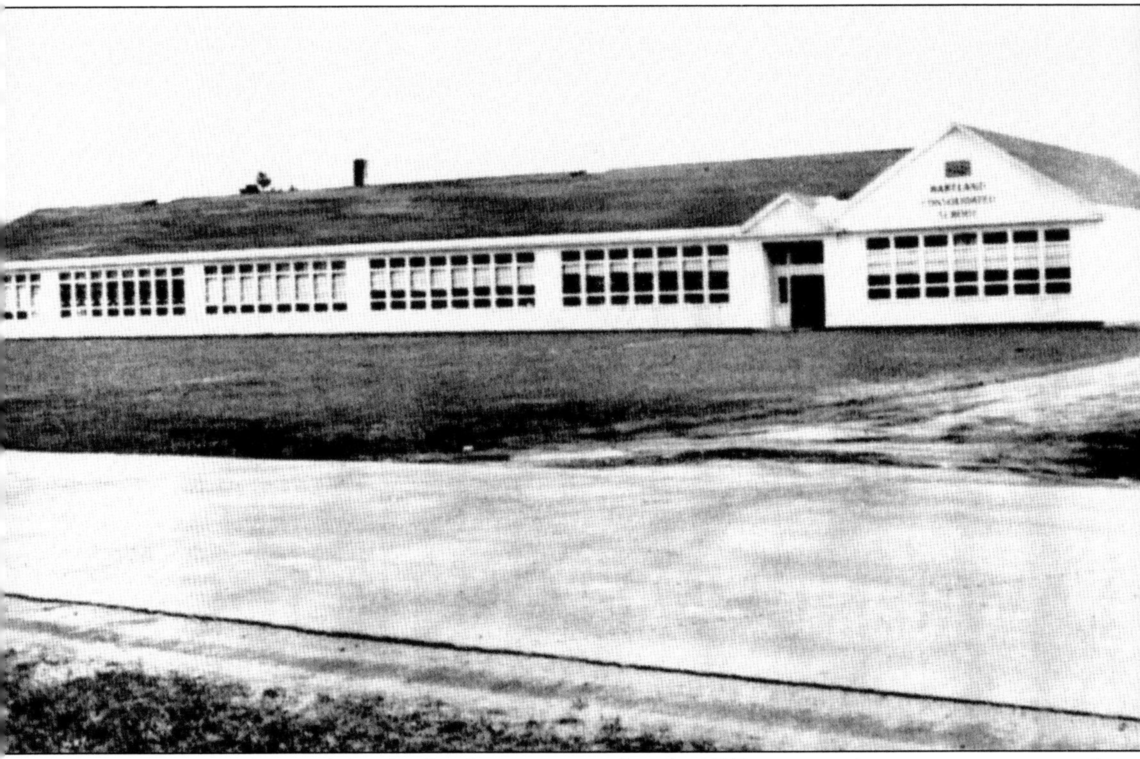

The Hartland Consolidated School, as it appeared in the 1950s, was similar to many constructed in that era across Maine. Energy concerns since that first construction has eliminated the numerous large windows. The building received a large addition in 1999 with a new gymnasium and classrooms.

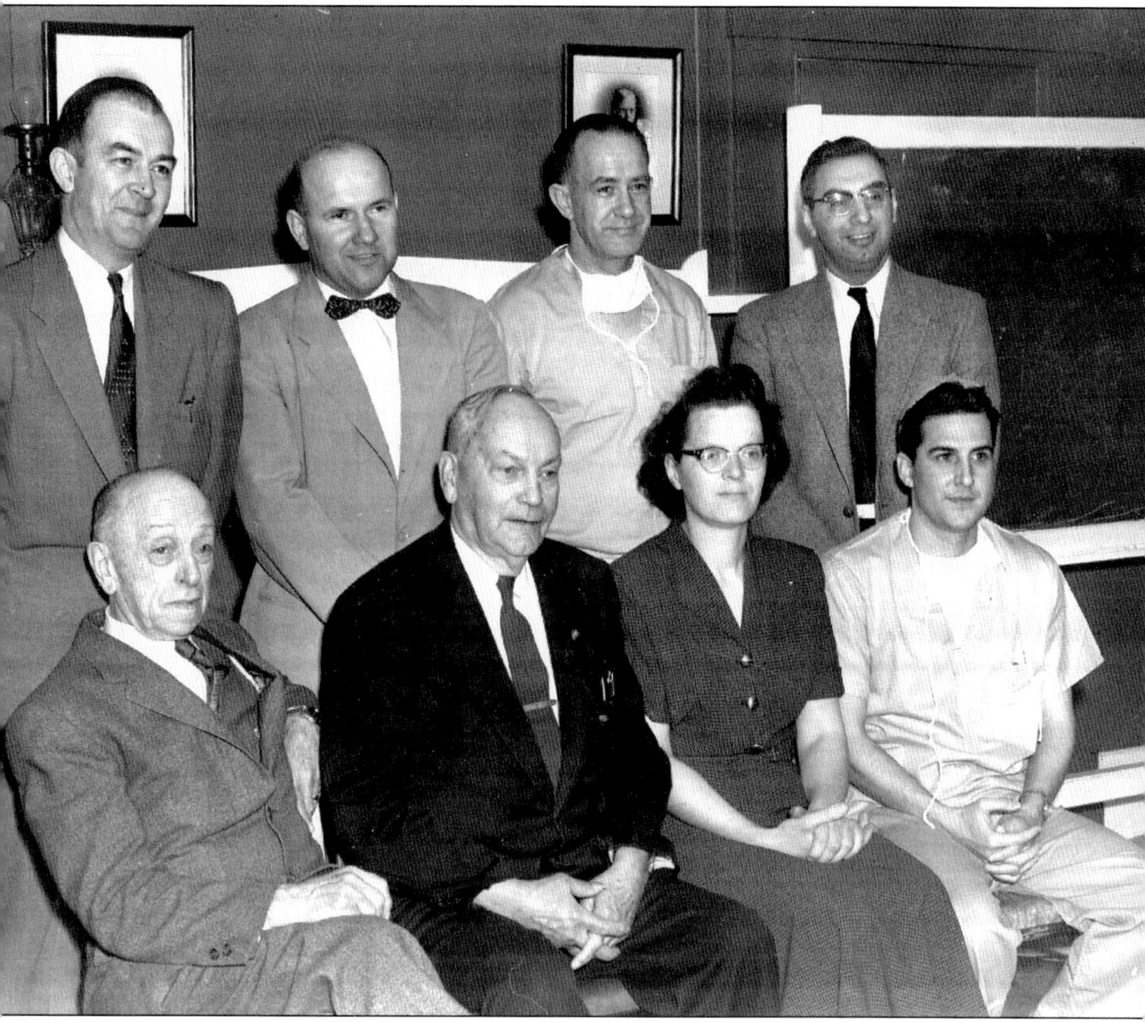

Eight doctors were serving Hartland and the surrounding area at Scott-Webb Hospital in 1956 including, from left to right, (first row) E. D. Humphrey, M. A. Webber, Marion Strickland, and Julio A. Gomez Rangel; (second row) P. W. Burke, R. F. Gloor, P. R. Briggs, and E. R. Nawfel. All the doctors were medical doctors except Nawfel, who was a doctor of dental medicine.

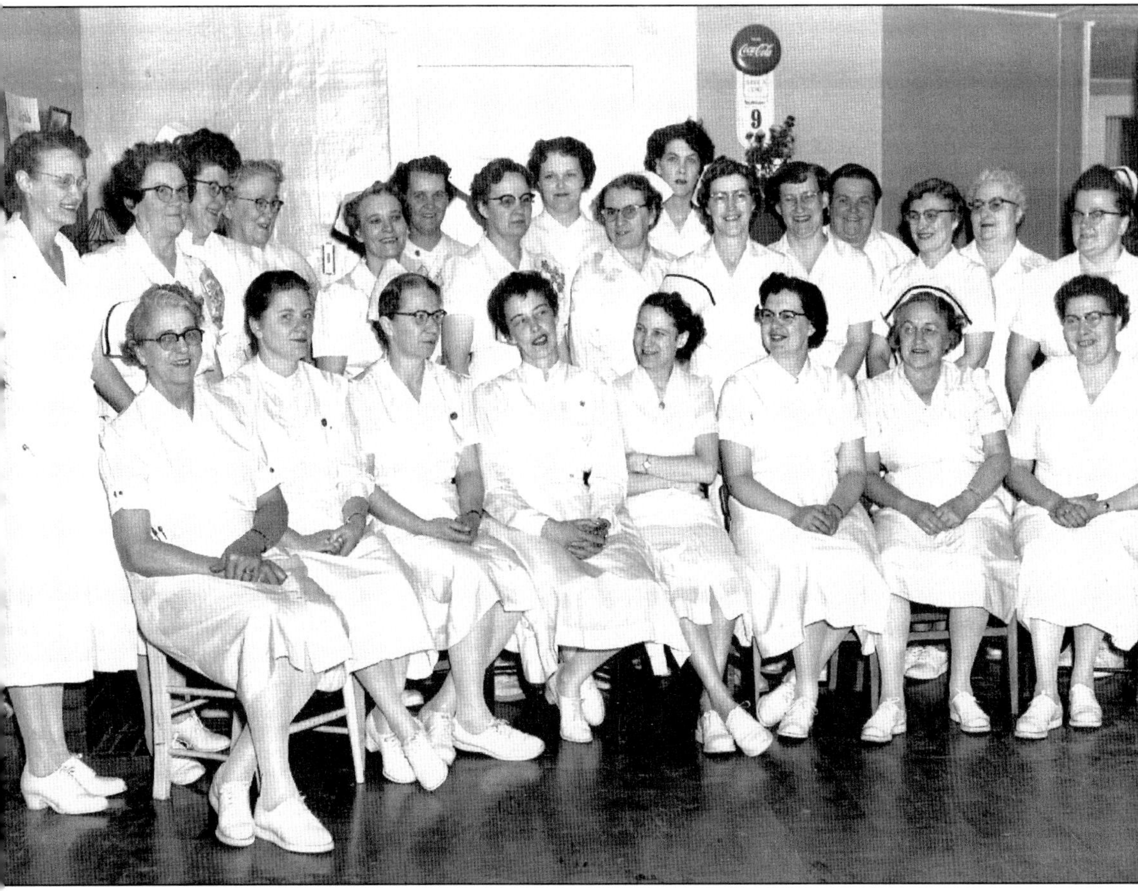

Scott-Webb Hospital was the only hospital within a 25-mile radius for many years until Pittsfield's Sebasticook Valley Hospital opened in the 1960s. Most any nurse who resided in the area worked at Scott-Webb Hospital at one time, including several members of this group in 1956. From left to right are (first row) Grace Webber, Ida Briggs, Emily Spear, Madeline "Tillie" Ball, Arlene St. Peter, Eunice Harper, Bessie Nickse, and Lucille Hanson; (second row) Grace Marble, Bessie Field, Erline Humphrey, Annie Adams, Evelyn Nichols, Thelma Brooks, Rhoda Nelson, Ruth Tibbetts, Irma Stedman, Ada Randlett, and Norma Temple; (third row) Phyllis Woodman, Glenice Hanson, Marilyn Merrow, Augusta Hayden, and Ellen Kelley.

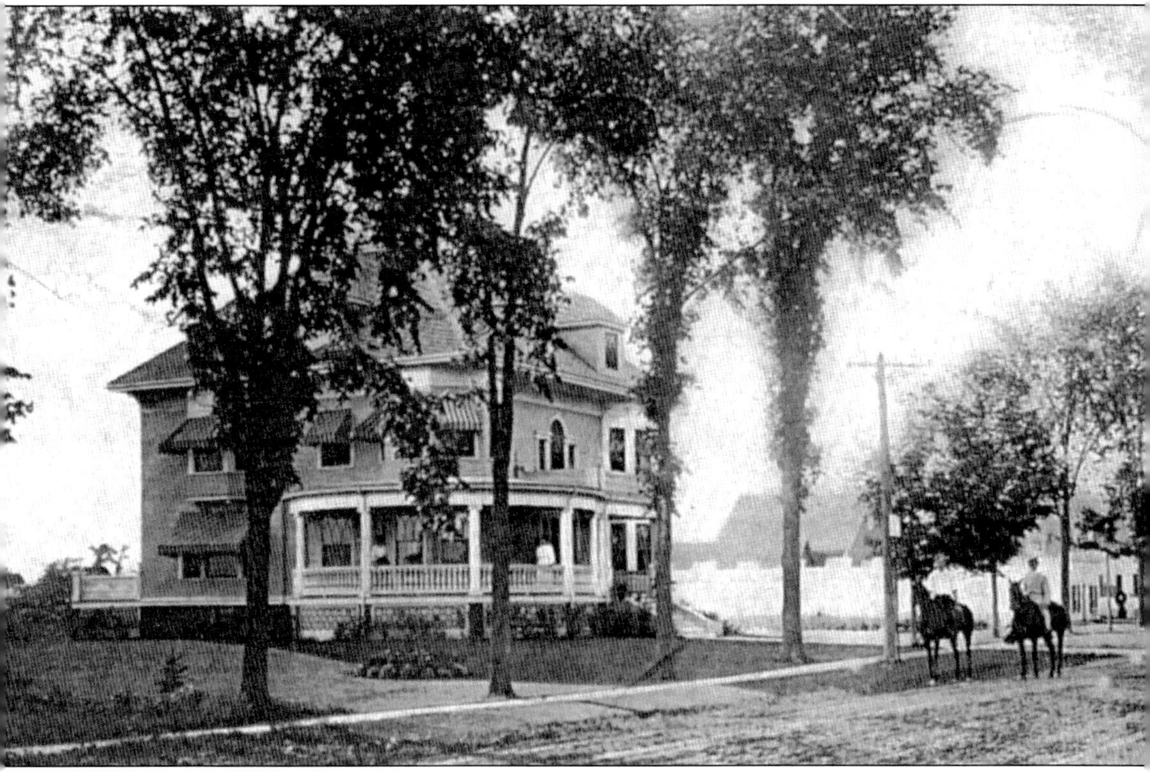

The Mary Fuller residence on Elm Street was a grand home in its early days. Fuller was a descendant of Hartland's original settlers. Her daughter Dr. Jenny Fuller, an early advocate of women's rights, also lived on Elm Street. Today the Fuller residence houses a boarding home for the developmentally disabled. The street was true to its name in the early part of the 20th century, with many stately elms.

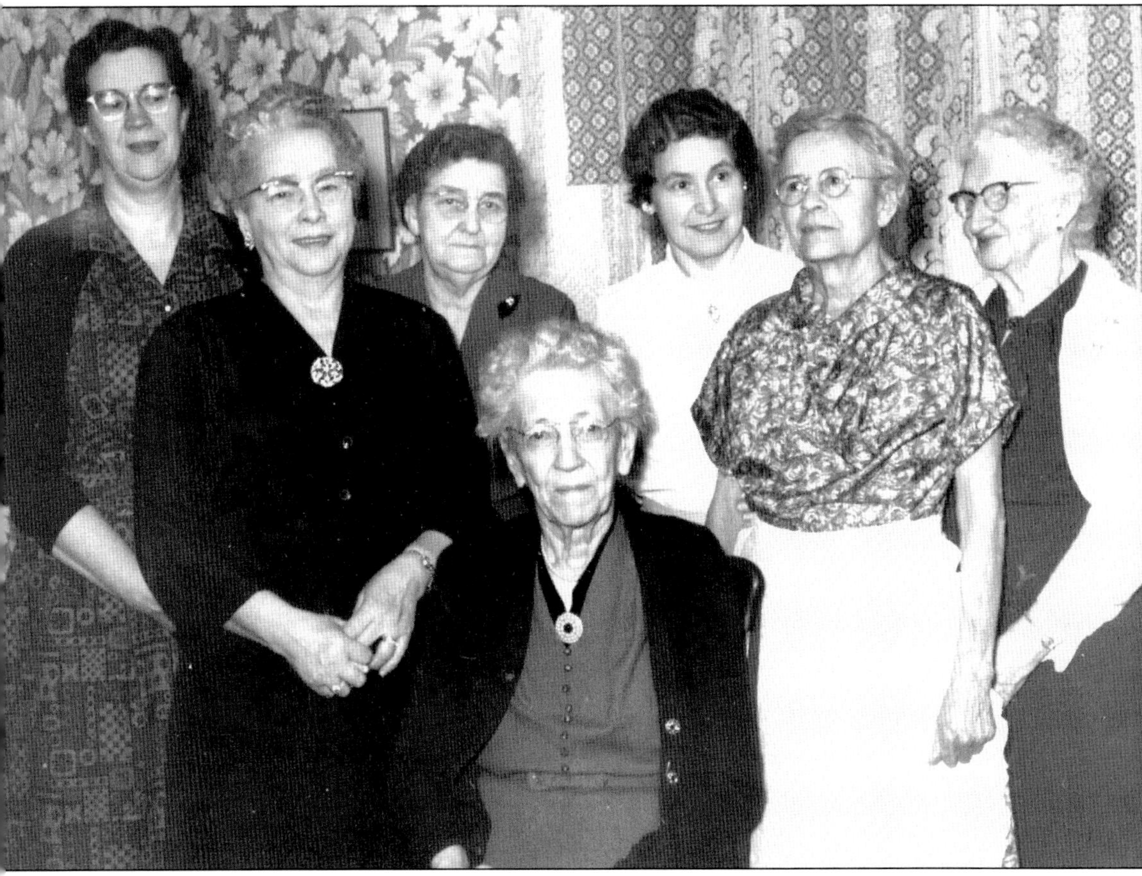

The Rebekah Lodge is the women's division of the Independent Order of Odd Fellows. Past noble grands of the Hartland Rebekah Lodge gathered on this occasion to celebrate the 87th birthday of Mae King, seated. Standing from left to right are Beulah Huff, Leta Libby, Alice Randlett, Elizabeth Fisher, Vanessa Pickens, and Mary Coston Smith.

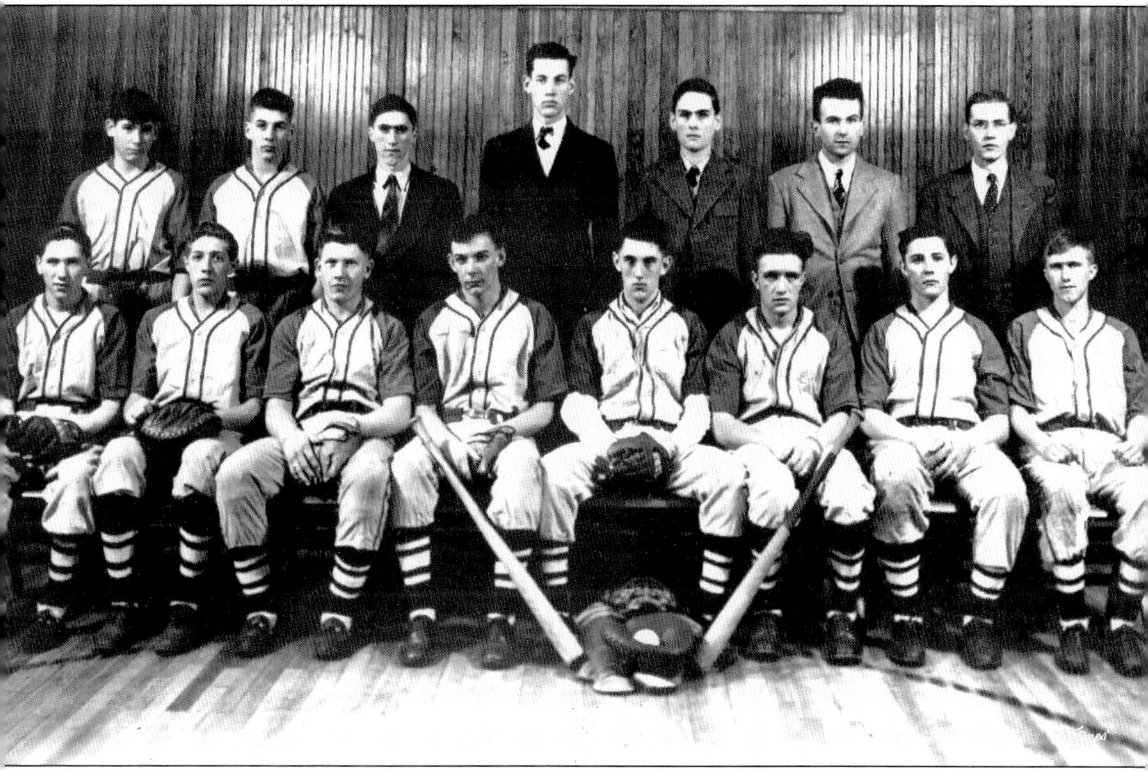

In the 1940s, this group represented Hartland Academy in baseball including, from left to right, (first row) Paul Neal, Linwood Wheeler, James Snow, Kenneth Pelkey, Arthur Chapman, Edmund Seekins, Raymond Lucas, and Philip Estes; (second row) Halver Stedman, Lloyd Cookson, manager Ivan Estes, Roger Jordan, unidentified, Stanley Dyer, and Richard Pippin.

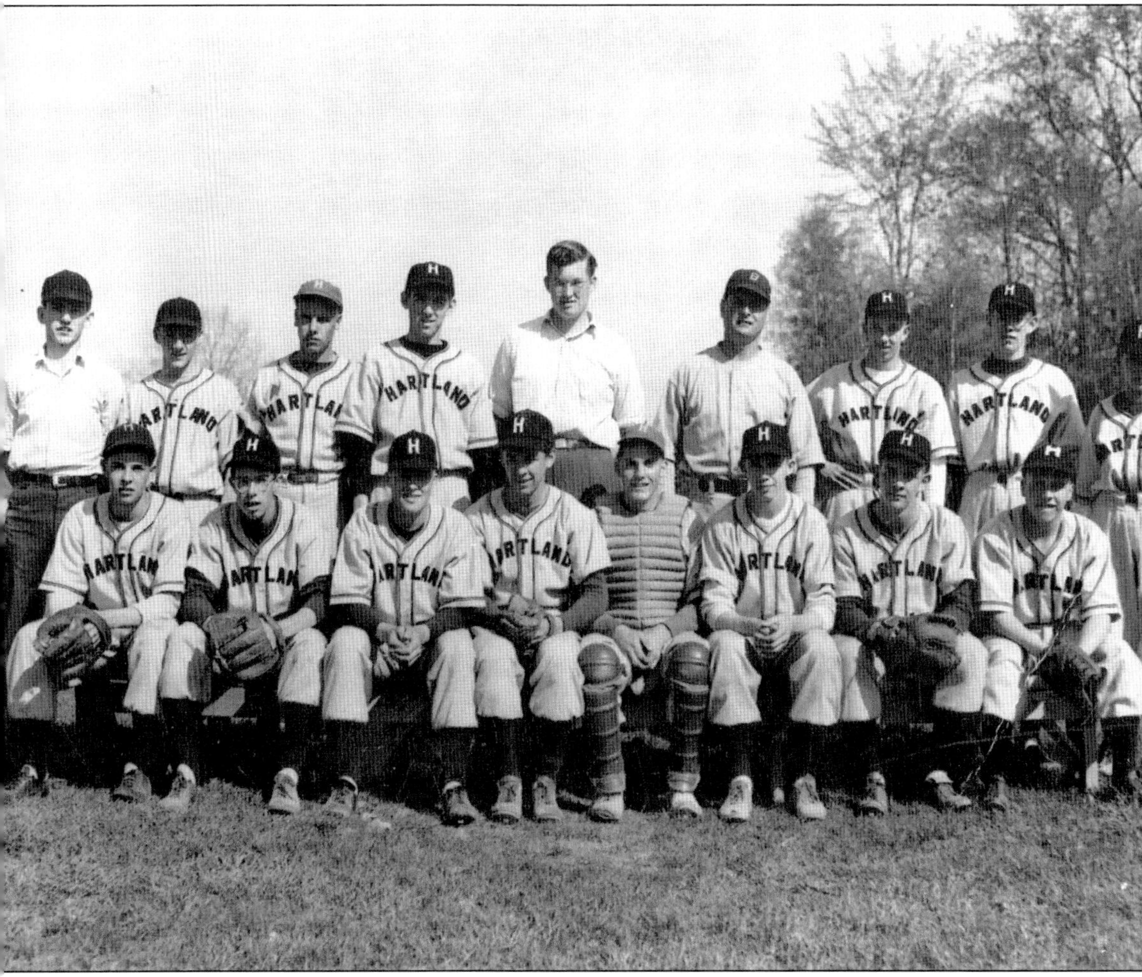

A Hartland Academy baseball team is seen here in the 1950s. From left to right are (first row) Dan Snowman, Ken Southard, Jim Jamieson, Tom Williams, Blaine Tibbetts, Ted Strombeck, Ray Martin, and Pete Taylor; (second row) assistant manager Phil Gardner, Bob Lucas, Donnie Deering, Vaughn Stedman, manager David Huff, coach Hank Washburn, Phil Emery, Clark Connelly, and Izzy Martin.

Three

Castle Harmony
The History of Wild Goose

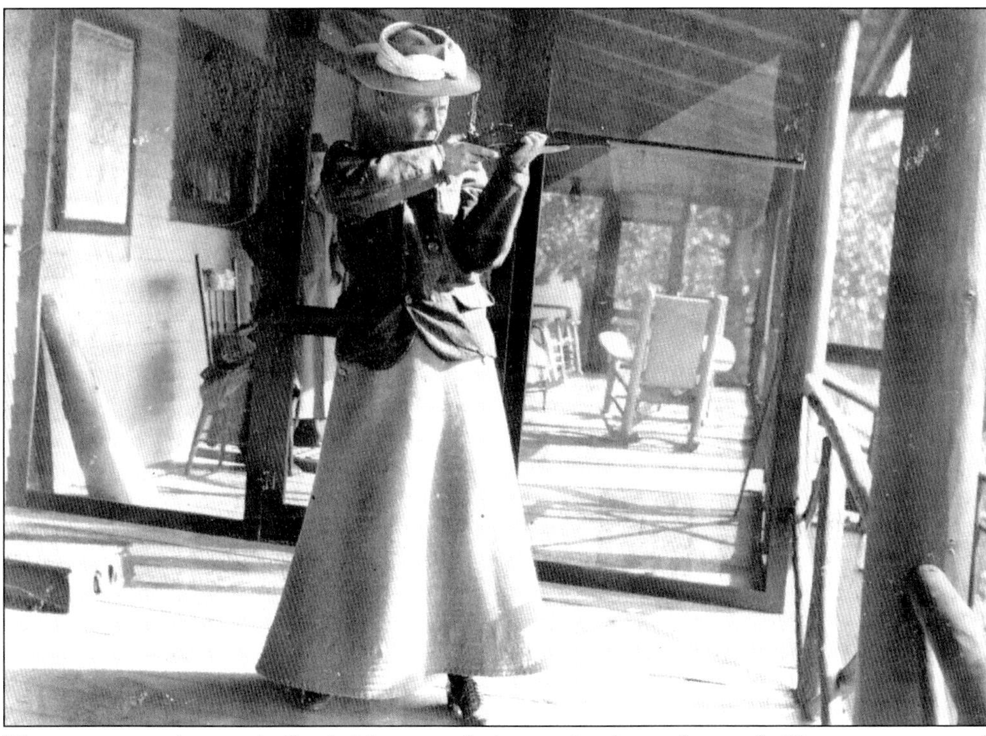

The sportsmen that made Castle Harmony their vacation home for nearly 70 years were not all men, as this image of Mrs. E. T. Bigelow in October 1902 demonstrates, as she takes aim from the porch of the wooden castle. The castle and the cove, called the Bay of Galashiels, were named in honor of Archibald Linn, owner of the woolen mill at Hartland, who helped the original Madawaska Club find a site for the members to construct a new hunting lodge at the outlet of Main Stream, also known as the west branch of the Sebasticook River.

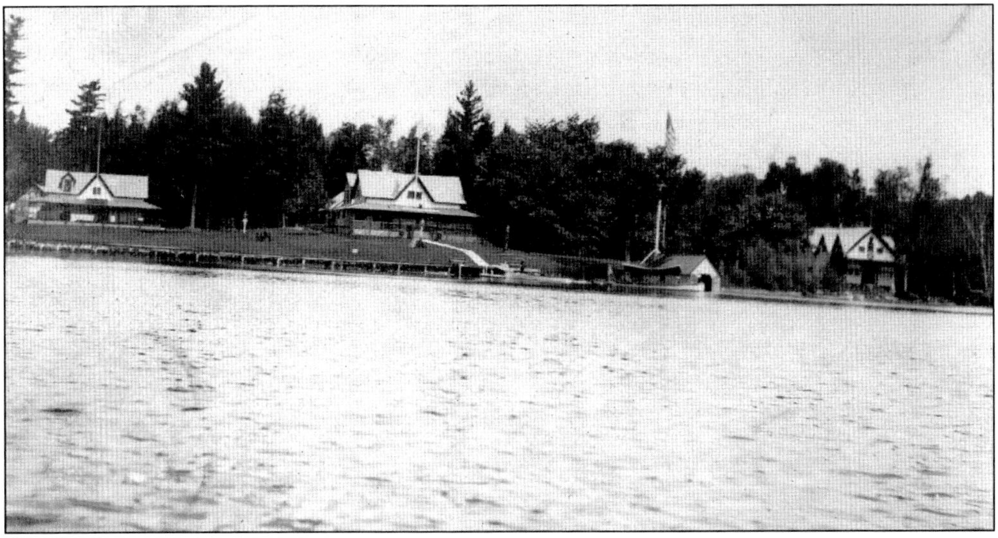

Castle Harmony has been a landmark on the Harmony shore of Great Moose Lake. It was founded in 1873 when the Madawaska Club outgrew its quarters in Pittsfield, nearly 20 miles south. The men's hunting and fishing club would stay in Pittsfield's Lencey House and use a building outside of town as headquarters for their sporting pursuits. The "men of means" from Massachusetts needed more land and wildlife to continue their regular retreats, eventually including whole families in their travels. The building was the main "castle," several more buildings were added to accommodate their growing numbers and the staff it took to maintain their luxury-living style. Members commented the search for new land was a "wild goose chase." The name stuck, and the Wild Goose Club was born. The club would occupy the land and buildings into the 1930s.

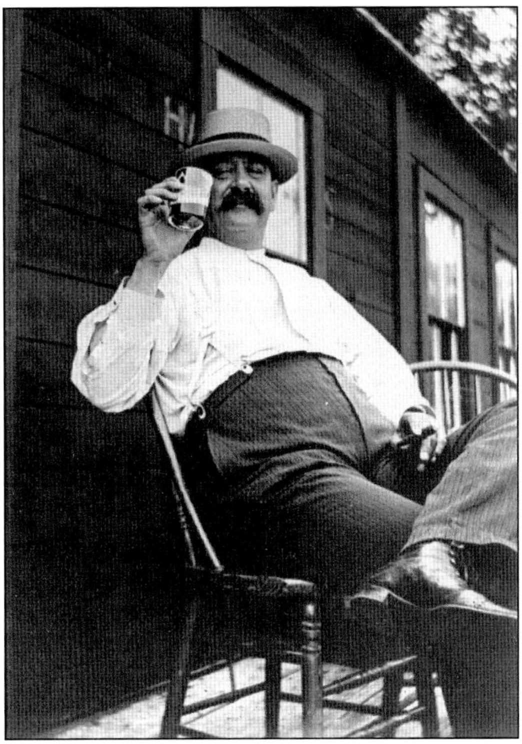

George W. Hastings apparently inherited the title commodore, holding the title at Castle Harmony and at the Commodore Club on the Hartland shore. All the members of the club would hold a title or rank in the Wild Goose Club. George Hastings is believed to be the son of Henry Hastings who first came in search of the new land in Harmony.

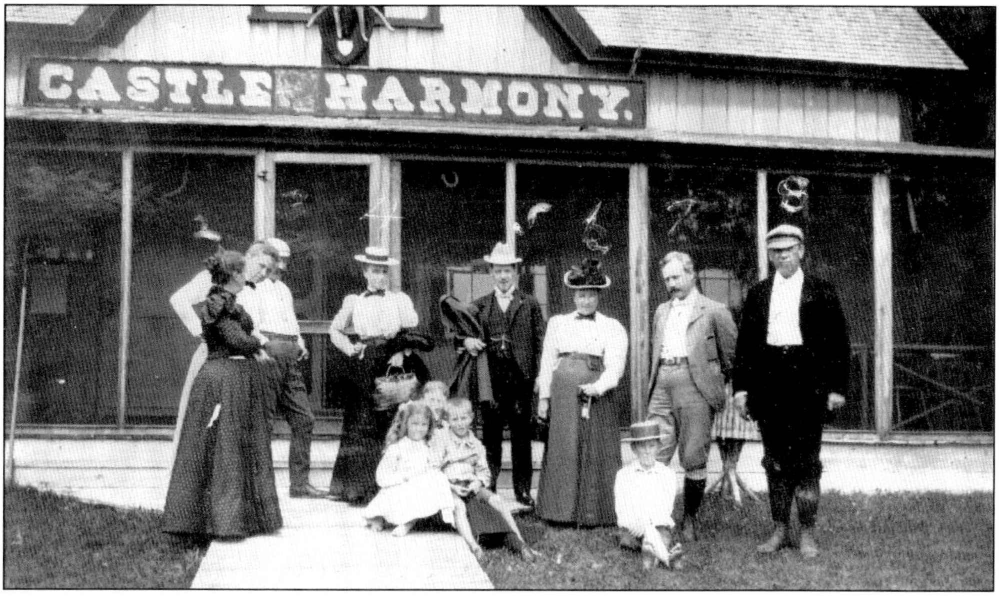

Posing under the Castle Harmony sign on the porch steps was an ongoing tradition for the visiting members of the Wild Goose Club. In 1898, this group demonstrates the styles worn at the club in that time period. All of the photographs left behind by this group were faithfully numbered and identified. Members present include (1) Mrs. Renfrew, (2) Mrs. Hall (3) T. VanValkenburgh, (4) Mrs. Davidson, (5) H. T. Hayward, (6) Mrs. A. M. Silsbee, (7) William Hall, and (8) James Renfrew. The children are not identified.

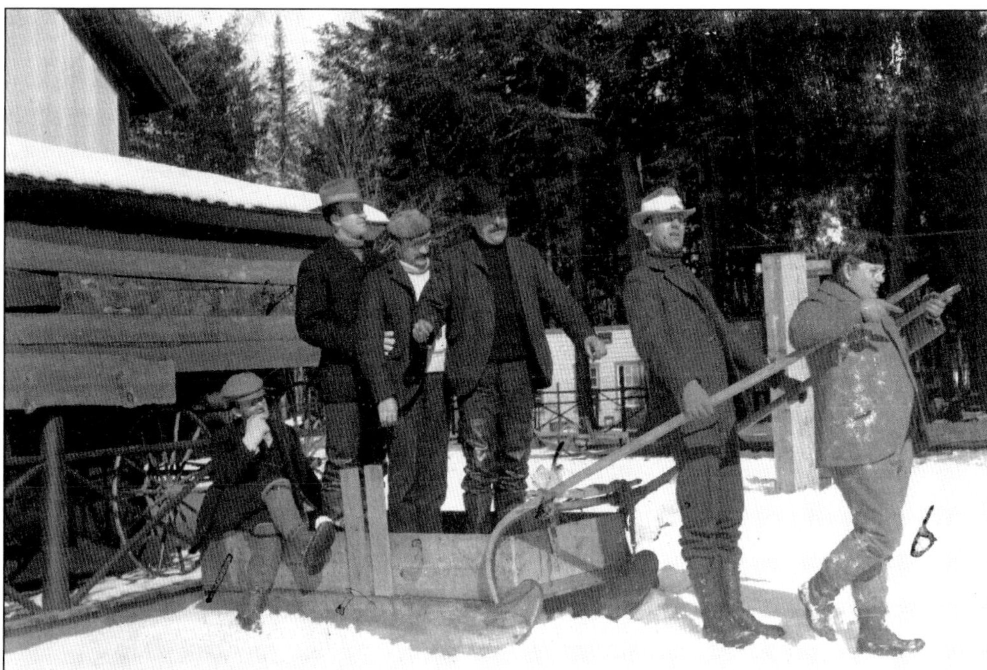

Club members were not above "horsing" around as this bit of play with one of the club's sleds shows in March 1902. Members involved in the horseplay include, from left to right, Charles H. Warren, L. Williams, R. L. Hall, B. W. Wells, C. H. Cole Jr., and W. T. Jeremy.

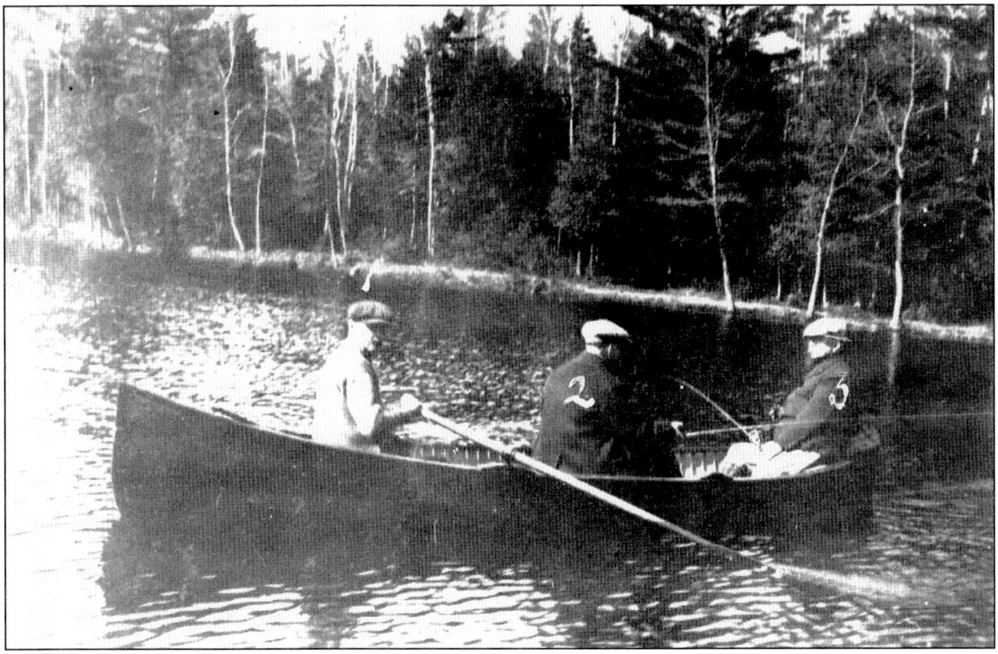

Canoeing in May 1921 was a far cry from the canoeing the second generation of Wild Goose Club canoeists discovered when the aged hunting camp became a boys camp from 1955 to 1995. Canoeists in the earlier expeditions include, from left to right, Charles Ricker, H. A. White, and C. F. Murphy.

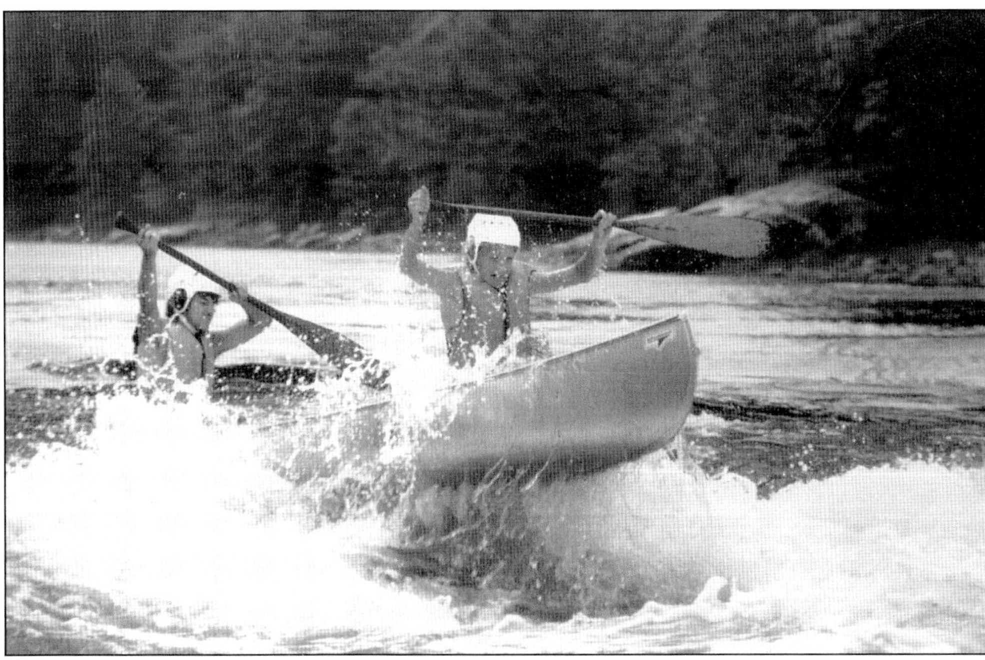

The second generation of Wild Goose Club participants at the Wild Goose for Boys, which operated for 40 years on the site, found a faster canoeing experience.

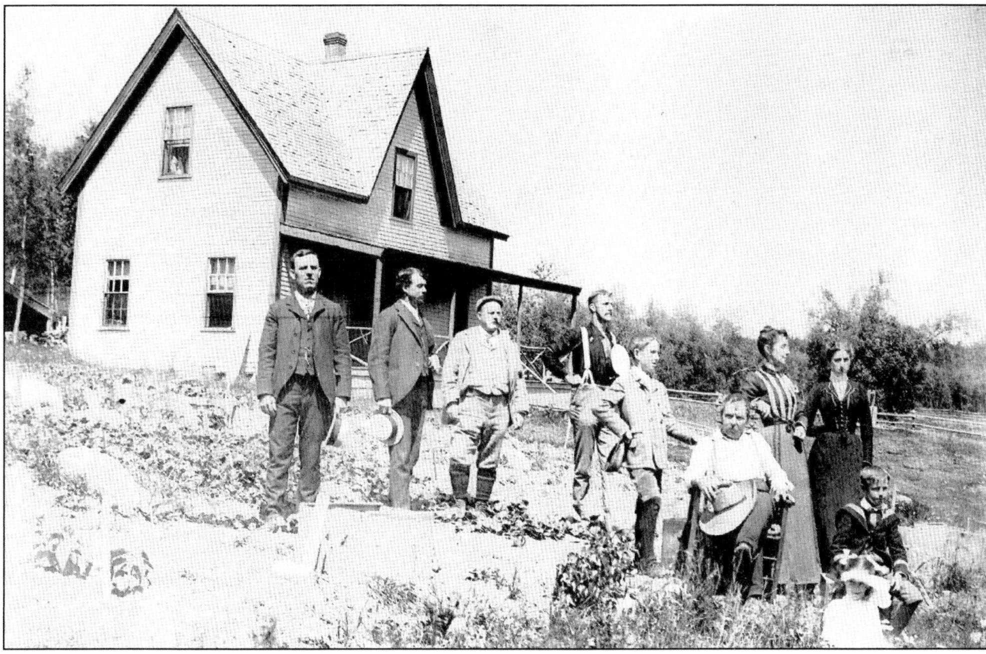

Around 1903, Castle Harmony was undergoing some renovations. To accommodate the work crew and some of the castle guests, the club used a guest house on Castle Road. Staying at the house from left to right are Andrew Curtin, ? Fraser, G. F. Manning, F. A. Linnell, Clyde Harvey, Arthur Harvey (seated), Mrs. Harvey, and Emma Merrill. The younger children in the front left are not identified. Curtin and Fraser were reported to be from Medford, Massachusetts, and were installing plumbing at the castle.

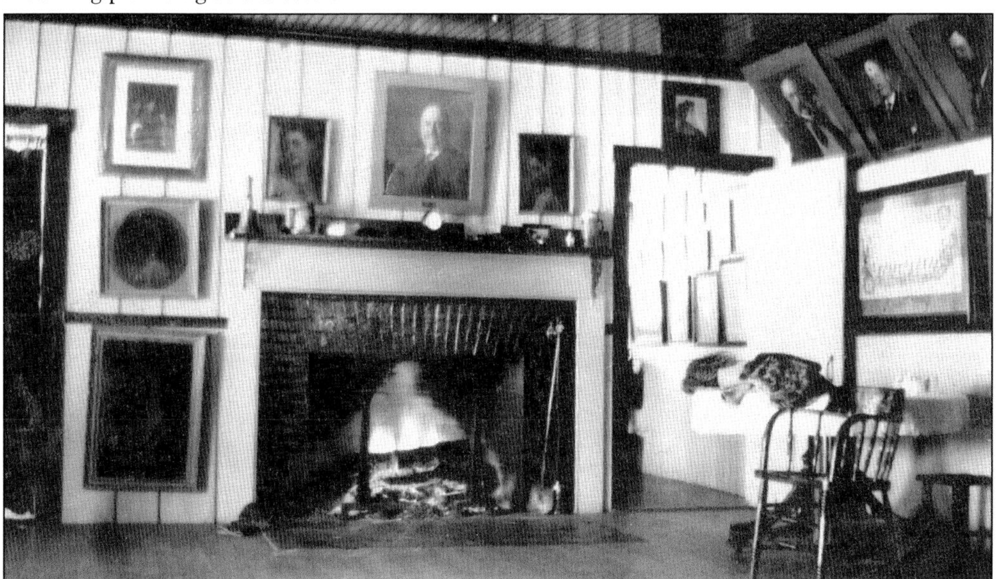

The interior of the main lodge at Castle Harmony has changed very little since its original construction. Many of the old portraits of the early club members still hang and were enjoyed by hundreds of boys who attended the Wild Goose for Boys camp. Newer pictures of the many summers with boys have been added to the walls.

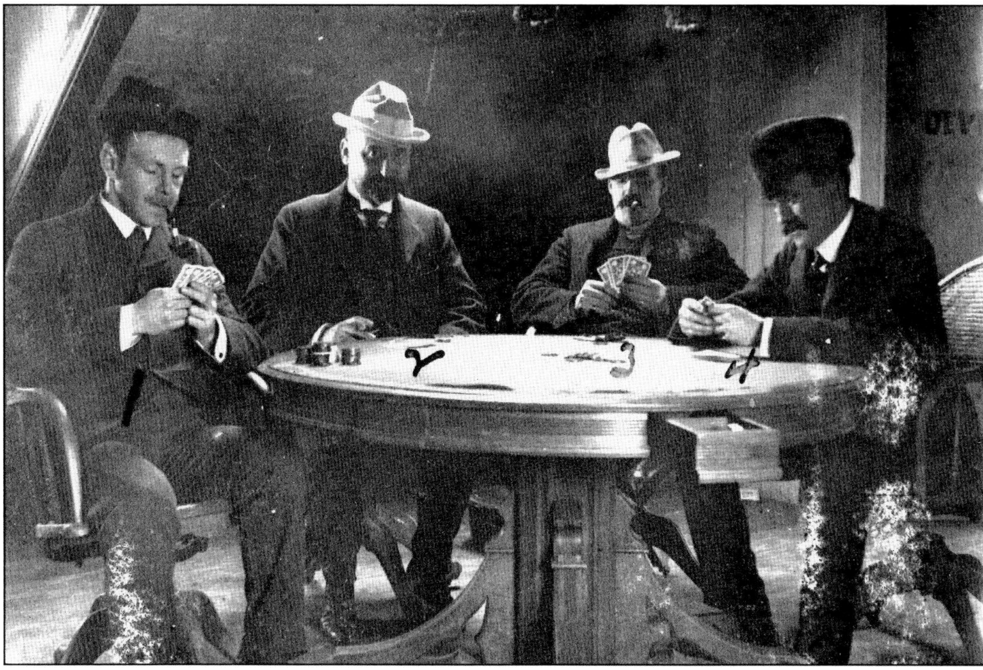

The library at Castle Harmony still holds the same library table used by many generations, beginning in March 1901 with a poker game including, from left to right, C. B. Gleason, George W. Hastings, George F. Parker, and R. L. Hall.

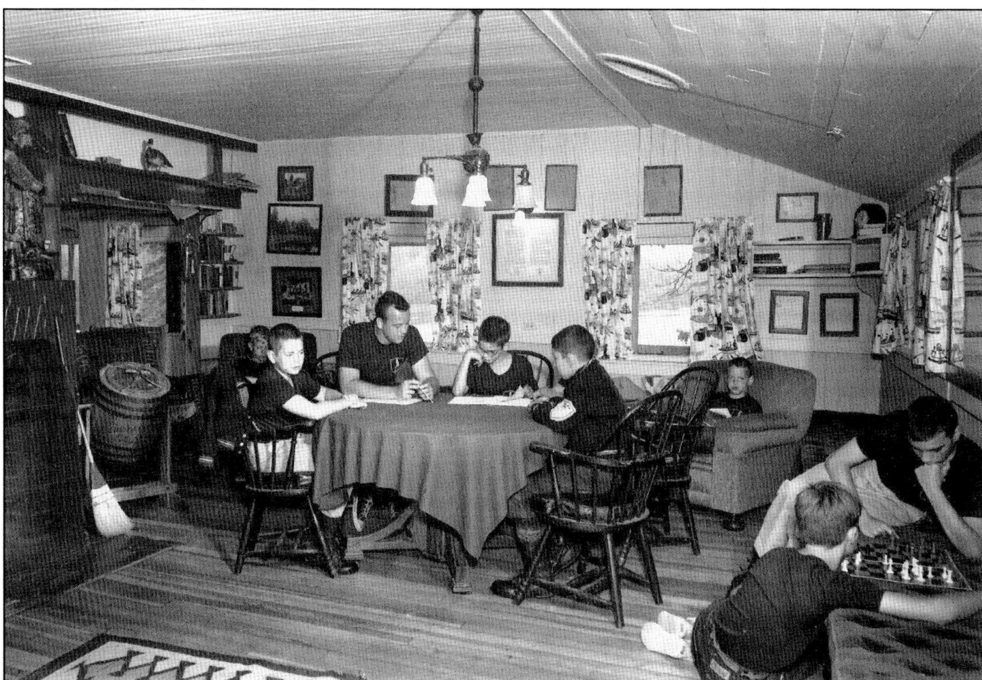

By the 1960s, poker was not a game appropriate for the library of Wild Goose for Boys. In this group, longtime counselor Charley Martin works with some boys at the library table while others play games.

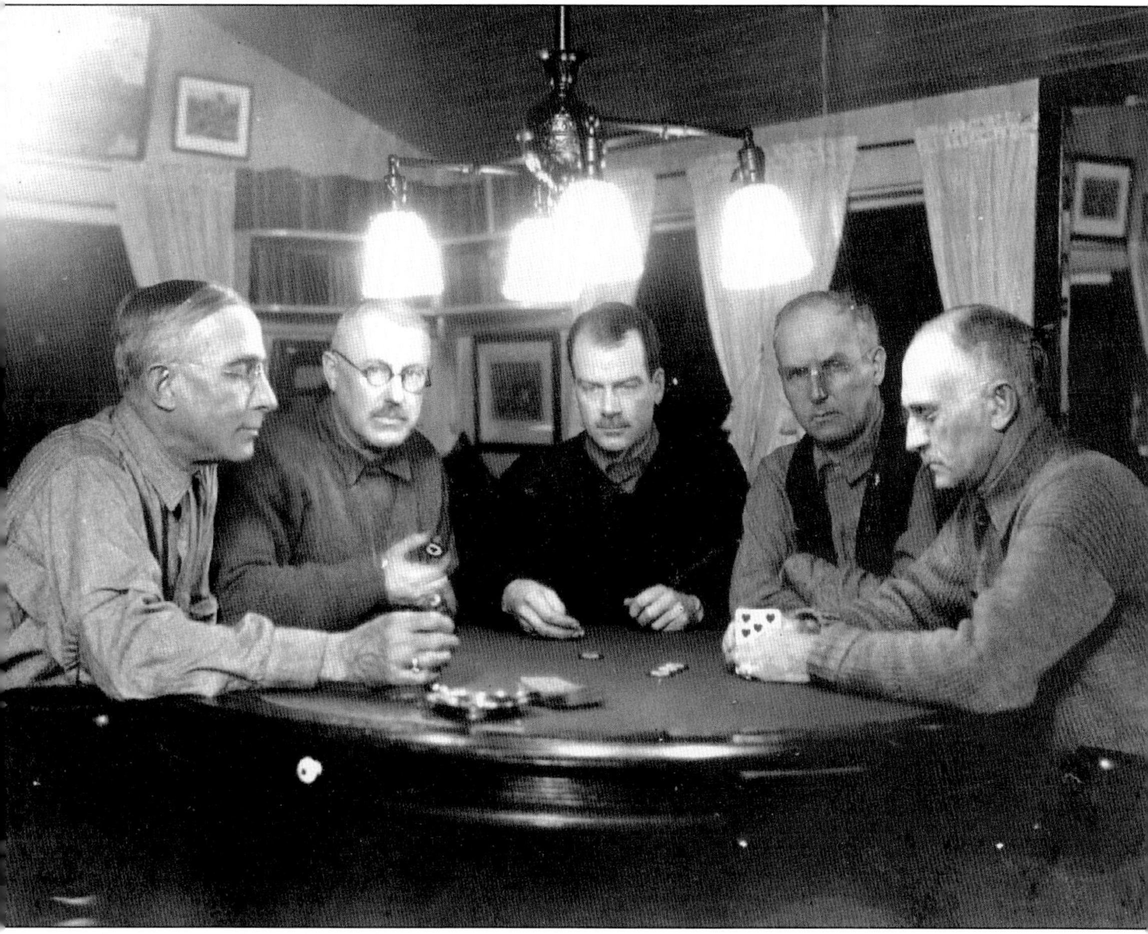

In February 1921, the poker tradition was ongoing for members of the original Wild Goose Club in the library at the same table. This group included, from left to right, Arthur Boardman, J. W. May, I. F. Marshall, Dr. C. B. R. Chase, and R. L. Hall with the addition of some brighter lighting for the time period. Electricity reportedly came to the castle around 1921.

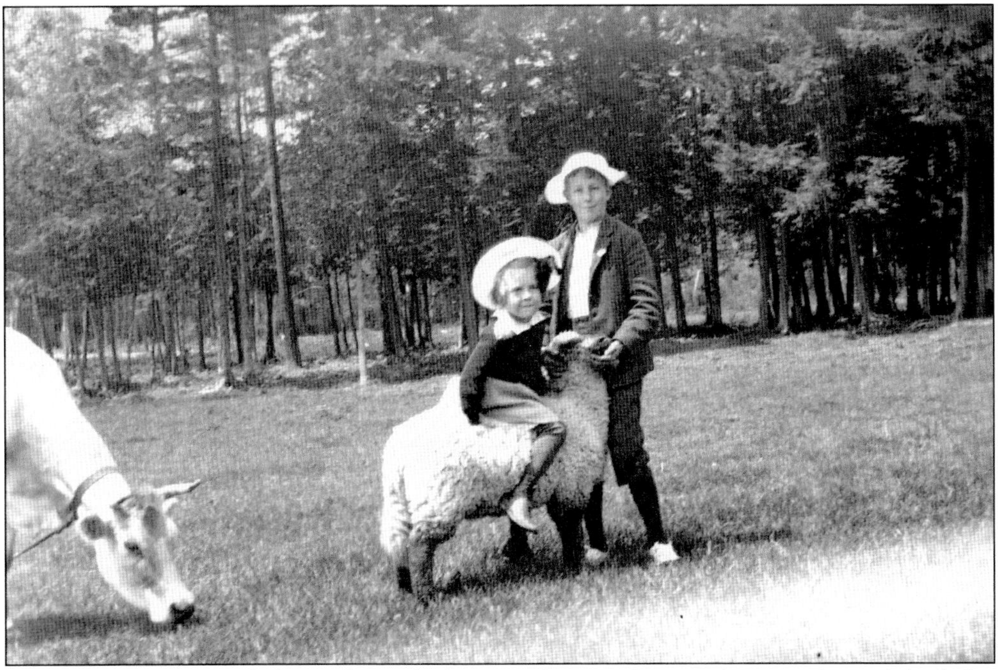

To maintain an active lodge with ample dairy products and meat, the caretakers of the lodge kept cows and sheep, a garden, and other animals. The animals were too much for Betty Bigelow and Clyde Harvey to pass up in 1903.

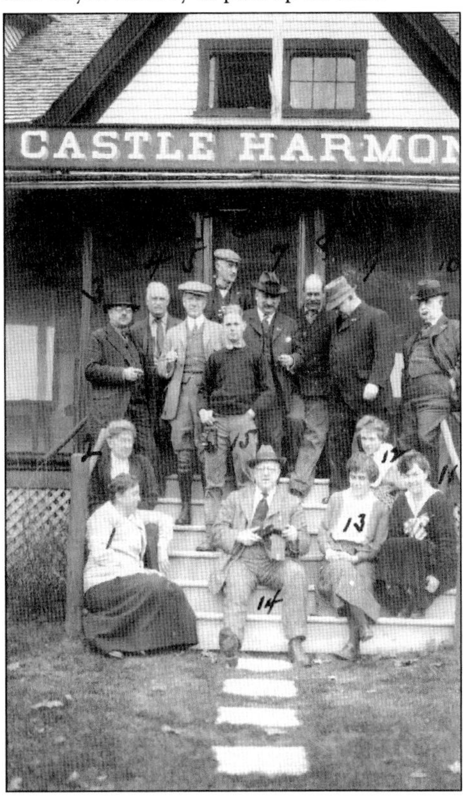

By 1917, members had aged and new members likely added to the club as they again posed for a picture. The faithful photographer again numbered and identified the members including, from left to right and clockwise, (1) Mrs. Meigs, (2) Mrs. Rice, (3) S. P. Snow, (4) V. H. Hall, (5) William Sutton, (6) R. L. Hall, (7) G. W. Hastings, (8) E. T. Bigelow, (9) G. Rueter, (10) Harry Rice, (11) Mrs. Keyes, (12) Barbara Hall, (13) Betty Bigelow, and (14) Dr. Meigs.

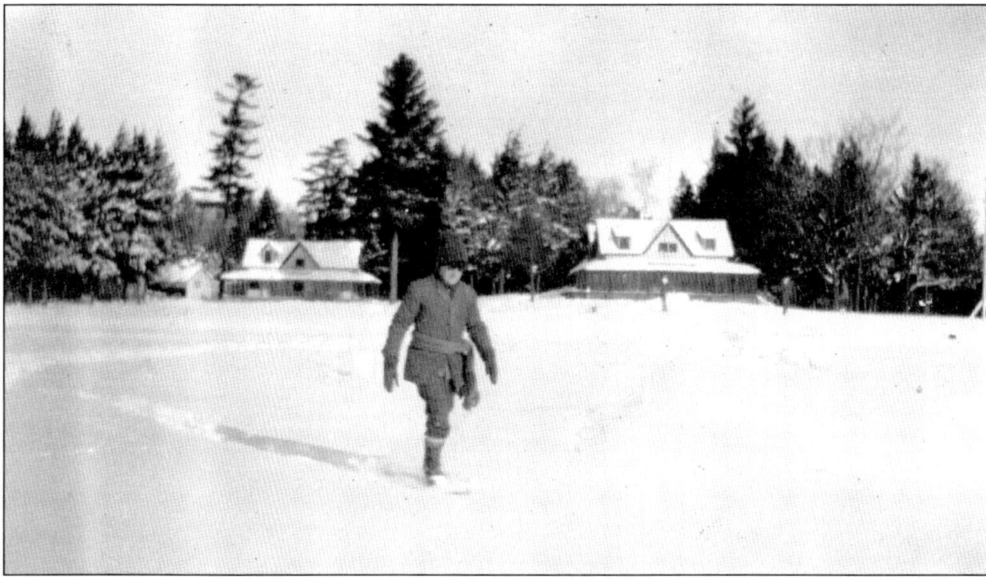

Winter weather and an iced-over cove did not deter the members from making the trip to Castle Harmony and the wilds of Maine, as this January 1917 picture shows. The ice allowed more access to the lake and ice fishing as well as traveling from the Hartland train station or the club's Wild Goose landing on the Harmony-Mainstream line. Early in the history of the club, members traveled by a Concord coach from the rail line at Pittsfield. It was not until 1886 that members could transfer to the Hartland line. Once in Hartland, they could travel by boat up the river and lake, but it would be another 15 years before the line was extended to Mainstream village following the east shore of the lake. The additional line shortened the boat ride with the use of a special rail stop to accommodate club traffic near Northeast Cove.

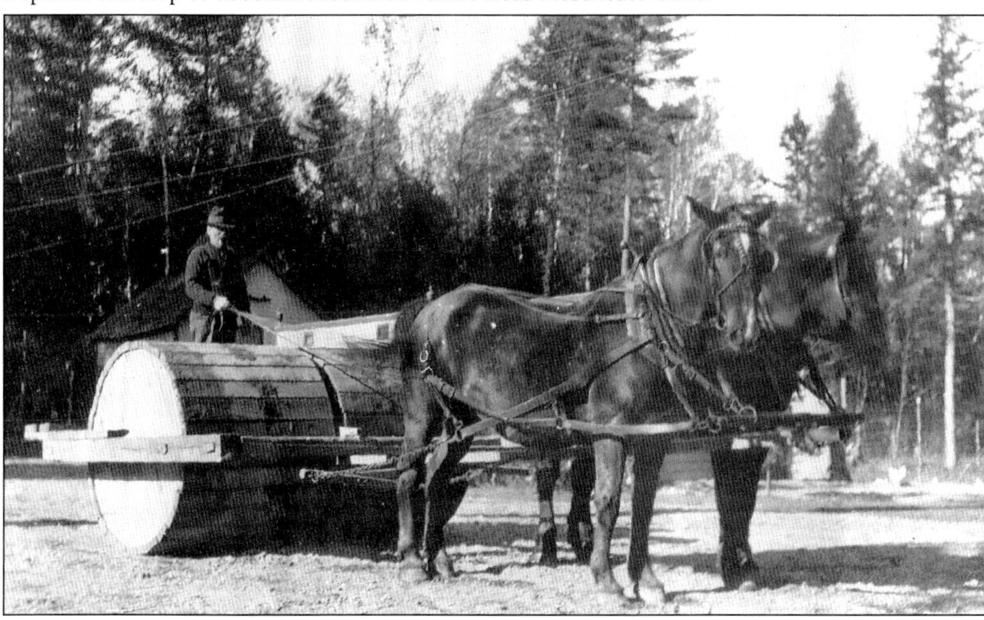

Ivan Lombard was the Harmony road commissioner in 1921. He poses for a picture for a Wild Goose Club photographer at Castle Harmony after working on the road in October with his team and roller.

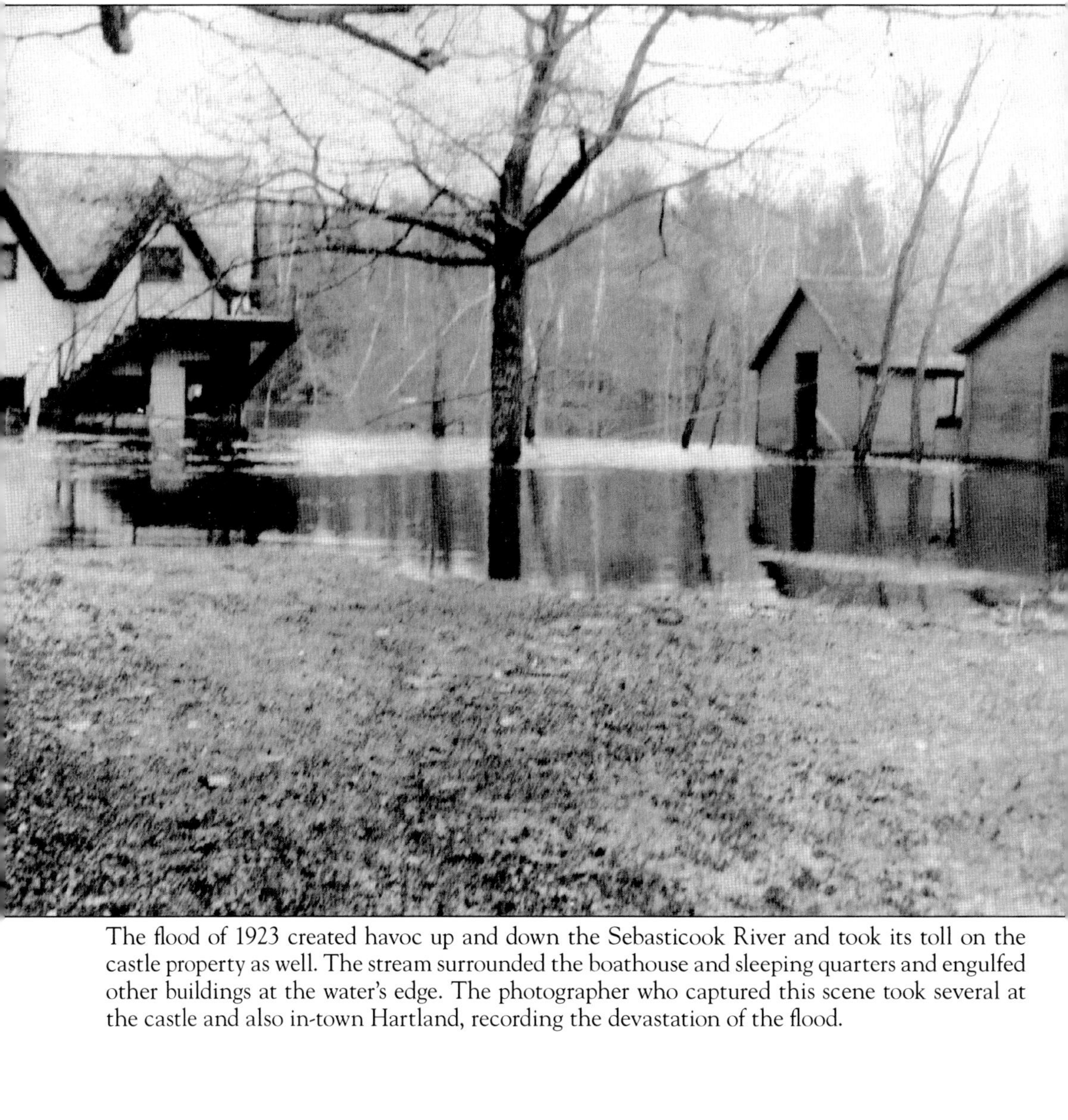

The flood of 1923 created havoc up and down the Sebasticook River and took its toll on the castle property as well. The stream surrounded the boathouse and sleeping quarters and engulfed other buildings at the water's edge. The photographer who captured this scene took several at the castle and also in-town Hartland, recording the devastation of the flood.

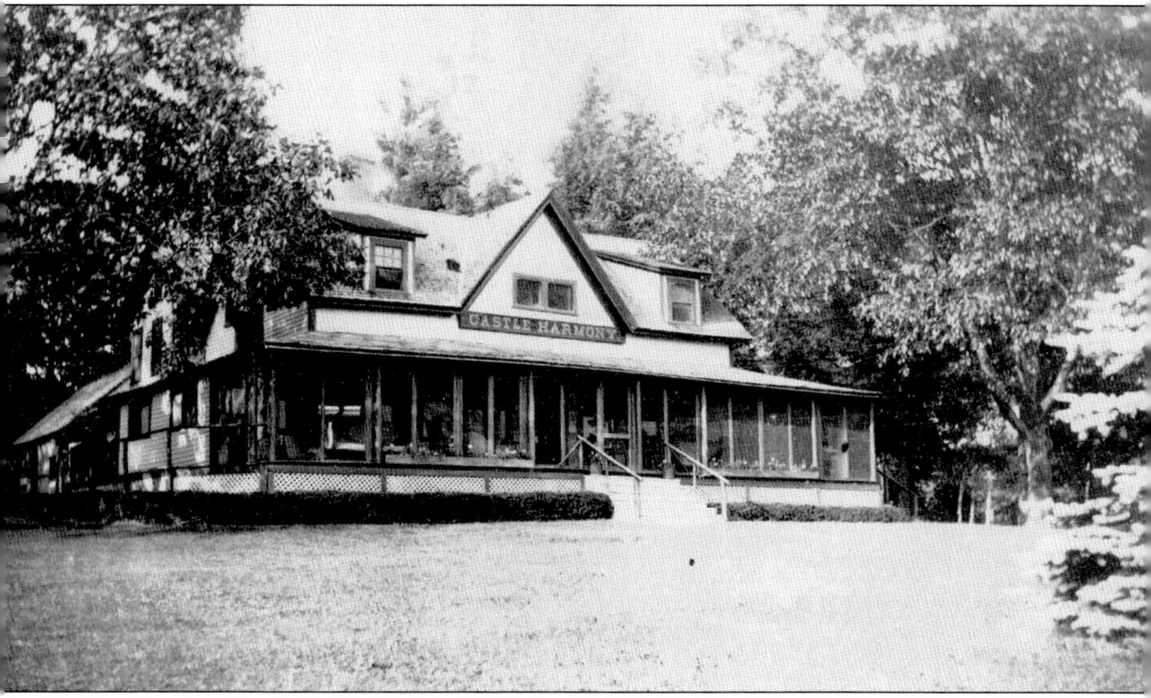

By the 1930s and early 1940s, the castle had taken on much of the appearance it has today with a screened-in porch, and expansive and manicured lawn. The club met its end around 1933, in the midst of the Depression, when the once well-to-do members could no longer justify or afford its expense. The club's ownership continued to the last surviving member W. L. Hayward according to the Tontine charter of the group. It was sold to a private owner in 1947 and sold to William and Lorna Trauth in 1955, who operated the second generation as Wild Goose for Boys, a summer camp for boys from around the world. The Trauths felt a special bond to the property and its rich history, maintaining many of the original possessions, records, and photographs to share that history.

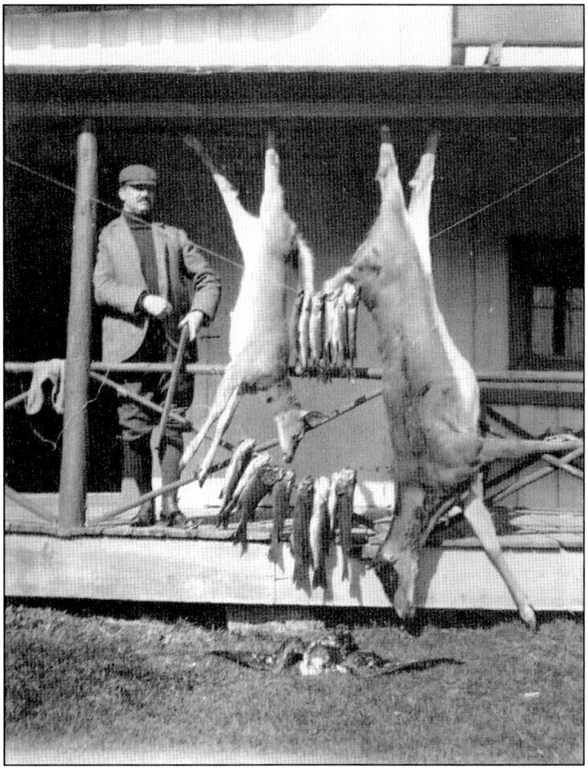

Hunting and fishing were the primary sports at Castle Harmony. Many pictures from the time and records about the "campaigns" of each successive year tell a story of abundant game. The pictures corroborate many of those tales until one realizes that in a single year, each sportsman would pose with the catch of the day. That was the case with this image. The deer and fish remained the same as the photographer snapped picture after picture for each participant to have his own copy, preferably with him in it as the proud sportsman. With that in mind, it was only necessary to capture one sample from 1902 depicting Phil Dyer with the trophies.

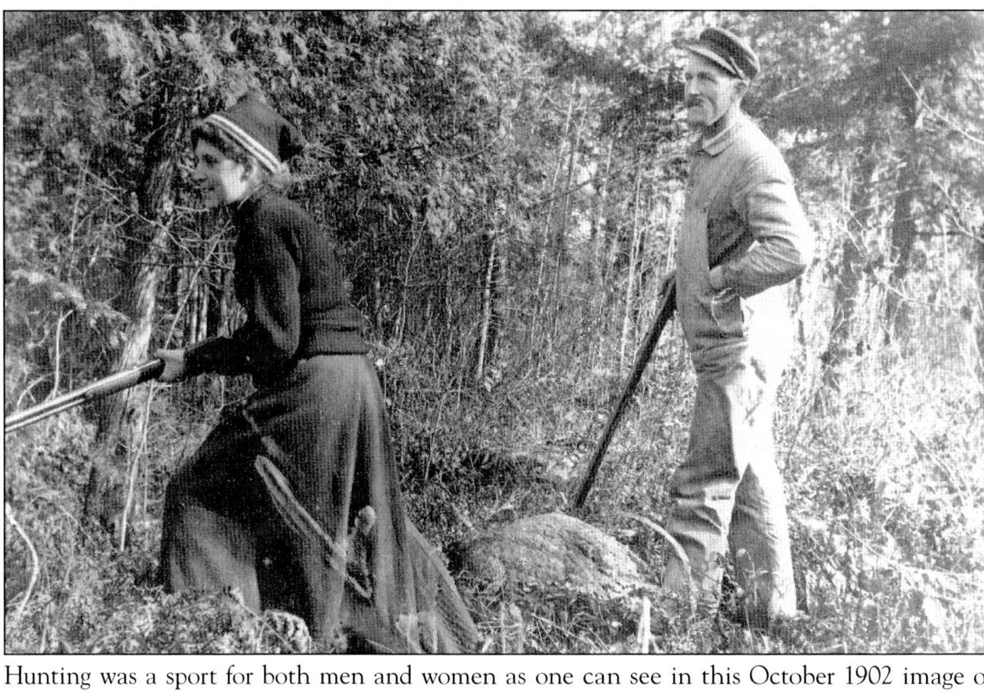

Hunting was a sport for both men and women as one can see in this October 1902 image of Mrs. S. Gleason and Frank Linnell. Women may have been ready for hunting and fishing, but their attire was not. Hunting and hiking through the underbrush, a shotgun under one arm and fighting a tangled skirt with the other must have been a challenge.

Gen. A. O. Davidson demonstrated that the fish were abundant and of good size in July 1898.

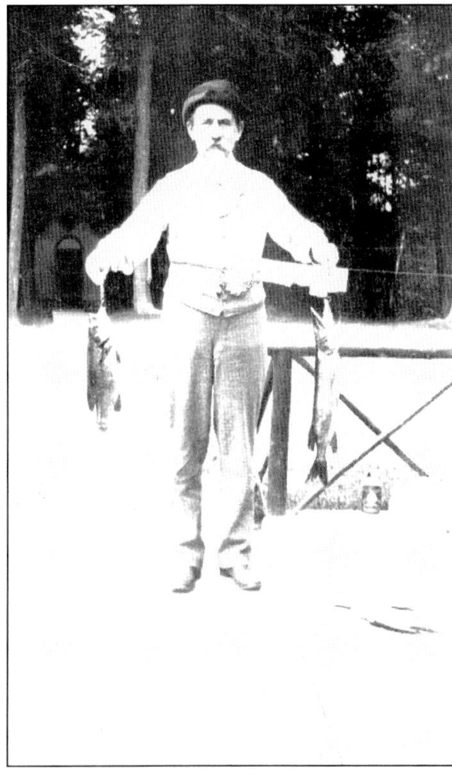

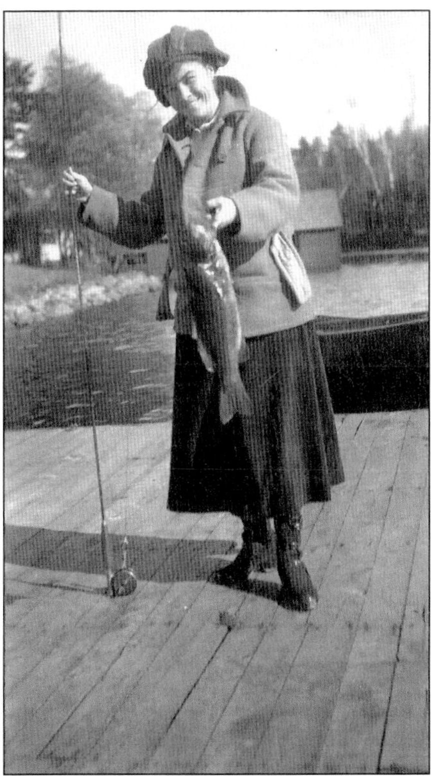

Not to be outdone by any of her predecessors, Mrs. Keyes proved she was an accomplished and proud fisher, in her long skirt and high button shoes, in this 1917 photograph.

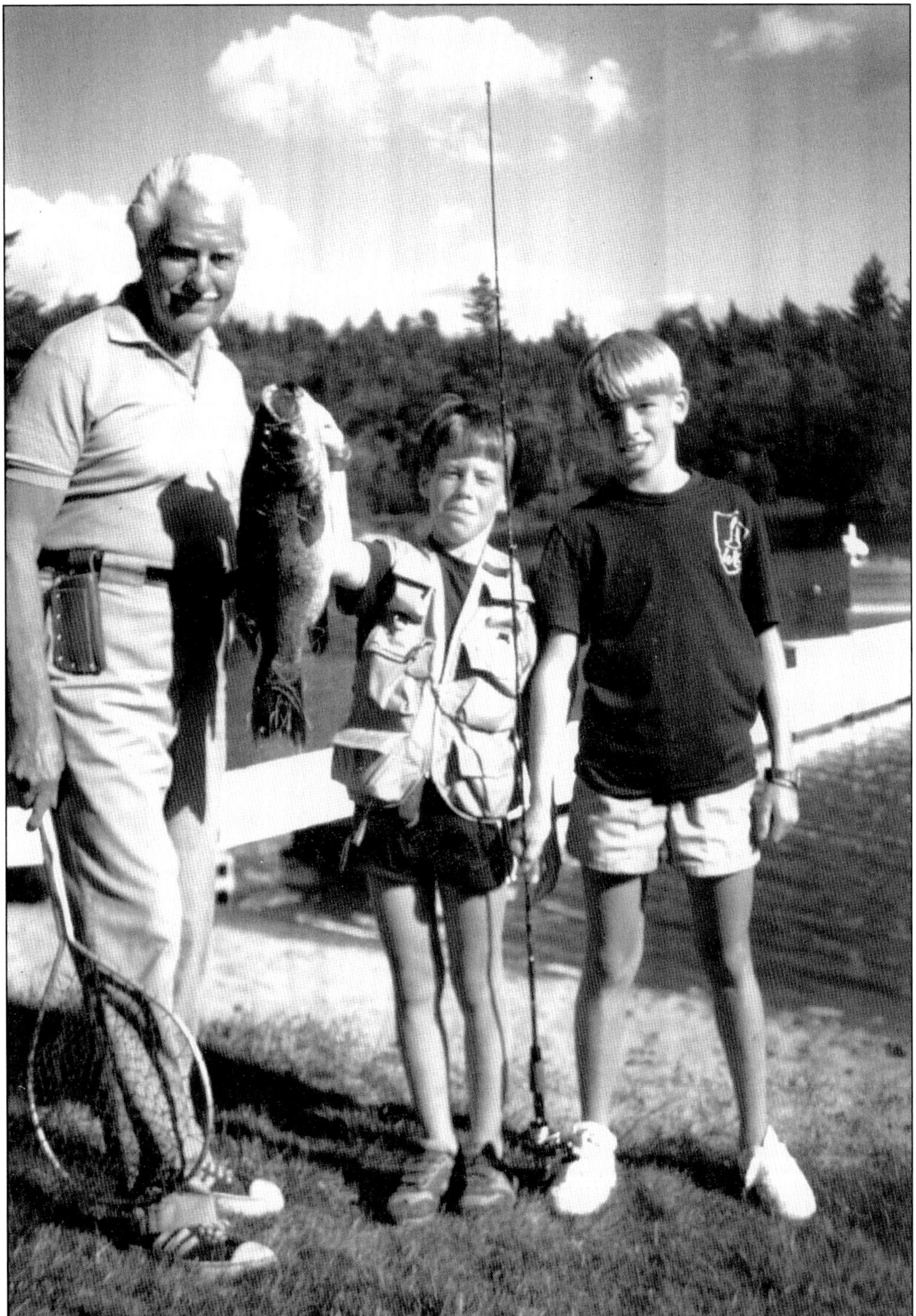

Fishing was still a favorite pastime when Wild Goose for Boys introduced new generations to the sport. Counselor Frank Jones posed for the camera with successful fisher George Wade holding the fish and Tommy Lippert enjoying the moment.

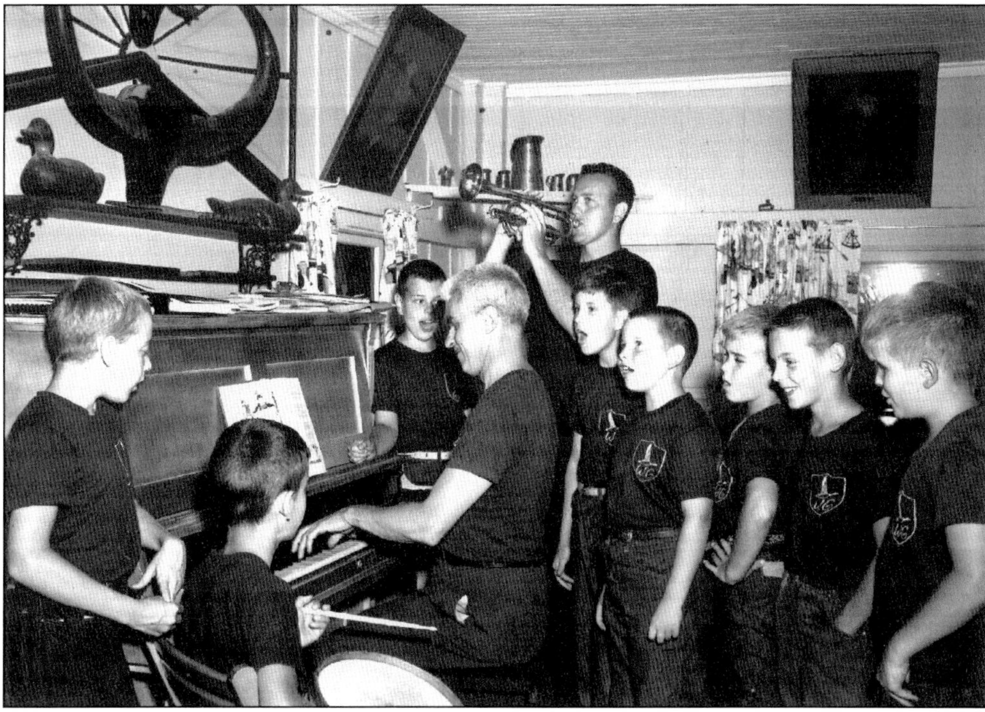

In an earlier shot of camp activities, Frank Jones plays the piano for a camp sing-along in the castle library.

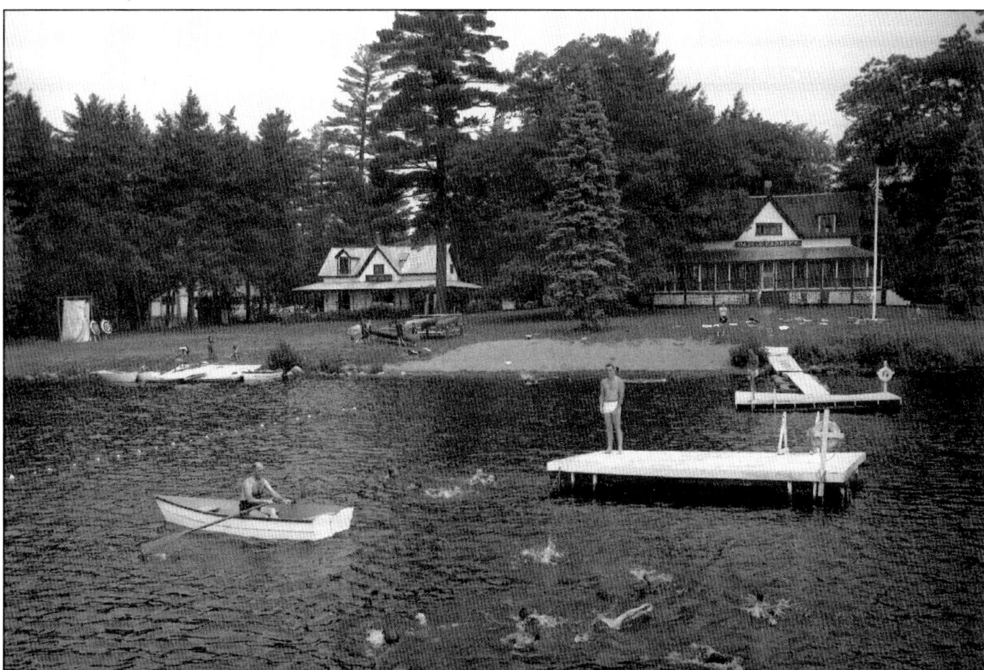

From its beginning in 1956 until closing in 1995, Wild Goose for Boys offered numerous outdoor activities for boys using the same grounds and building that an earlier, and older group of "boys" enjoyed for nearly 70 years.

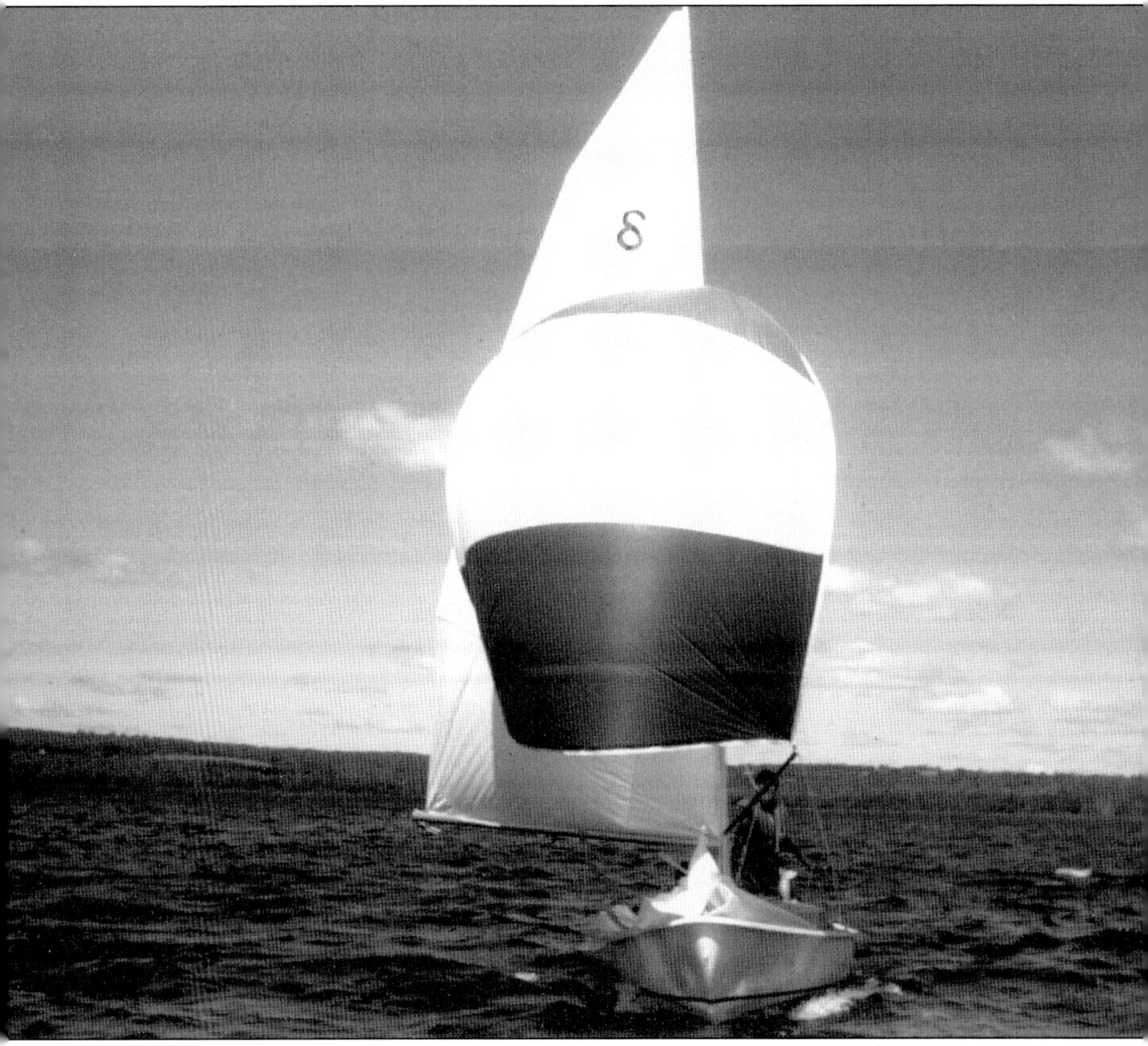

Wild Goose for Boys taught its members sailing; a skill that was a long ways from the motor launch the original Wild Goose Club members took such pride in bringing to Great Moose Lake.

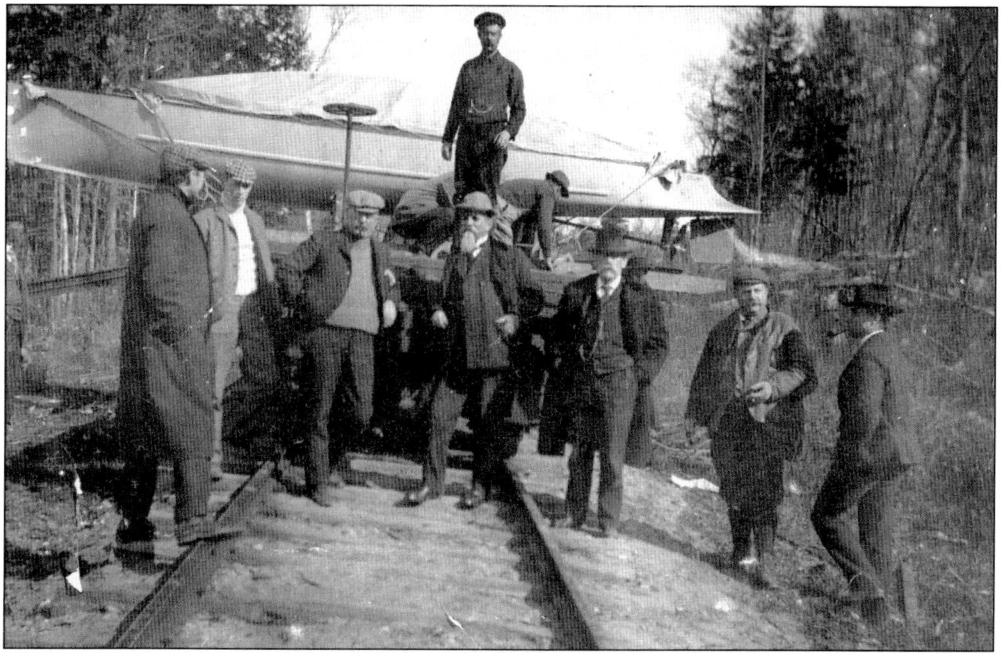

The rail line along the shore of Great Moose Lake was still new in 1903 when members of Wild Goose Club took delivery of a new motor launch, the *Gosling.* Once unloaded, likely at the club's landing near Northeast Cove, the launch was an attractive means of traveling between the club's two lodges on opposite sides of the large lake.

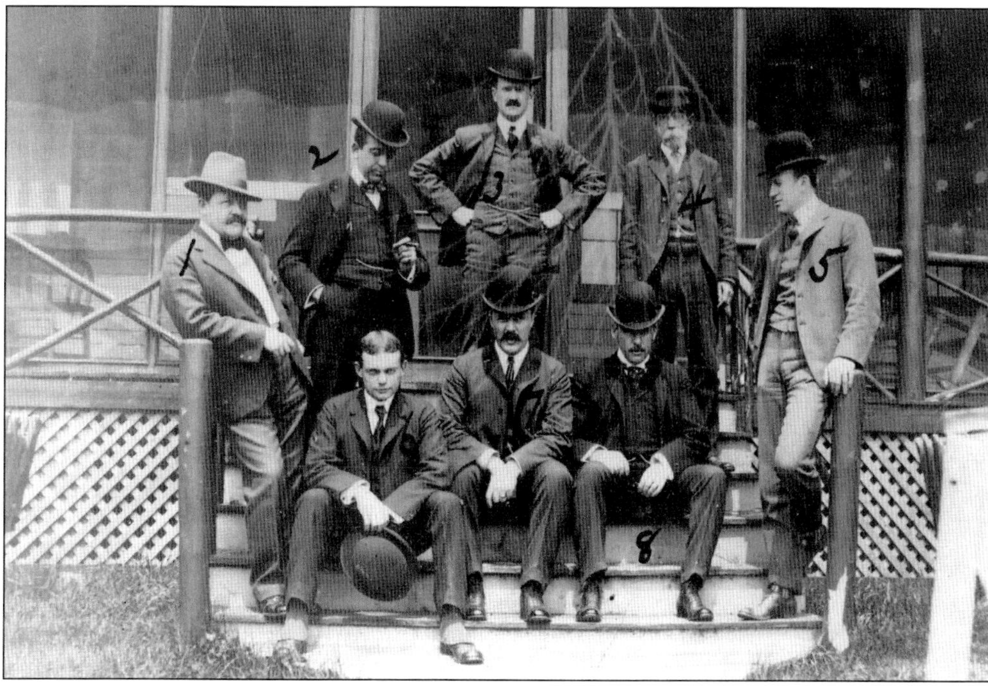

Among the members who likely assisted with the new motor launch in 1903 were, from left to right, (1) Allan Taylor, (2) F. P. Royce, (3) R. L. Hall, (4) J. K. Mannin, (5) L. Williams, (6) John Dearborn, (7) T. Woods, and (8) E. R. Champlin.

EDITION OF 1880.

The Wild Goose Club.

CREED

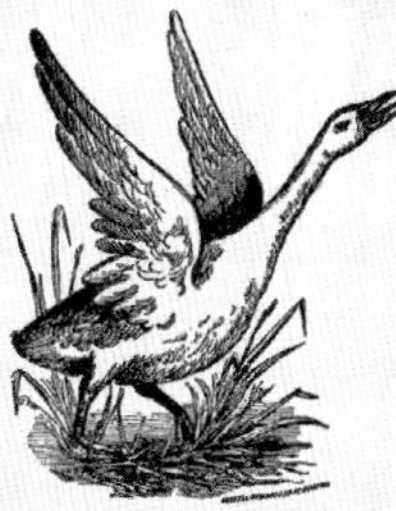

We believe that all men have the right to do as they please—if they can.

We believe that all men are born equal and handsome, but do not remain so any length of time.

We believe it to be the privilege of all men to enjoy health and pleasure.

We believe that good cheer, good digestion and good company are the greatest promoters of the same.

We believe Castle Harmony to be the most delightful place on earth and well equipped for the comfort of the body and edification of the mind. Therefore—

We, the Goslings of the "Old Wild Goose," in full assembly met—declare the objects of this Club to be: Health, Happiness and the Pursuit of Ducks—both wild and tame.

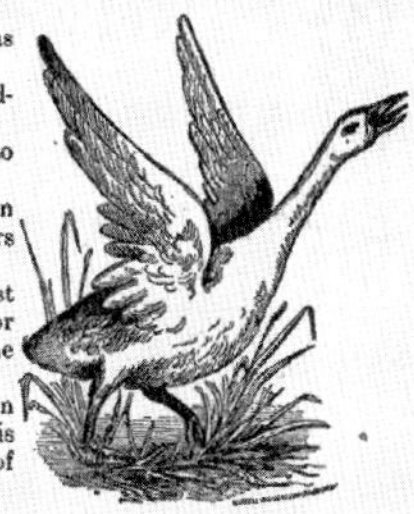

BY-LAWS

ARTICLE 1st.—The Wild Goose Club shall consist of Fifteen Ganders in full plumage; and every Gander shall be an officer with high rank and large pay.

ART. 2d.—This Club may hold real estate and personal property to an amount not exceeding one million dollars, which shall be held in trust by some members elected by the Club for the use and enjoyment of all its members for three thousand years.

ART. 3rd.—No member shall have the right at any time to dispose of or withdraw any funds or property of the Club, except his own carcass.

ART. 4th.—The Club House shall be known and called by the name of Castle Harmony.

ART. 5th.—No intoxicating liquors will be allowed upon the premises of the Club—"*except in case of sickness.*"

ART. 6th.—Any member or visitor who snores will be furnished with quarters in the Light House.

ART. 7th.—Drinking between drinks, and labor between meals, will not be allowed.

ART. 8th.—Eye openers, fog cutters, appetizers or night caps will never be permitted, that is—hardly ever.

ART. 9th.—No game will be allowed to be followed or taken upon the premises of the Club except grouse, pigeons, ducks, rabbits, fish, poker, euchre and old sledge.

ART. 10th.—Any member who introduces a friend to the Castle, will be charged for what he steals.

ART. 11th.—The cost of living at the Castle for both members and visitors shall be $2.00 Entrance Fee, and $2.00 per day. No extra charge for the boats or horses and carriages of the Club. Any person who eats more than his own weight per day, will be charged by the pound.

ART. 12th—No fish shall be caught before dropping him a line, and each person must eat his own catch. No one will be allowed to eat another's fish, or vice versa.

ART. 13th.—That this Paradise may not be broken up by the Daughters of Eve—it is ordered—that Ladies shall not be allowed to run loose in the domains of the Club without a Keeper, or so muzzled that they cannot do injury to the innocent Ganders and Goslings.

ART. 14th.—The members must be addressed on all occasions by their Club title. Violation of this rule will be punished by fine and imprisonment.

ART. 15th.—These by-laws may be amended or altered by giving three years' notice in all the weekly papers in the State of Maine. The members suggesting any alteration must pay for the Seidlitz Powders for the crowd upon the opening of the meeting called for that purpose, and produce a certificate of good moral character from the Commodore.

P. S.—Indulgences and permits to violate these By-Laws may be obtained on application to the Burgomaster.

MEMBERS.

HENRY HASTINGS, COMMODORE.

Names.	*Club Title.*	*Names.*	*Club Title.*
H. C. PRESCOTT,	BURGOMASTER.	E. M. STODDARD,	EMPEROR.
WM. E. FRENCH,	QUARTERMASTER.	ROBERT H. BUTCHER,	PARSON.
A. B. BUTTRICK,	TIPSTAFF.	HARRIS PUSHOR,	PRINCE.
A. LINN,	GALASHIELS.	A. O. DAVIDSON,	ASTRONOMER.
JACOB PFAFF,	COUNT.	D. W. C. FARRINGTON,	JUDGE.
A. PUTNAM,	BONIFACE.	NATHAN HOLBROOK,	ELDER.
EDWARD HASTINGS,	SCRIBE.	D. W. LAWRENCE,	BULWARK.

Honorary Members.

D. D. STEWART, - - - HIGH CHANCELLOR. | D. A. GLEASON. - - ATTORNEY GENERAL.

EDWARD WARE, - - - - - - - - - - - FALSTAFF.

Dated this day, 1880, at Castle Harmony, Port of Galashiels on the "Great Moose Lake," in the "Pine Tree State."

The Wild Goose Club posted its creed and bylaws in 1880, demonstrating the tongue-in-cheek fun the group enjoyed from the beginning as well as the numerous titles conferred on members.

Four

HARMONY
THE VILLAGE

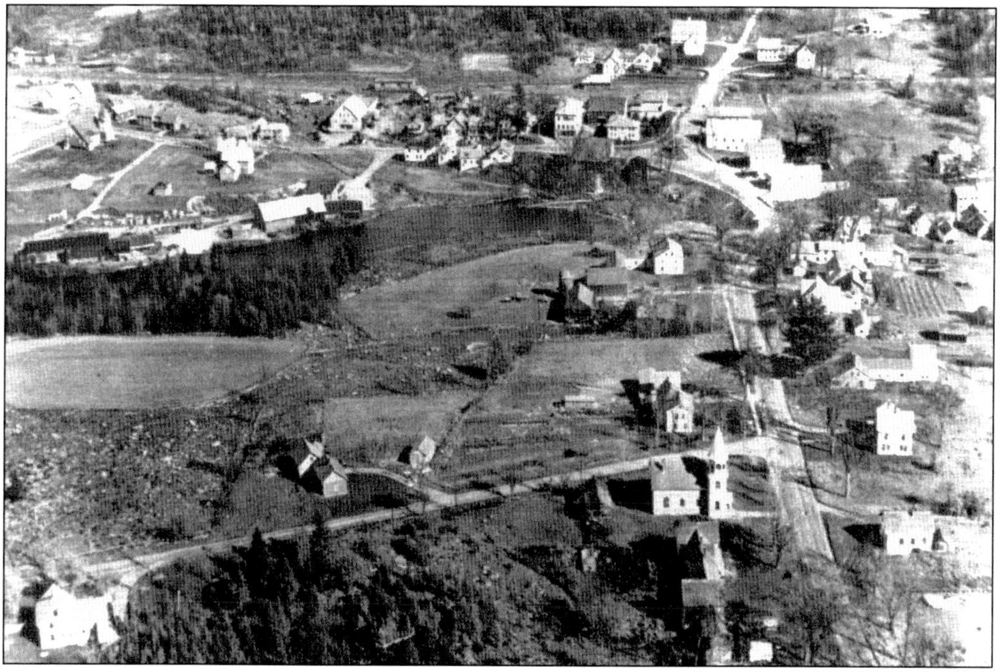

Harmony, as seen from the air in 1940, depicts a New England village anchored by its school, church, and general stores. The small rural community was first surveyed in 1790, and the first permanent settler, Trustum Hurd, was in the area west of Higgins Stream by 1796. Like other communities bordering Great Moose Lake, the earlier settlers did not arrive by water, but rather overland from settlements on the Kennebec River or farther west in New Hampshire. One early settler swamped his own road from Athens over Lord's Hill to reach the village area, a distance of more than five miles. The name Harmony was not chosen until 1803, because of the good feeling the settlers felt among their fellow inhabitants.

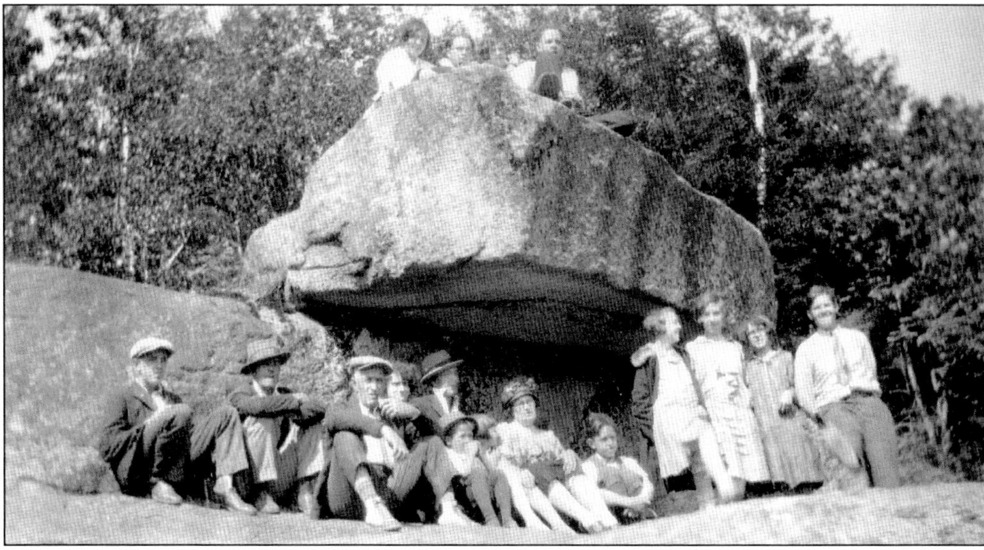

A popular Harmony landmark is an outcropping of ledge that overlooks Great Moose Lake. The ledges at Devil's Head have been a popular picnic site and hiking destination for more than 100 years. It is reached from either St. Albans or Harmony over long-abandoned roads. Likely in the early years, the roads were more accessible by horse and wagon. But as settlers left the mountain for the comforts of the village or lower land, the road was eventually a rough ride reserved more for hikers, snowmobiles, or now all-terrain vehicles. Few of the long established families have not been to Devil's Head to pose on the rock itself, as members of the Seekins family did in this image from around 1920.

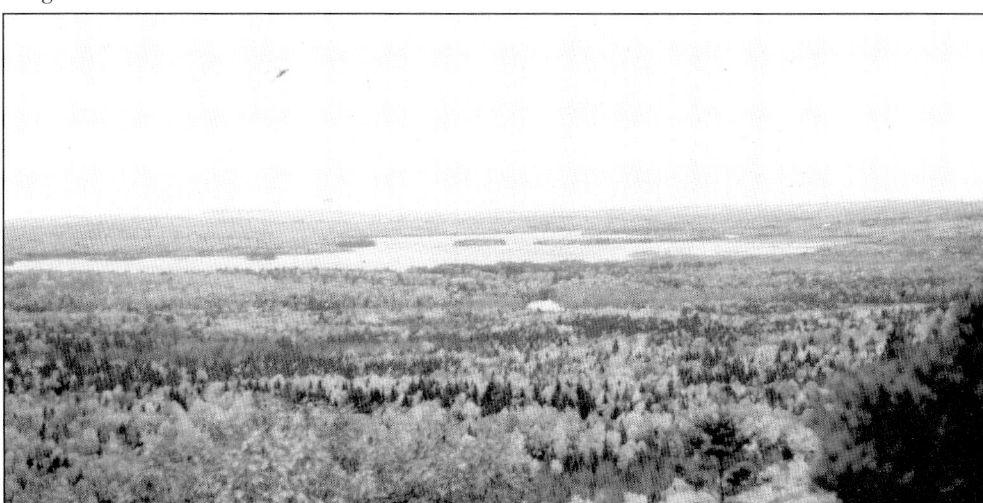

The view from Devil's Head is the goal when hikers or all-terrain travelers make their way up the rough road. The view takes in the entire length of Great Moose Lake from the river outlet to the southeast (left) and the western shore of the lower lake, to the Narrows in the center of the view that provides access to the upper lake to the west. In the 1800s, the lake was apparently three lakes with water access connecting them. The dam added at the outlet in Hartland changed the lake's character, apparently eliminating the low water in the Narrows, and eliminating farmland on the northern end in Harmony. The maintenance of the dam over the past 40 years has kept the water level at a more constant level.

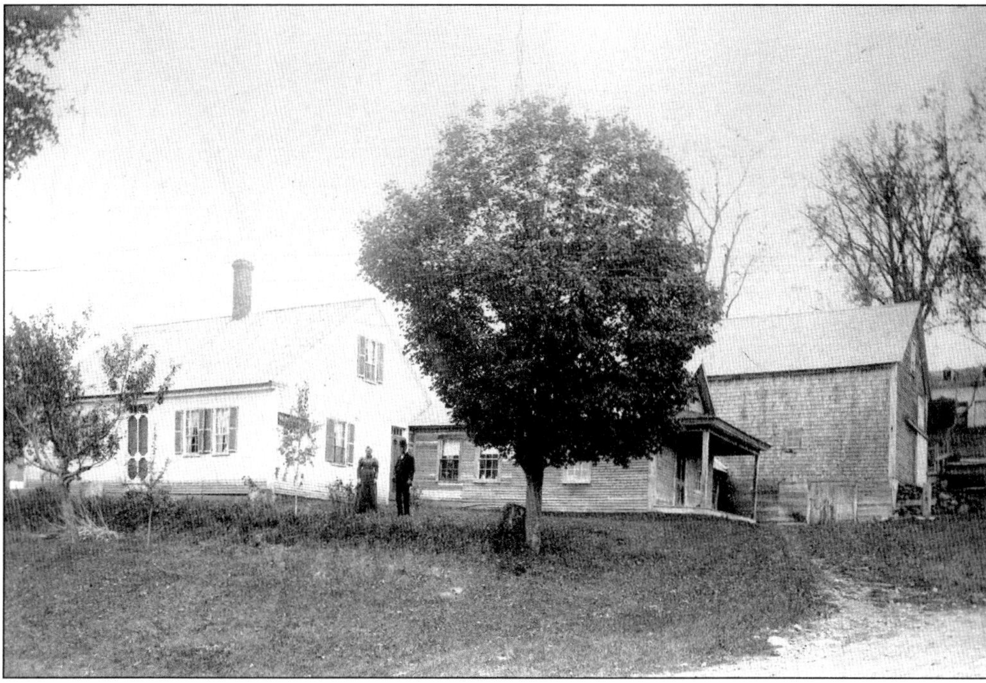

The first frame house in Harmony was owned by Dr. Charles McLaughlin, and is still in use in the village. The people seen here are believed to be Emma Longfellow McLaughlin and the doctor.

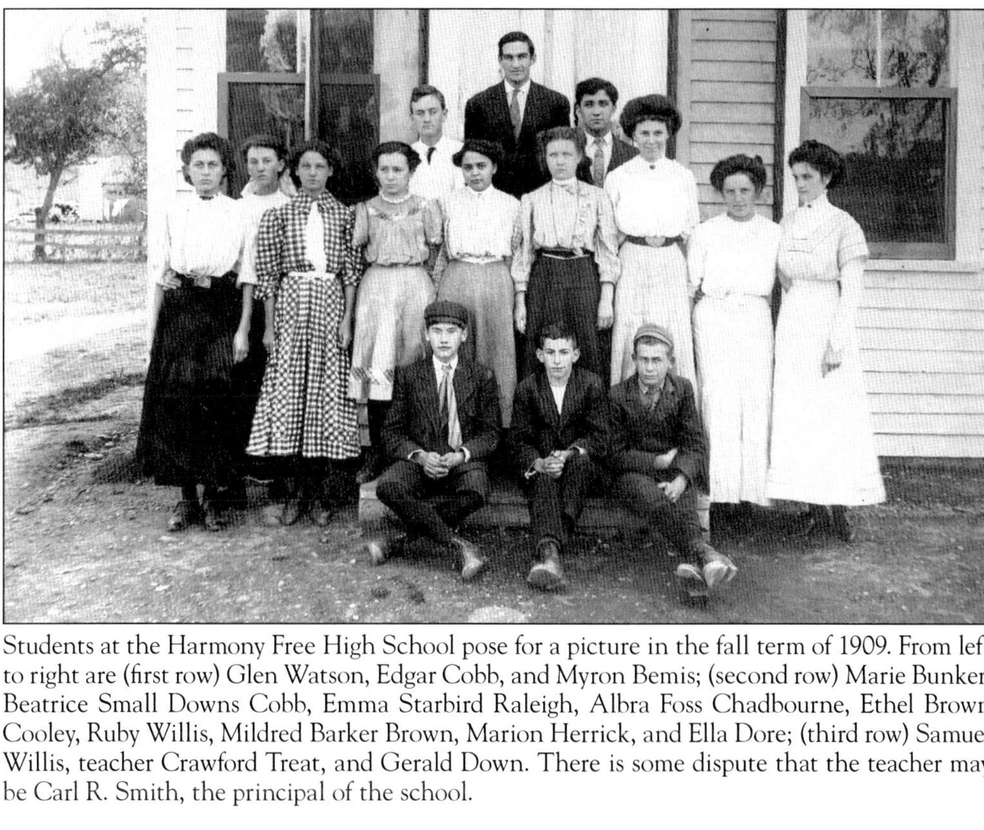

Students at the Harmony Free High School pose for a picture in the fall term of 1909. From left to right are (first row) Glen Watson, Edgar Cobb, and Myron Bemis; (second row) Marie Bunker, Beatrice Small Downs Cobb, Emma Starbird Raleigh, Albra Foss Chadbourne, Ethel Brown Cooley, Ruby Willis, Mildred Barker Brown, Marion Herrick, and Ella Dore; (third row) Samuel Willis, teacher Crawford Treat, and Gerald Down. There is some dispute that the teacher may be Carl R. Smith, the principal of the school.

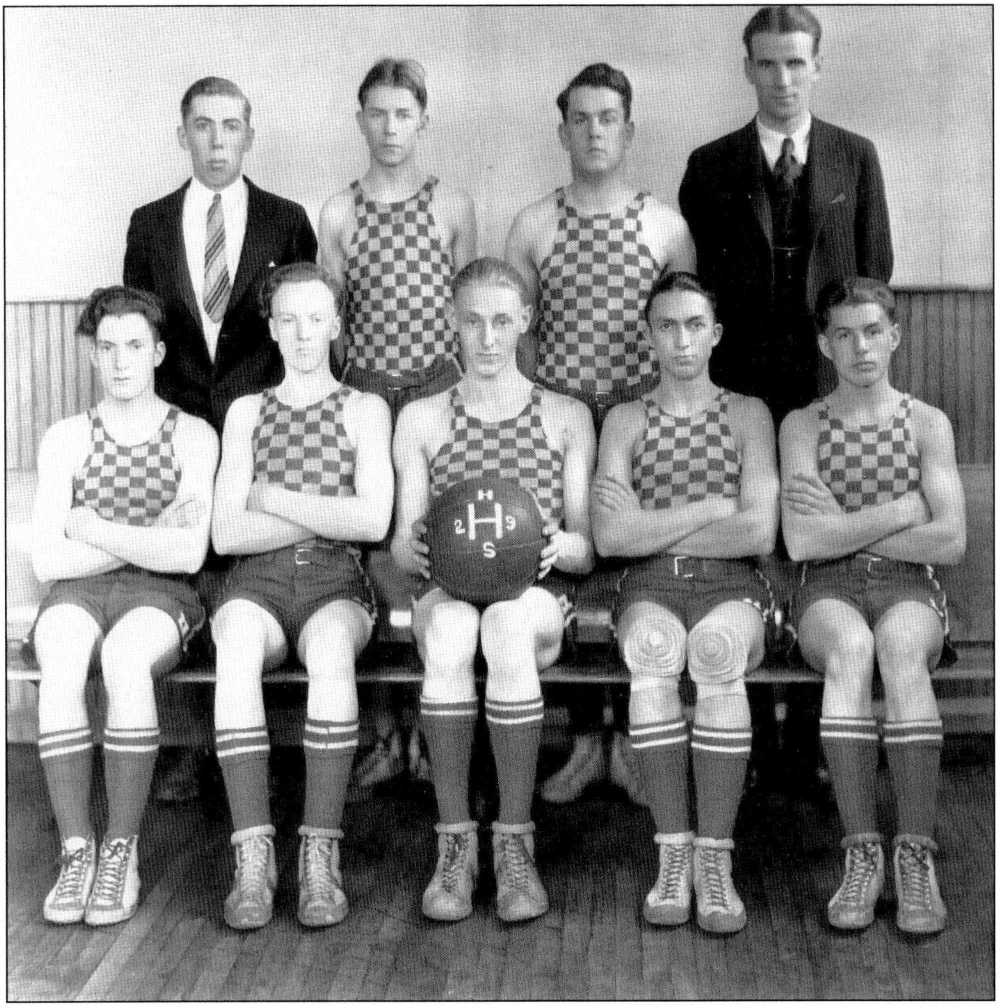

The Harmony High School basketball team of 1929 includes, from left to right, (first row) Julian Rawding, Fred Curtis, Floyd Robinson, Don Micue, and Francis Deering; (second row) manager Raymond Parsons, Marble Reed, Roy Nickerson, and coach John Abbott.

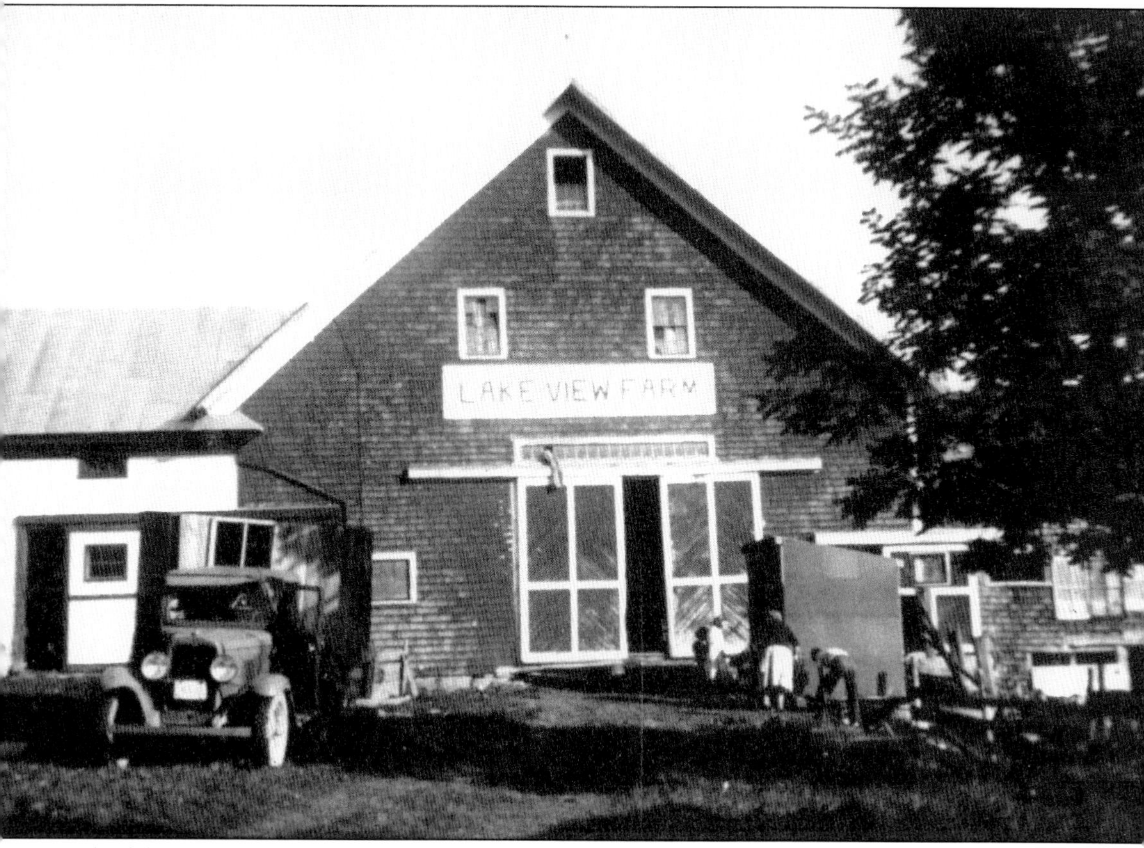

At the lake, Walter "Buck" and Lois Tripp operated Lakeview Farm in the 1930s and 1940s. The property includes 250 acres, with two and a half miles of shore land on the upper lake. In the 1952, Elden and Margaret Perkins purchased the farm and eventually developed a popular campground at the shore. A subsequent owner later subdivided the land into lots where several new camps and homes have been built. A nephew of Lois Tripp recalls when his aunt would drive her 1929 Buick to Castle Harmony daily to deliver milk, butter, and eggs.

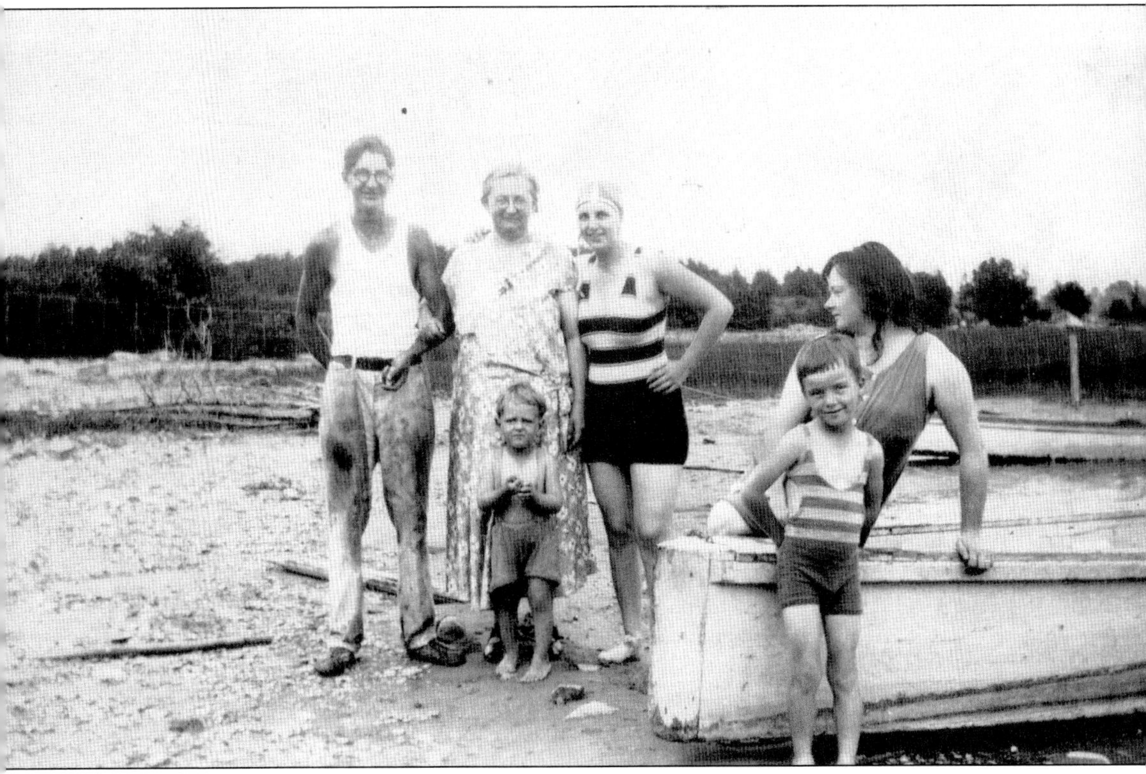

Water levels were much lower at the lake when Buck and Lois Tripp took family members to enjoy a day in the cove. Participants that day were Buck, Ethel Hight Tripp (Lois's mother), Lois, nephew Ken Stickney in front, and Irma and Phillip Brown at the bow of the boat. Ken's family would later be among the first camp owners on the Bunker Road on the Upper Lake in 1949, where Ken spends his summers today.

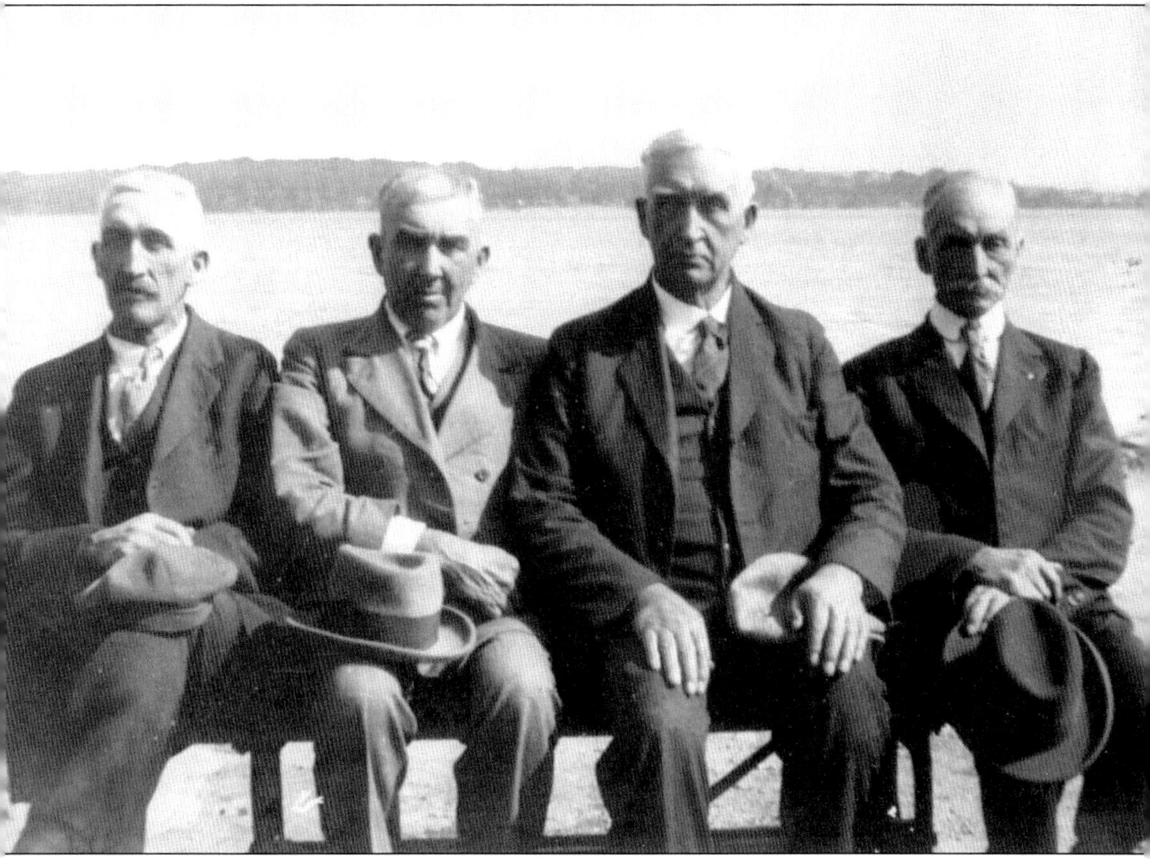

The Hight brothers are descendants from the earliest settlers in the area, and joined Buck and Lois Tripp at the lake for a family gathering in the 1930s. From left to right the brothers are Pliny, Clement, Cassius, and John Hight. Their father farmed land on the northern shore of Great Moose Lake in the 1800s, and lost a large section of fields to the rising water from the dam at the outlet in Hartland.

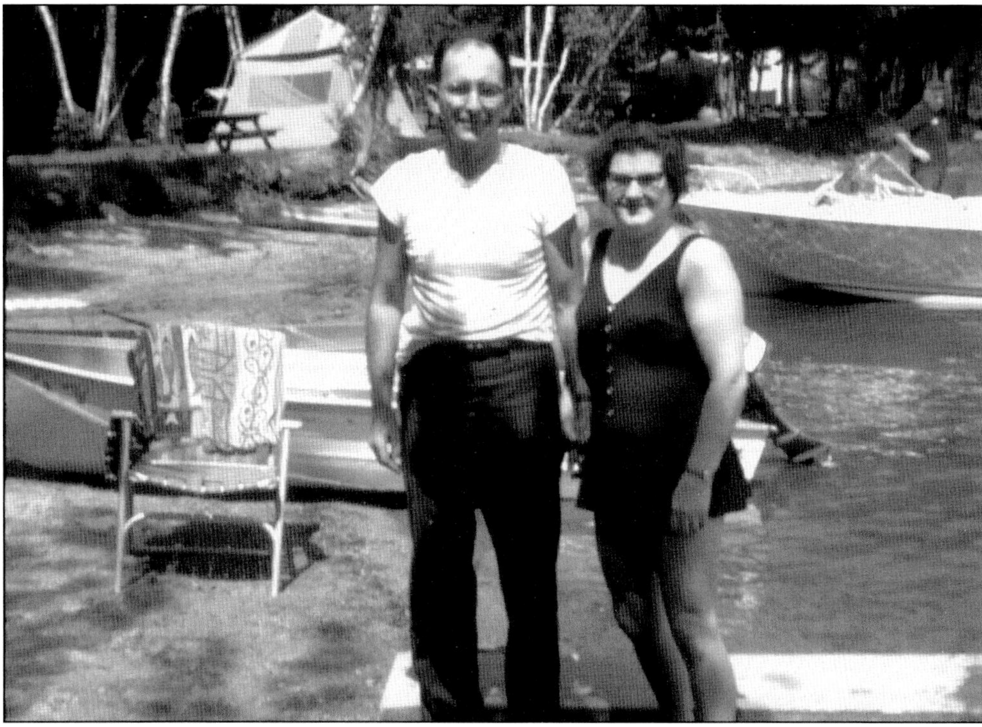

Elden and Margaret Perkins started a campground in the 1950s in conjunction with their farming at Lakeview Farm. The campground came to be known as Perkins Cove despite the established name of Lakeview Farm. Beginning with four cabins, they ultimately added three cabins and 14 campsites, making for a busy shoreline for many summers. The business eventually built to the point that Elden only worked out in the off-season, a time when Margaret was a schoolteacher and principal.

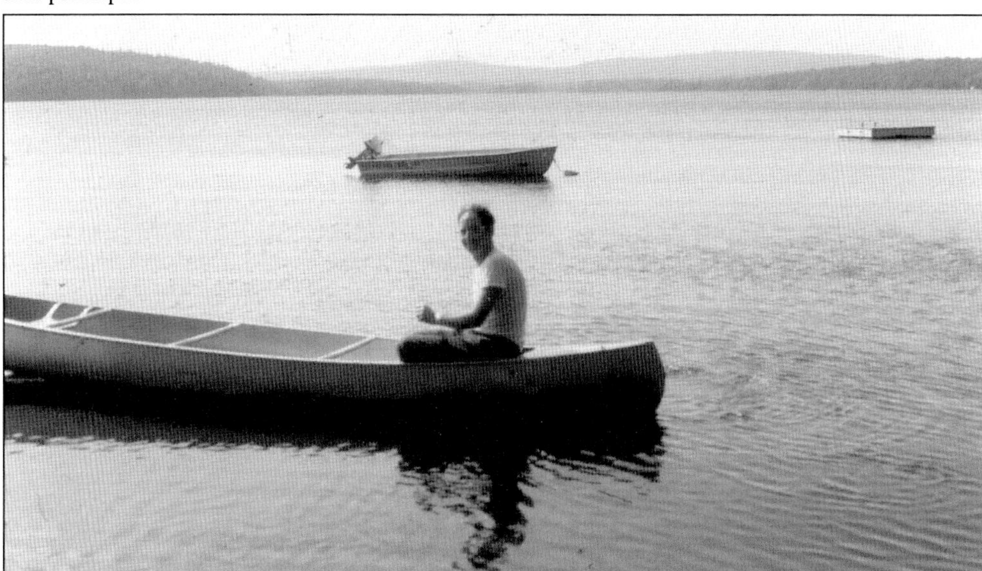

Elden was a hands-on business owner, often enjoying the canoeing and boating with his campers. In the picture, the expanse of the smaller upper lake is evident behind him.

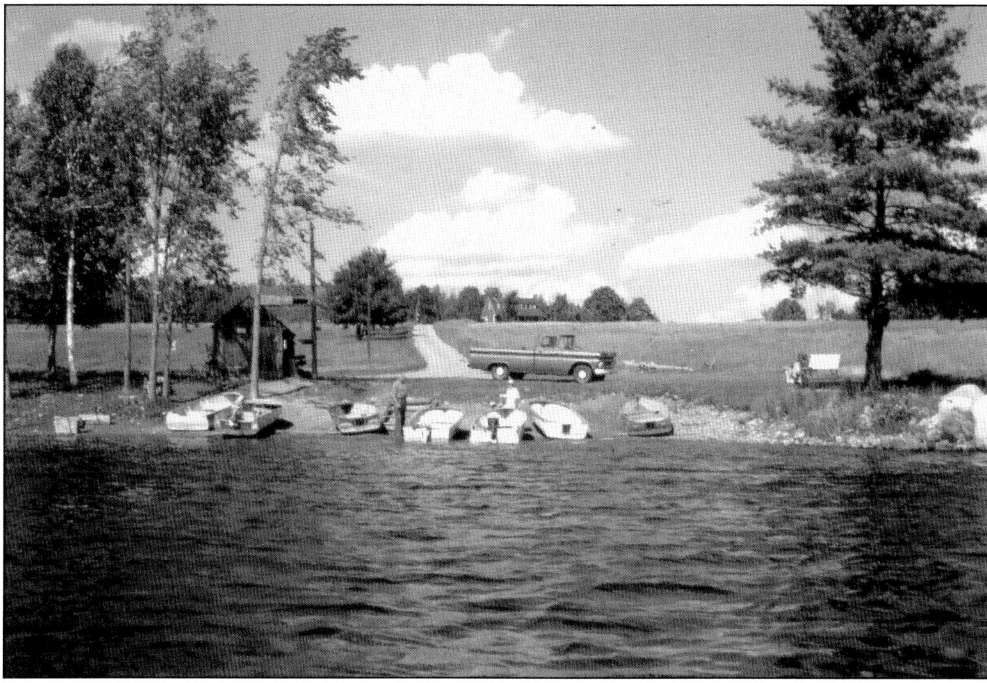

Around the point from Perkins Cove was "Zeliff's landing" or the "Moose Pond Lodge" of the Perkins' neighbors Horace and Sal Zeliff. The Zeliffs operated cabins on the lake in the 1950s and often referred campers to the Perkinses when the new operation opened. John and Connie West operated West's Cabins in Pickerel Cove in the same time period.

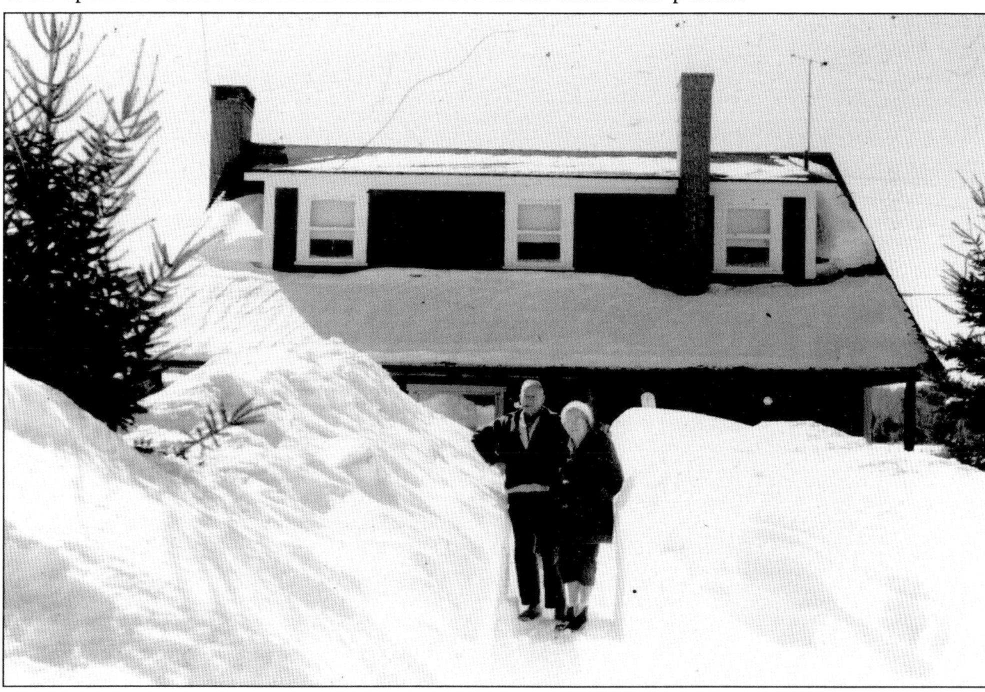

Horace and Sal Zeliff are dwarfed by the snow in front of their lakeside home in Harmony following a storm in 1963.

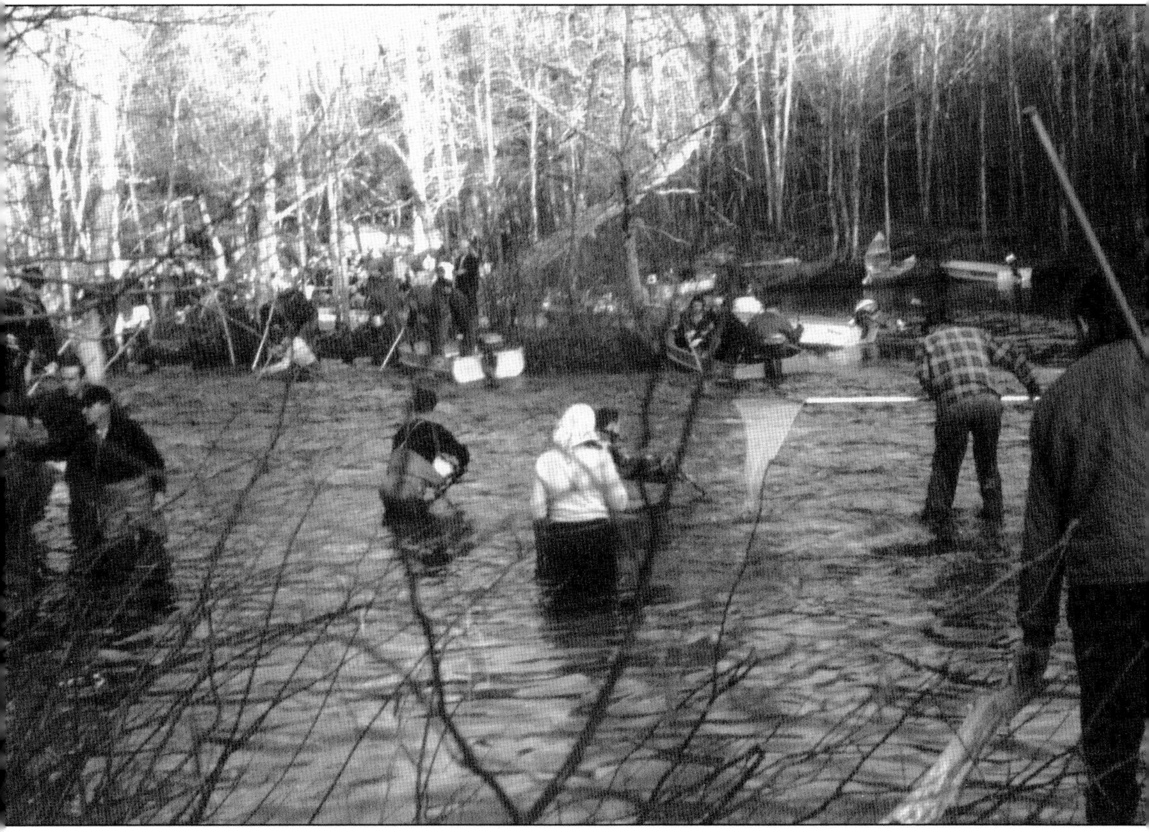

Stories from Main Stream during smelting season can be hard to believe until one sees proof of the chaos in this picture from the collection of Dale Perkins. The stream is a particularly popular spot for netting or dipping smelts during the spring run, and it is not unusual to see dozens, if not more than 100 people with their boats, canoes, waders, and buckets trying to take their limit of the small and tasty fish. During some seasons, locals have been known to set up impromptu hot dog stands to raise funds for various causes, if not personal gain.

Five

Athens
The Village

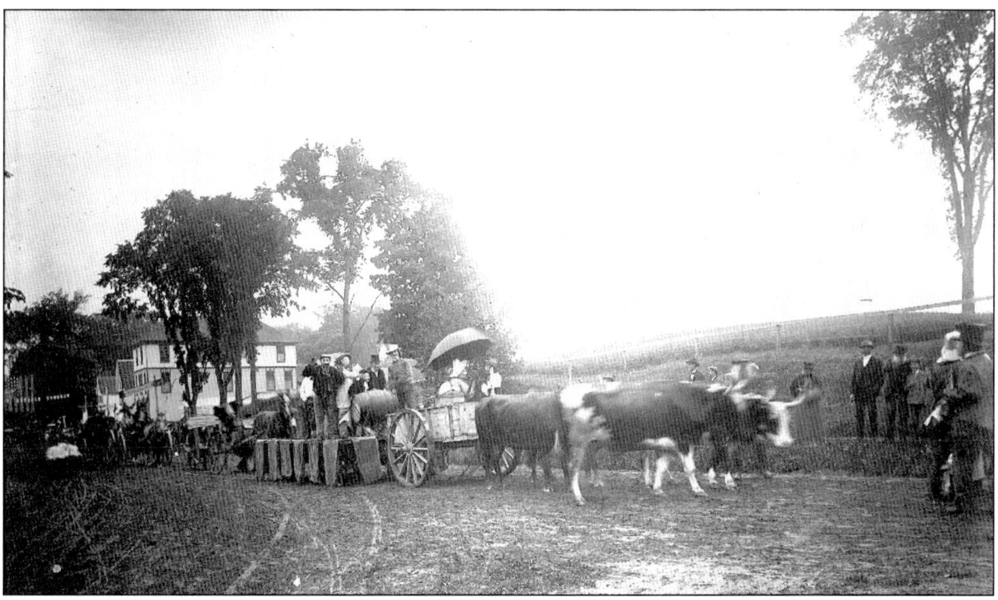

The early settlers to the communities around Great Moose Lake endured difficult overland travel from more established communities to the west to reach their new homes. That was the case in Athens, where some settlers drove oxen to reach the shores of Wesserunsett Stream, the surrounding hills, and eventually the other communities beyond. That trek was reenacted in 1904 with a team of oxen in the parade during the Athens centennial celebration.

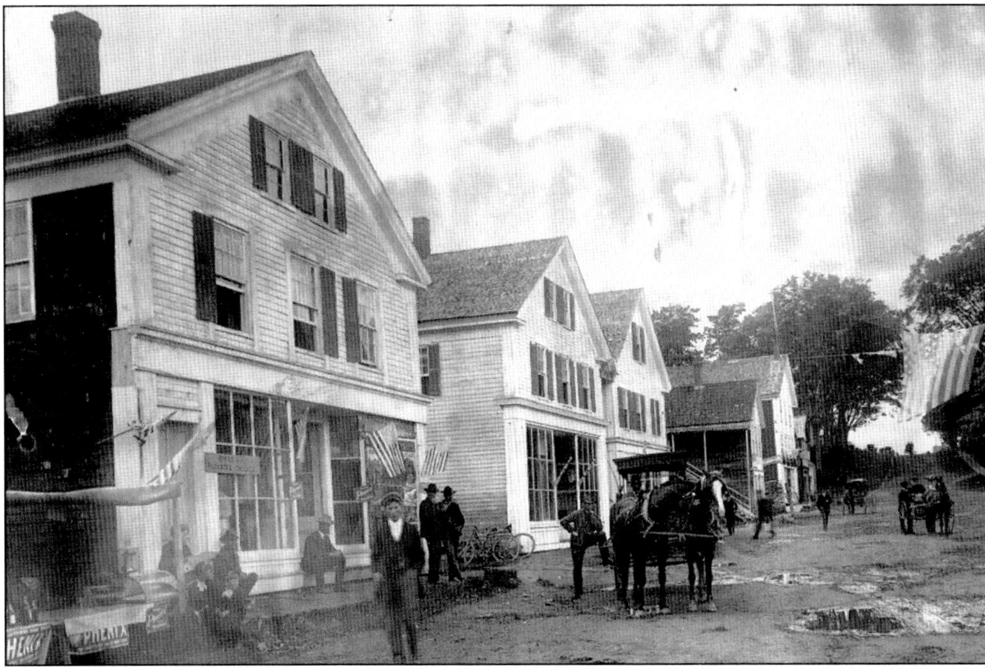

Main Street in Athens, was a busy and sometimes muddy experience in 1904. Like most rural communities of the time period, Main Street boasted many stores and businesses that created self-sufficiency for the community.

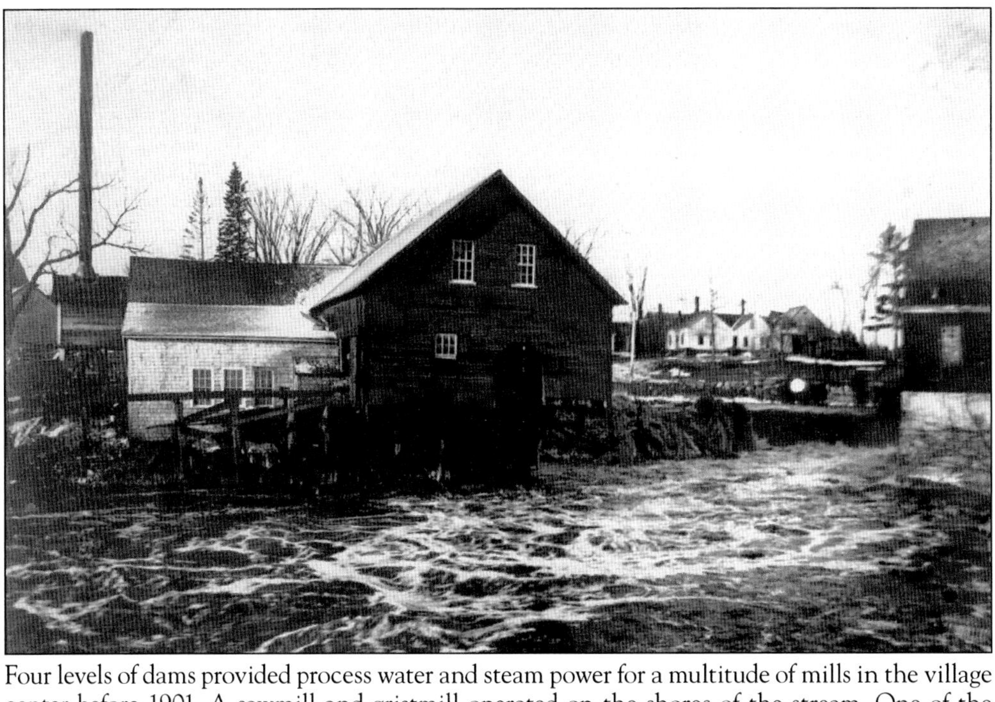

Four levels of dams provided process water and steam power for a multitude of mills in the village center before 1901. A sawmill and gristmill operated on the shores of the stream. One of the dams and the sawmill were destroyed in the flood of 1901, washing out the underpinning of the mill seen here looking north from downstream.

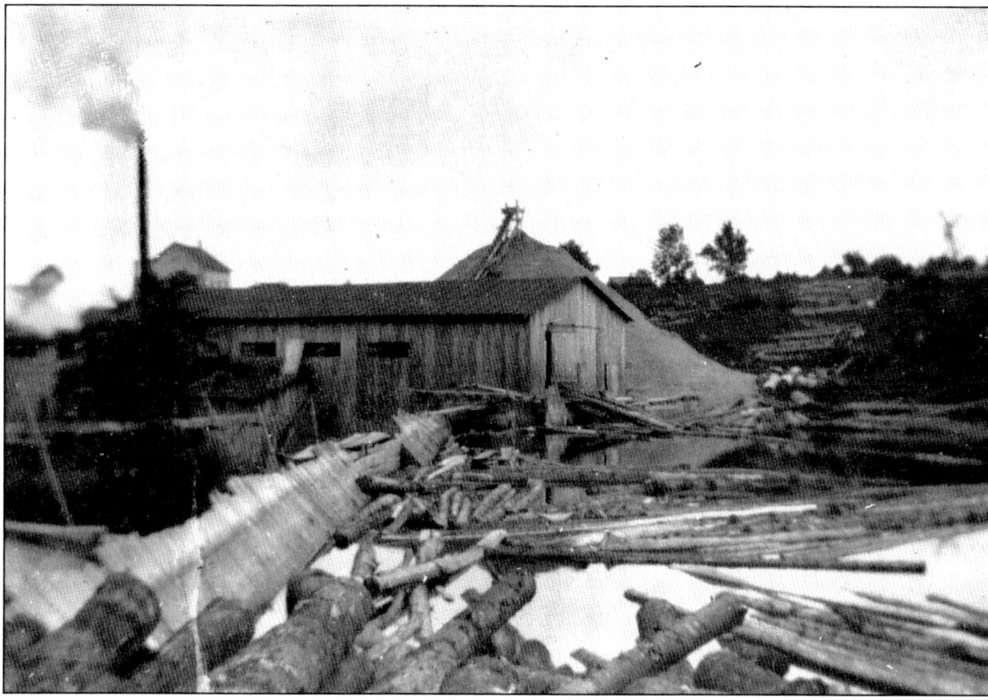

The west branch of the Wesserunsett comes from Wentworth (Ironbound) Pond while the east branch comes to the village from Smith Pond. The combined flow was harnessed by the dams including this one for Clark's sawmill.

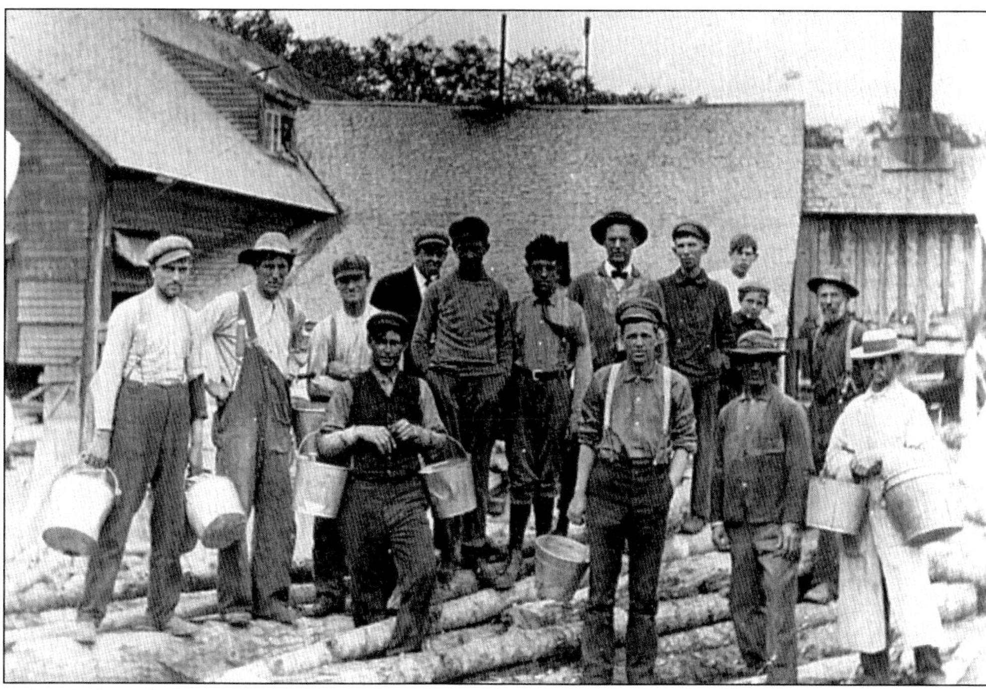

A hardy bunch of Athens mill workers stopped for this photograph, around 1900.

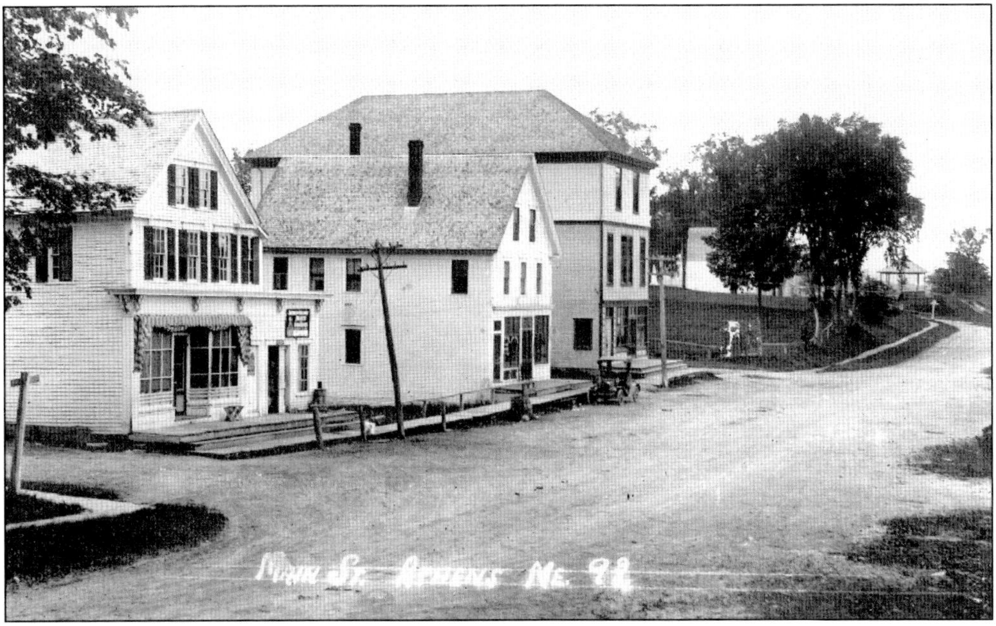

The east side of Main Street in Athens included a number of buildings in the early 1900s, including the large Odd Fellows hall at the southern end. The building was destroyed by fire sometime in 1931. Sanders and Flanders general store occupied the first floor, with the Odd Fellows and offices located in the upper levels. The telephone company operators were located on the third floor at one time. When phone service began in Athens around 1900, there were just three subscribers. Within five years, the business grew to 189 subscribers. The building immediately next to the International Order of Odd Fellows hall also burned in 1931. The building housed a post office and drug store.

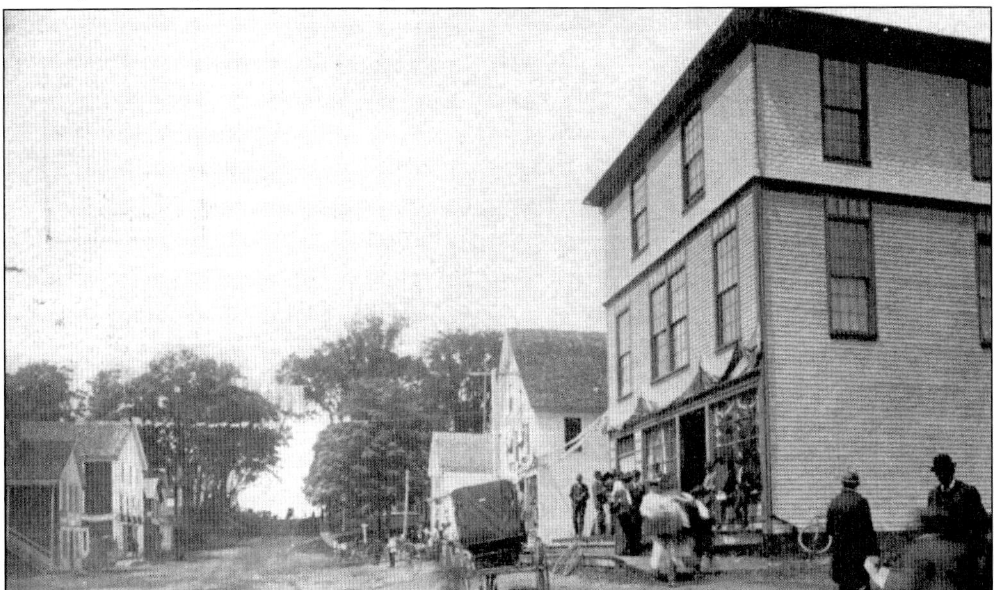

Around the beginning of the 20th century, the Odd Fellows hall was a bustling center of commerce. Horses were the primary mode of transportation and Athens was still a self-sufficient community.

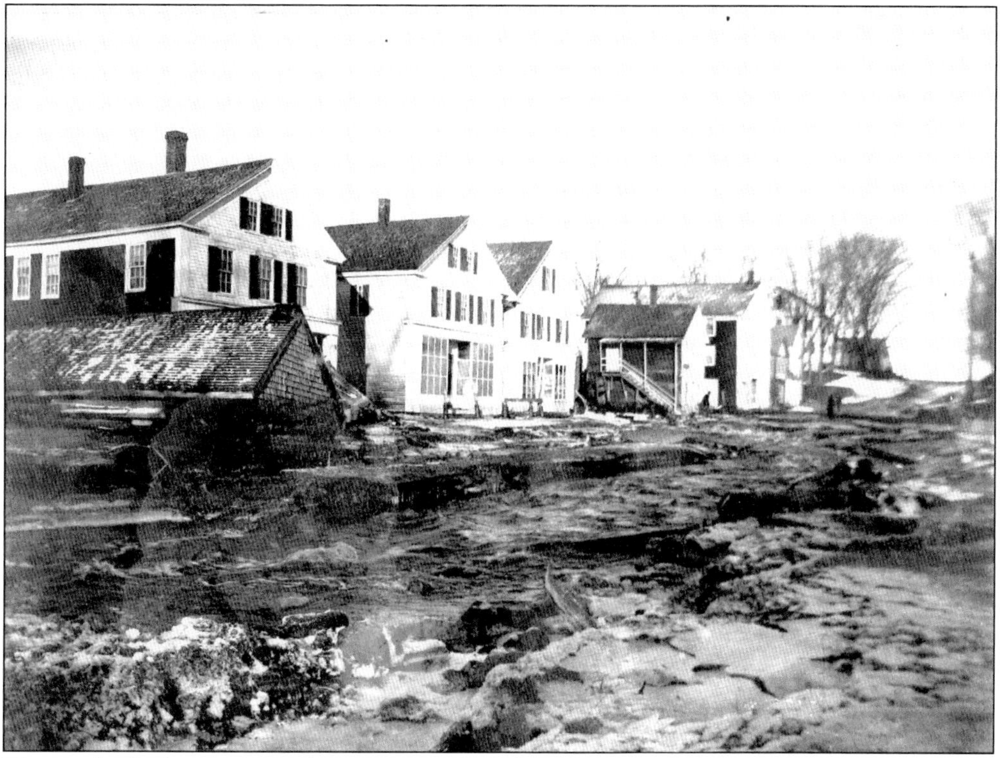

The roadbed of Main Street became a riverbed during the flood of 1901, which also destroyed many buildings in its path.

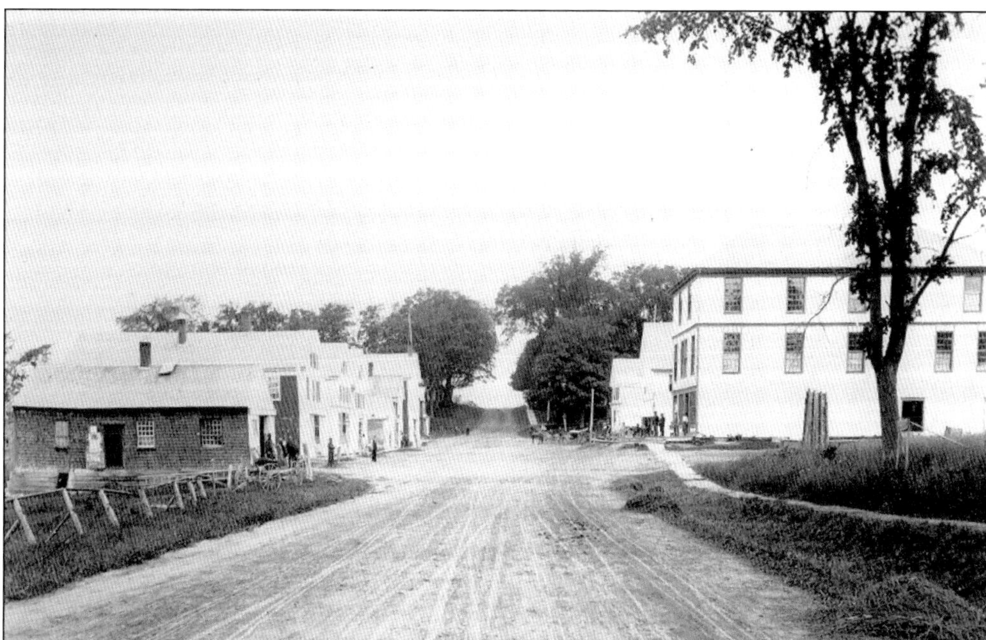

Main Street, now part of Route 150, looking north in the early 1900s included a blacksmith shop as the first building on the western side, where the telephone office is located today.

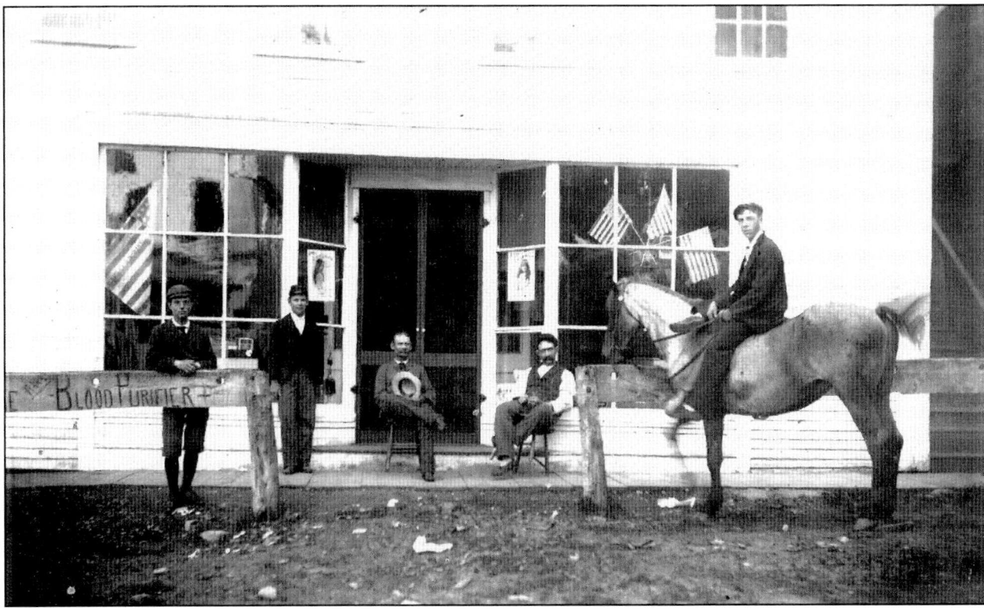

The Athens Store, shown here, has become the Country Store of recent times. This photograph was taken between 1896 and 1900, signified by the "McKinley for President" poster in the window. William McKinley was elected as the 25 U.S. president in 1896 and 1900.

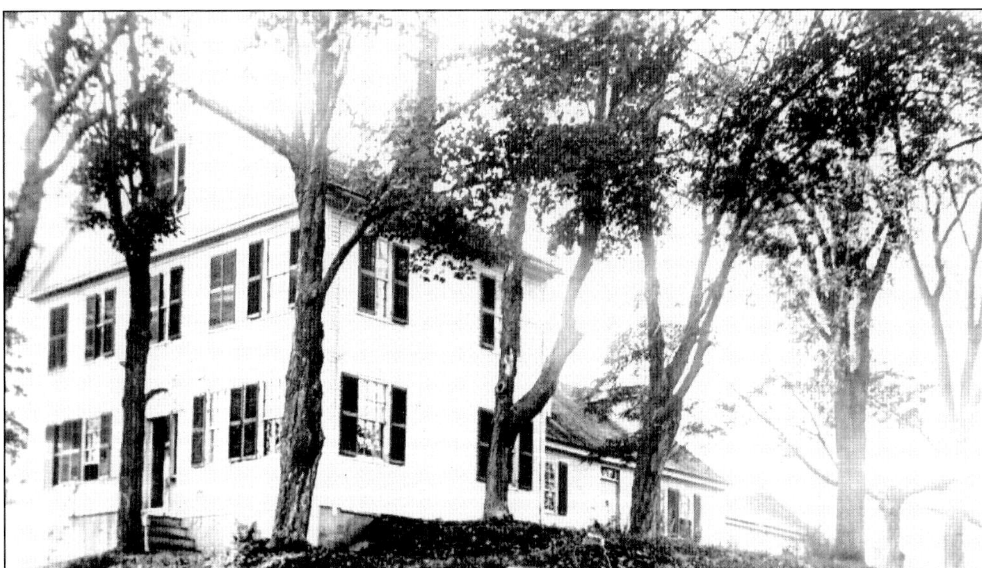

The Judge Greene home at the top of the hill on Main Street is one of the community's oldest homes. The Honorable Charles Greene who lived in the home was one of the original incorporators of Somerset Academy, the primary educational facility for the community from 1847 to 1967.

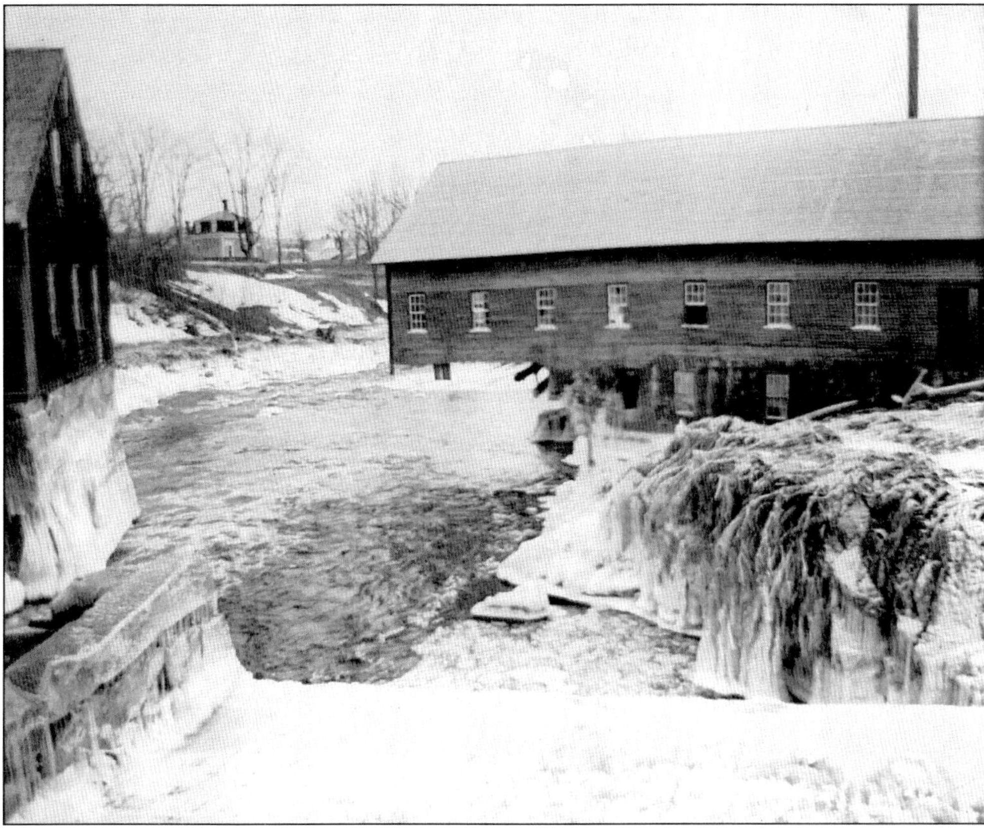

The Clark and Tobey Mill dominated the southern side of the bridge over the Wesserunsett Stream before part of it was destroyed during the 1901 flood.

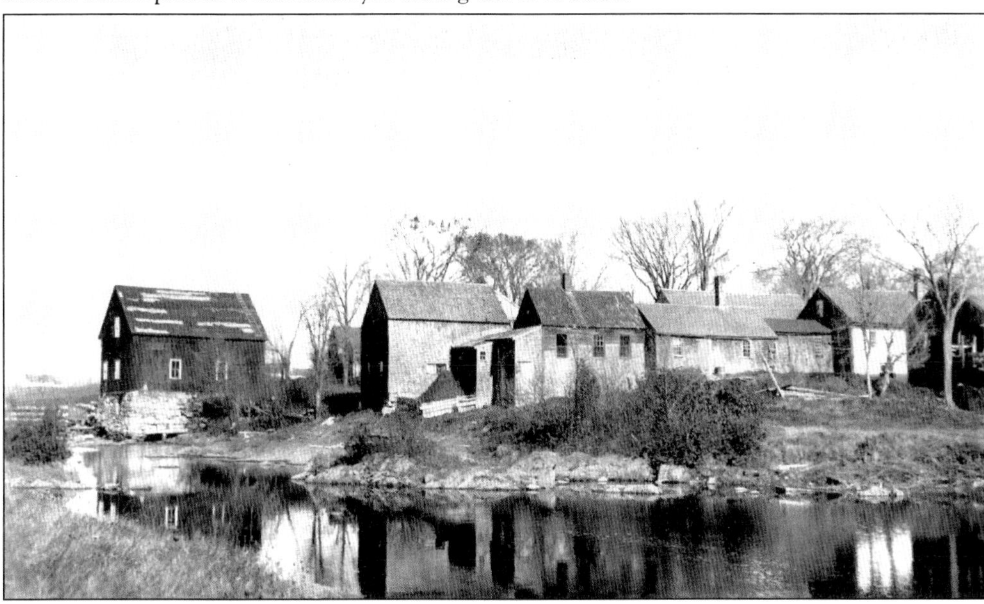

Upstream from the bridge, the backside of Main Street businesses are visible in the early 1900s. The large building at the edge of the stream was a box factory that specialized in creating coffins.

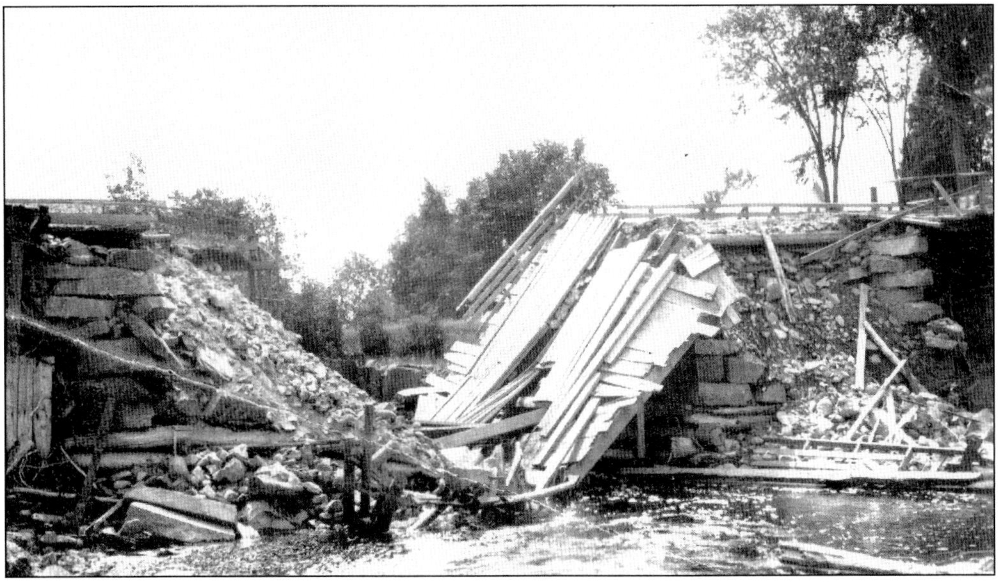

The bridge over the Wesserunsett Stream collapsed in the 1930s and was rebuilt.

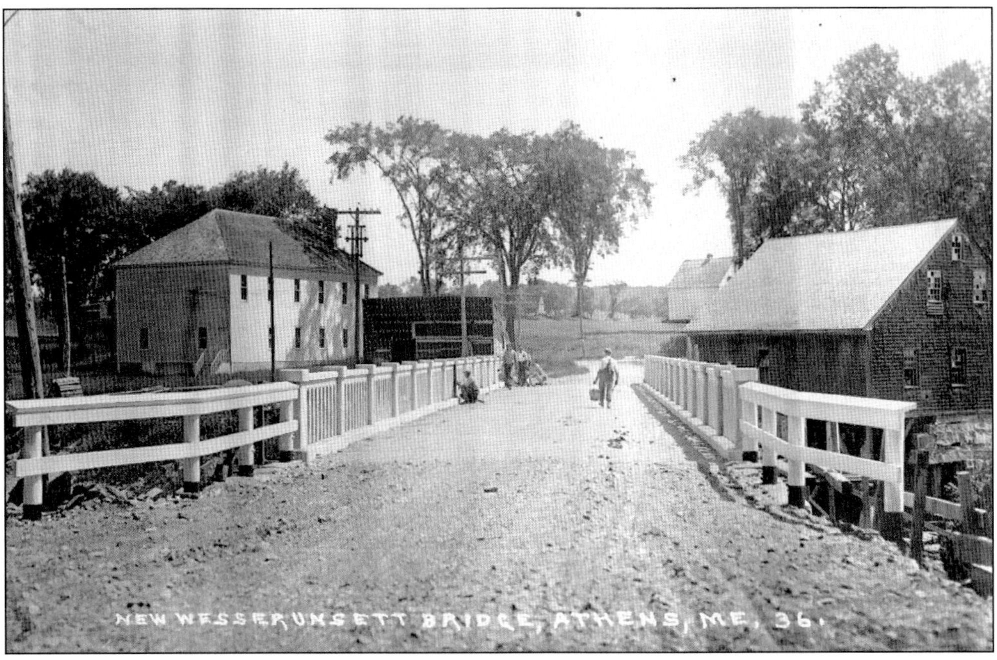

The bridge taking Route 150 to the southern end of Main Street was built around 1936. The Athens Grange Hall is visible on Main Street with a gristmill still visible south of the bridge. Samuel Hall was the original owner of the mill, but Tobey of Clark and Tobey later owned it. In the distance, the Ware cemetery is visible with a monument at its center. The graves and monument were removed when John Ware moved out of town.

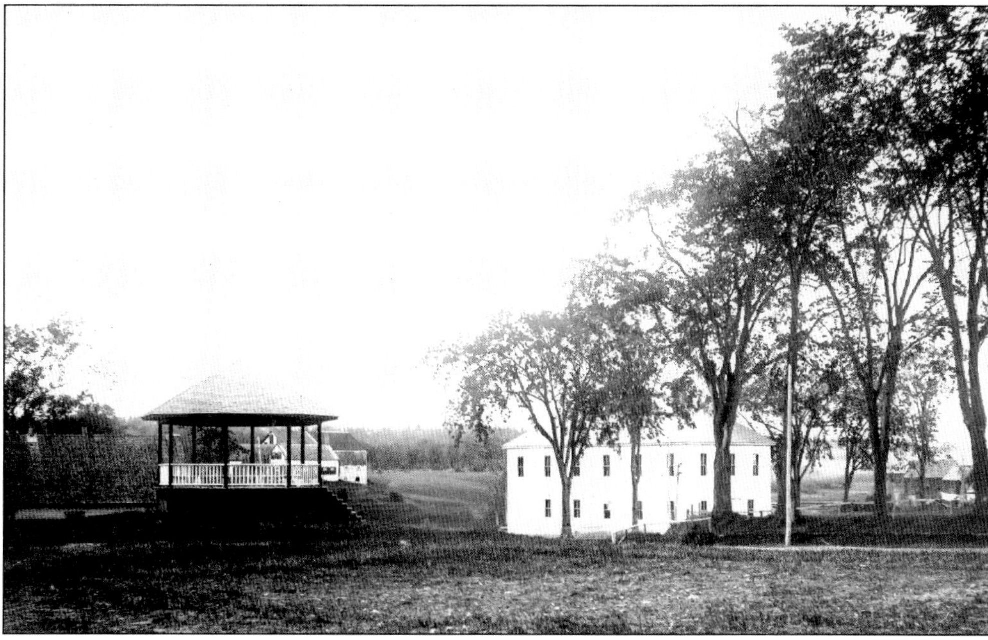

The town bandstand once stood with a view of Main Street and the Grange hall to the west. The same spot holds the town's elementary school today.

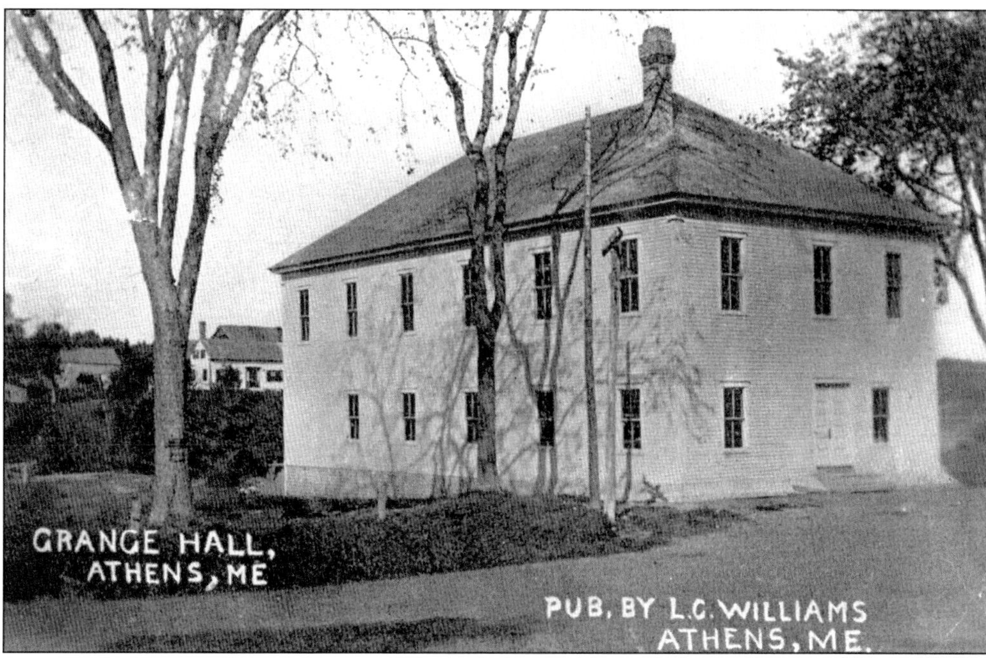

The Athens Grange Hall has been a prominent part of the community since the early 1900s. Initially, a meeting place for the Patrons of Husbandry, known more commonly as the Grange, the hall became a well-used hall for town and family celebrations and fund-raisers.

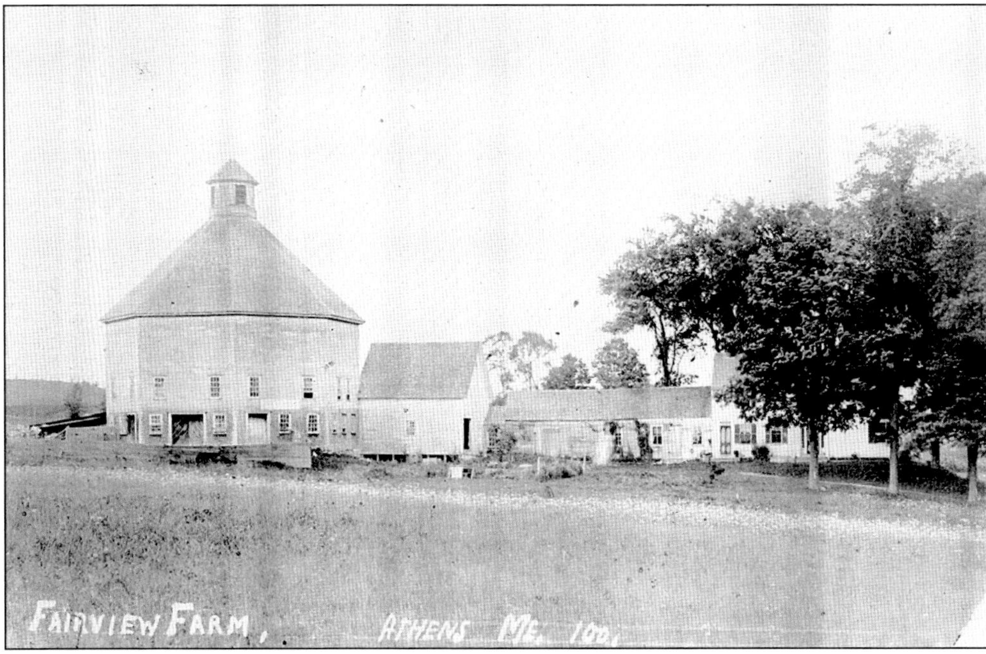

The round barn at Fairview Farm was a local landmark. It stood across from the fairgrounds behind what is now Jim's Variety. The house still stands, but the barn was torn down after it was determined too costly to make repairs. The structure was of Shaker design, engineered on the same idea as ship construction.

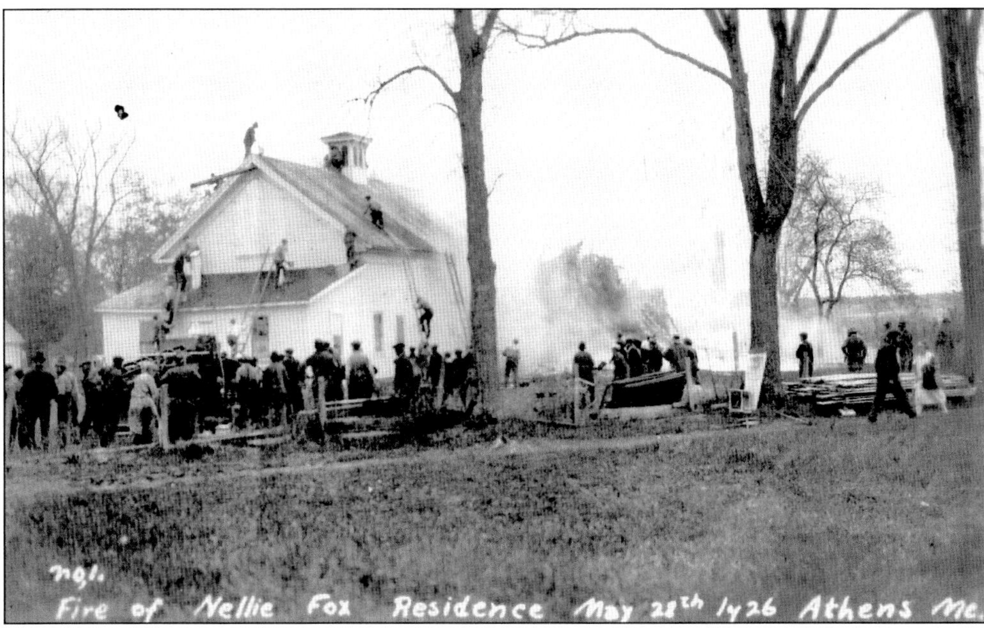

Many cameras from the early 1900s and into the 1920s took photographs that were reproduced as postcards. That may have been the reason postcards of the Nellie Fox fire of May 28, 1926, are in circulation. Postcards of that era captured landmarks, celebrations, and every day events as well as family events.

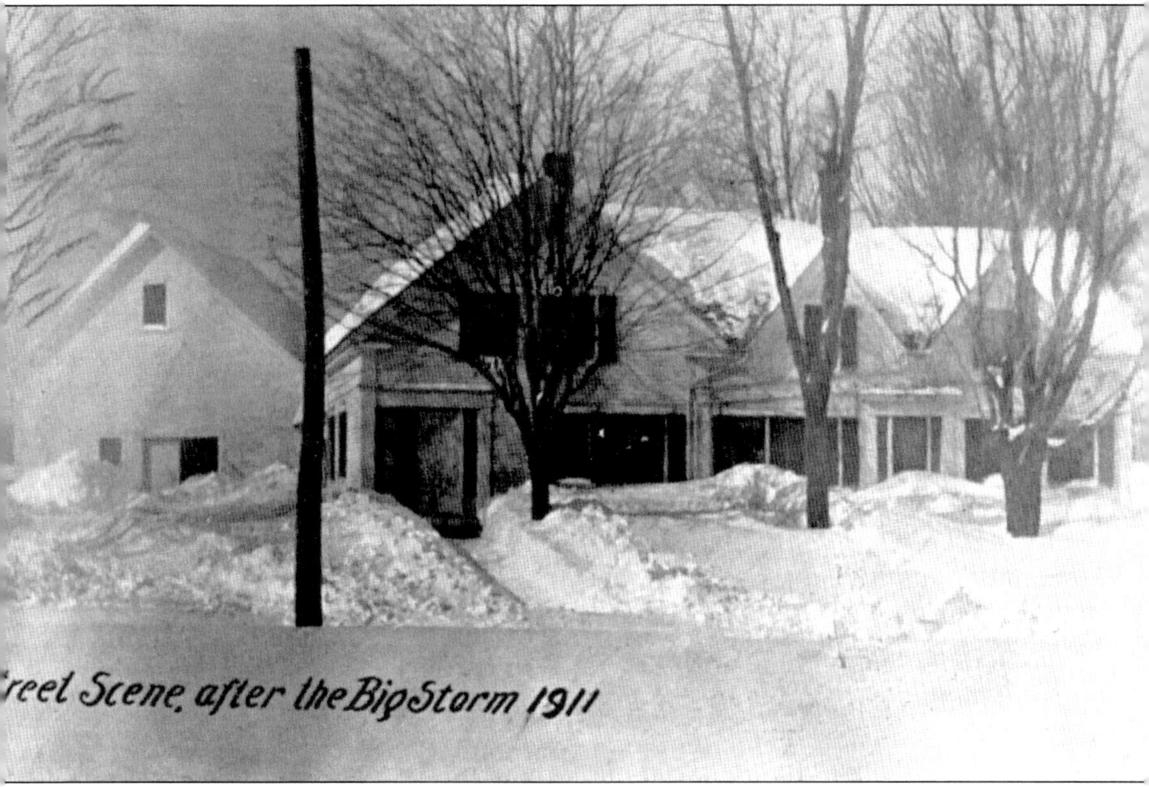

One of the earliest homes in Athens was captured on film following a snowstorm in 1911. Originally the home of Nahum Cook, it still stands today on Route 150 next to the bridge over Wesserunsett Stream.

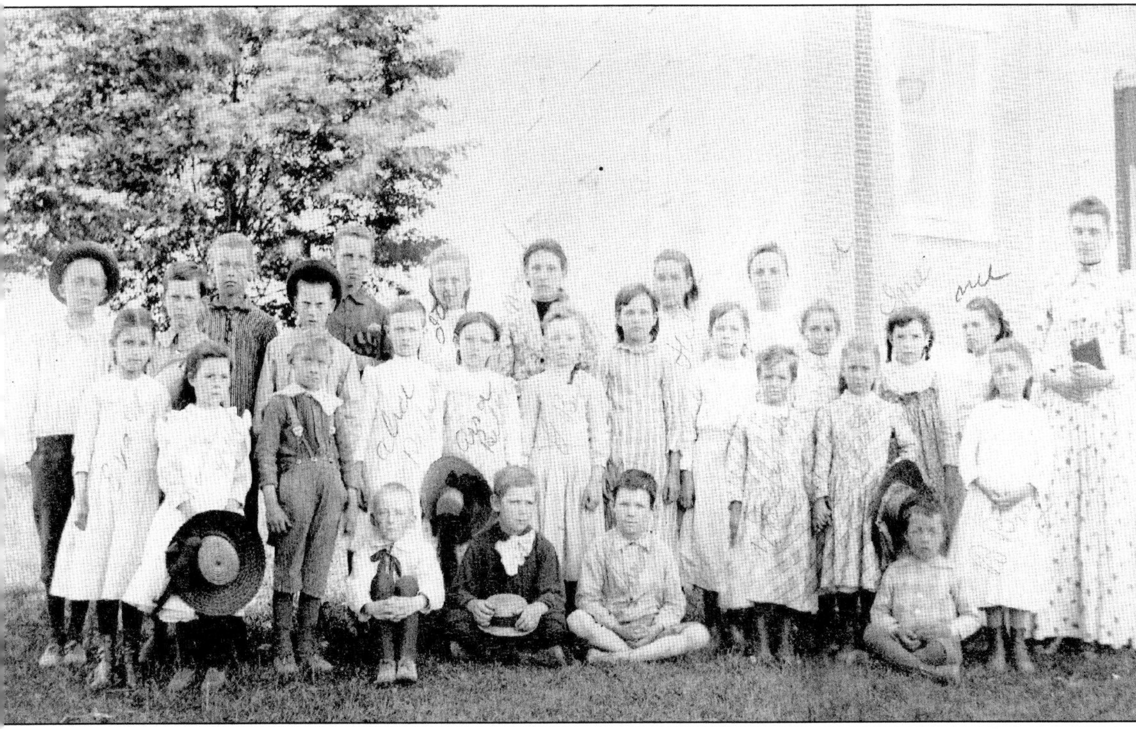

An early photograph of Somerset Academy, likely taken around 1900, demonstrates the various ages of students at the facility over the years. A school for all ages initially, in its final years, the school was the town's high school.

The Somerset Academy building was an impressive structure in its day, and is today an example of early construction techniques. The academy served the town of Athens for 120 years before the tiny local school was swallowed up by Maine's School Administrative District system and the town joined School Administrative District 59 based in Madison. The building is now on the National Register of Historic Places. The building holds the town office and the Athens Historical Society, and the local American Legion Post holds meetings there. The Somerset Academy's Board of Trustees is still active and awards scholarships to Athens students and contributes to projects at the Athens Elementary School.

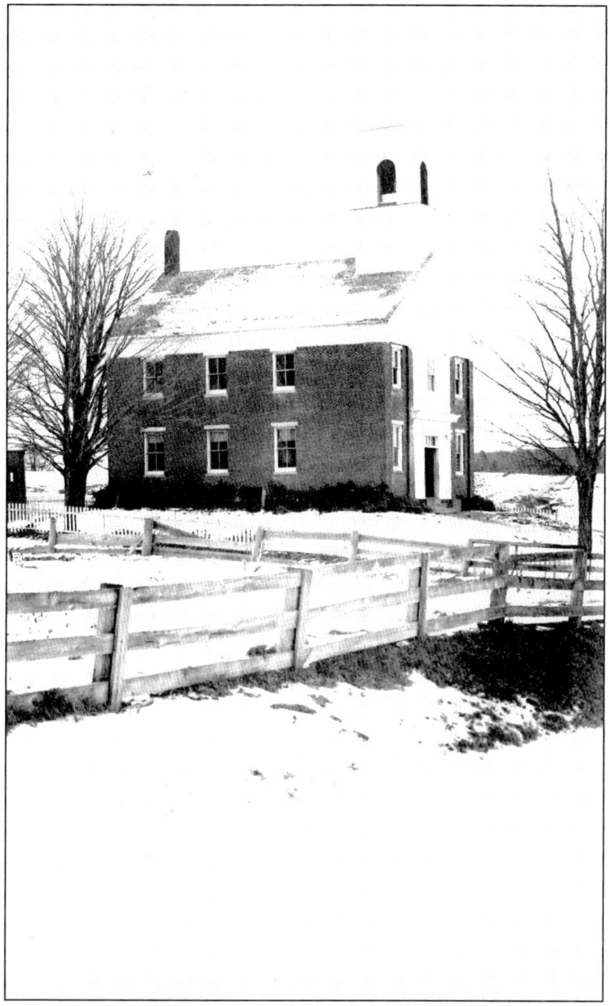

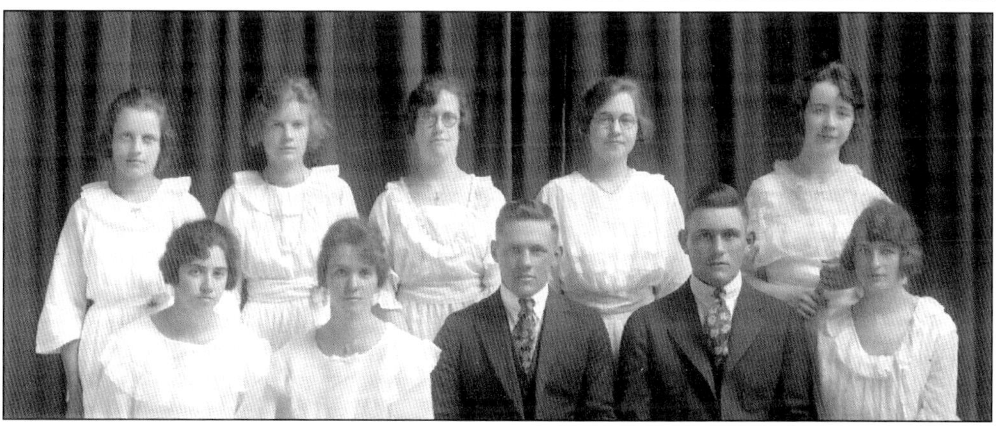

The Somerset Academy graduating class of 1926 had just 10 students. From left to right are (first row) Anne French, Lurline Small, Everett Tufts, Byron Weston, and Lucy Violet Slack Allen; (second row) Mary G. Russell, Nellie Mildred Russell, Helen Donahue, Fern A. Dennis, and Eleanor Troy Williams.

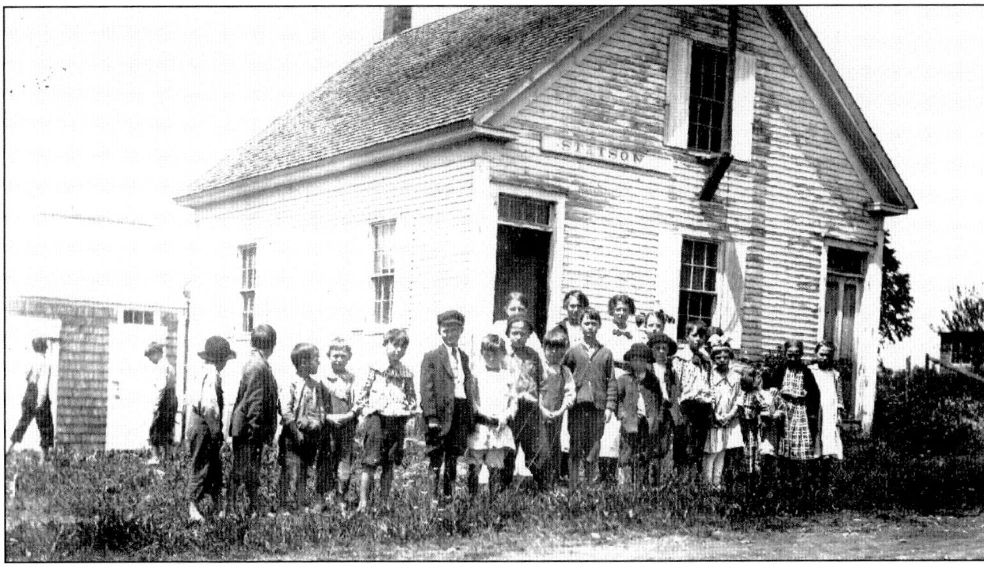

The Stetson School in West Athens, seen here with a class in the 1930s, began as a Seven Day Adventist Church after the Civil War and was used as a church and a school until 1936 when it burned. It was rebuilt and operated as a two-room school about 1937–1938. The property was later divided to become a home for one family, and the milk room for another's farm.

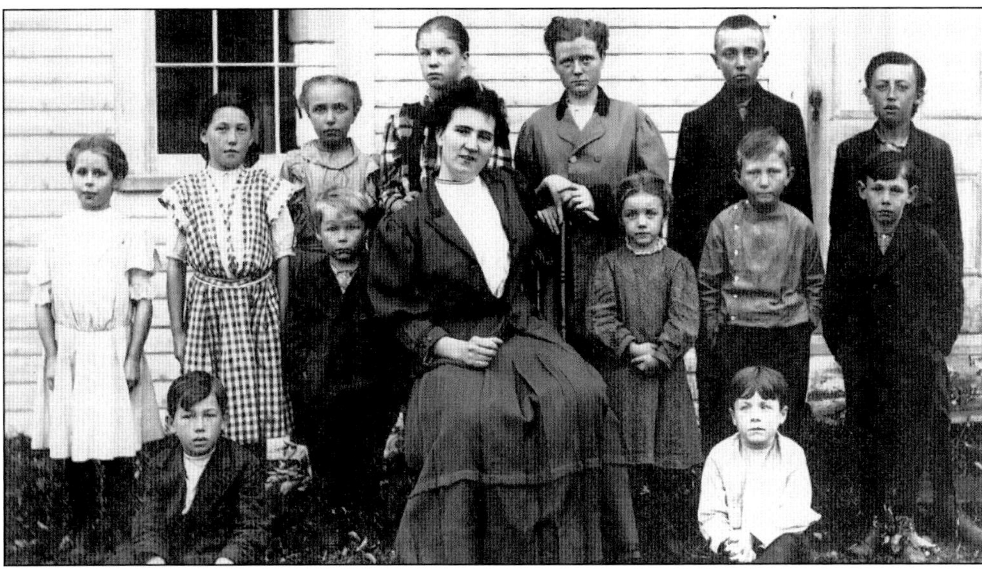

One room, multi-grade schools were the norm in rural Maine in the 1800s and in the early 1900s. The population of individual schools was similar to this group at the West Athens school. Students in the Athens district schools attended school from age 4 to 21, with the attendance higher in the winter months when the older children were not helping with farm chores at home. The West Athens Grammar School was one of the few district schools that survived in the 20th century. The students and teachers here are unidentified, but it is believed to include a number of members of the Avery, Kincaid, Brown, and Tuttle families. Many people from the area are familiar with a story about a feud between the Browns and Tuttles, but there is no current explanation for the alleged feud that may have developed as early as 1900. The school is still a home in West Athens.

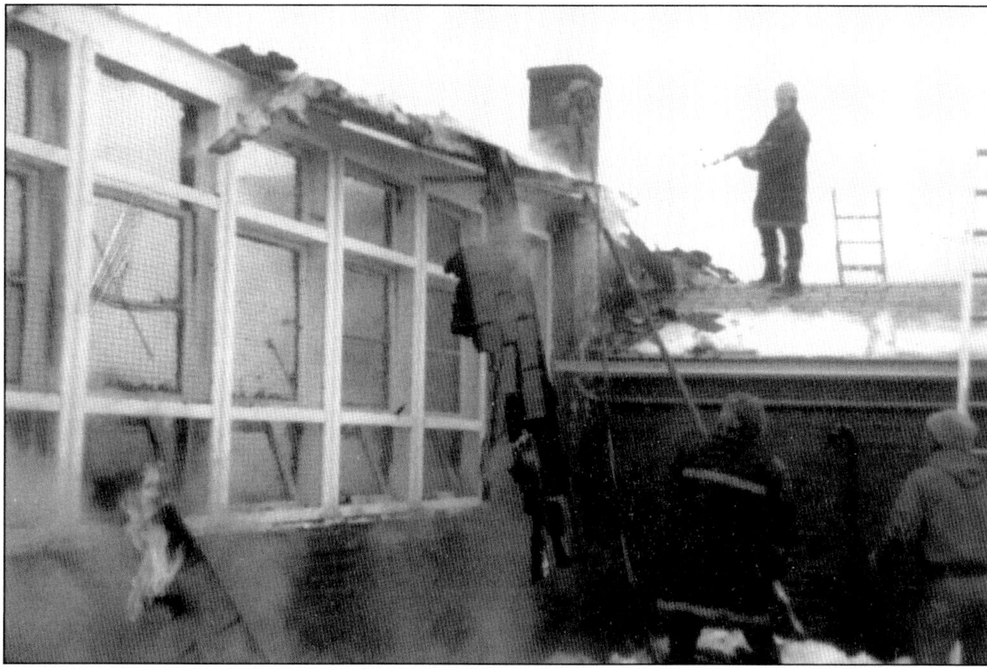

An activity in the utility room at the Athens Elementary School in 1981 set some paper on fire, destroying the school. Students attended school in a cluster of mobile classrooms until the new school opened in 1983.

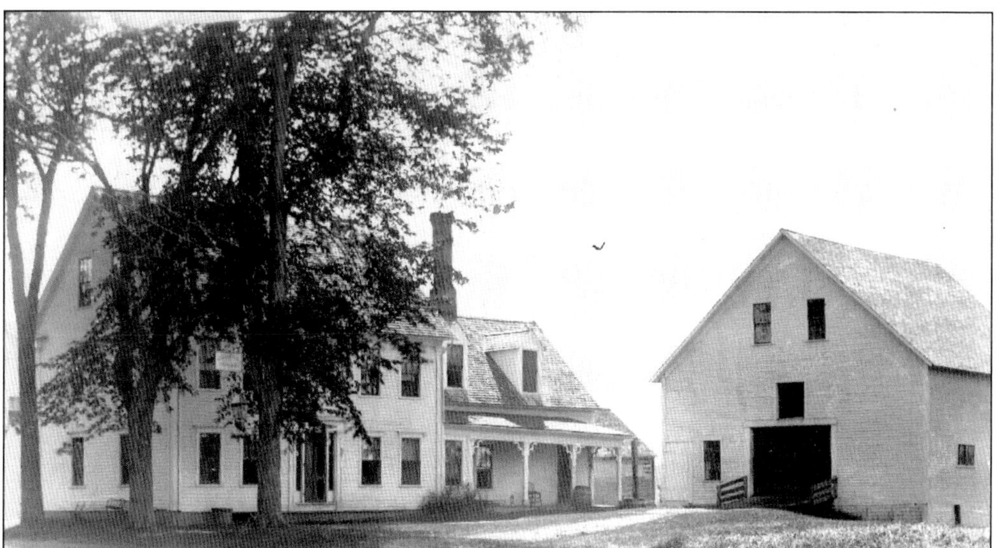

The Cook House, a large farmhouse across from the Ware estate and near the location of the present elementary school, served as an inn in the early 1900s.

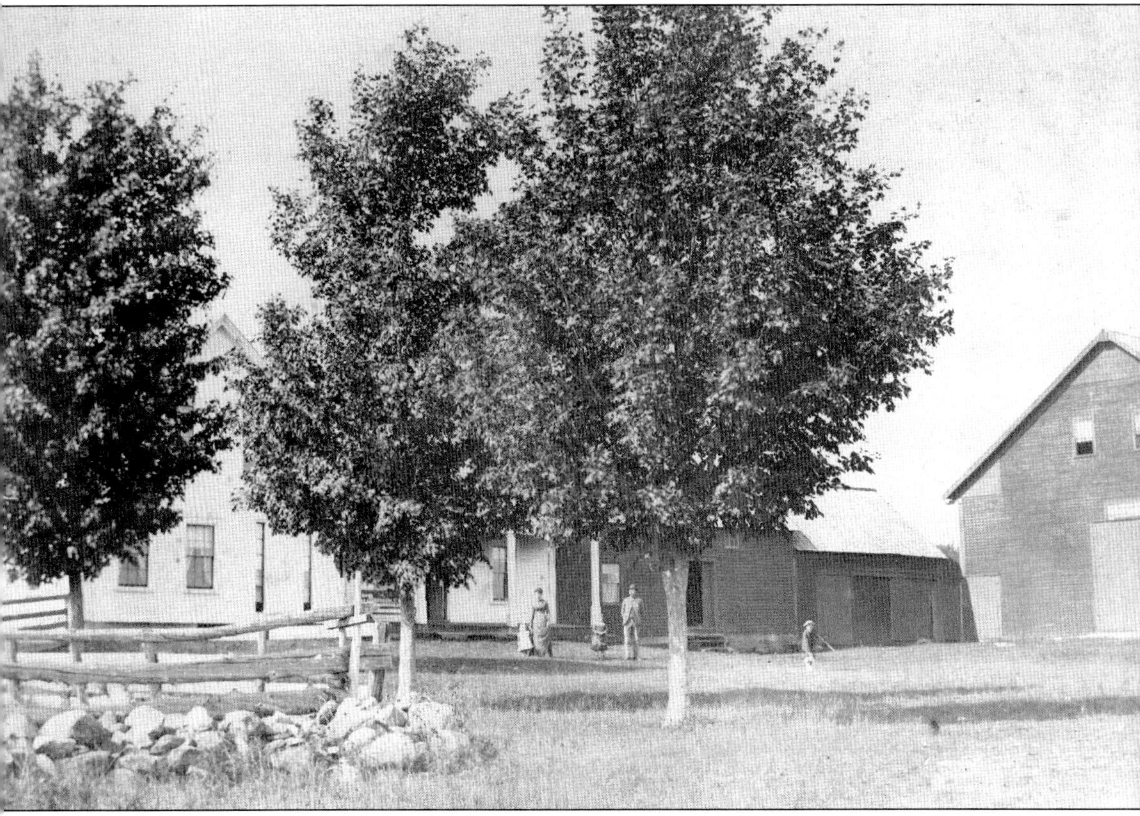

Simon and Nellie Fox with children Thomas, Eliza, and Jennie pose, around the beginning of the 20th century, in front of their farm home in the vicinity of Fox Hill. Simon is believed to be a descendant or relative of the one of the town's earliest settlers, Thomas Fox, who settled on Fox Hill in the early 1800s.

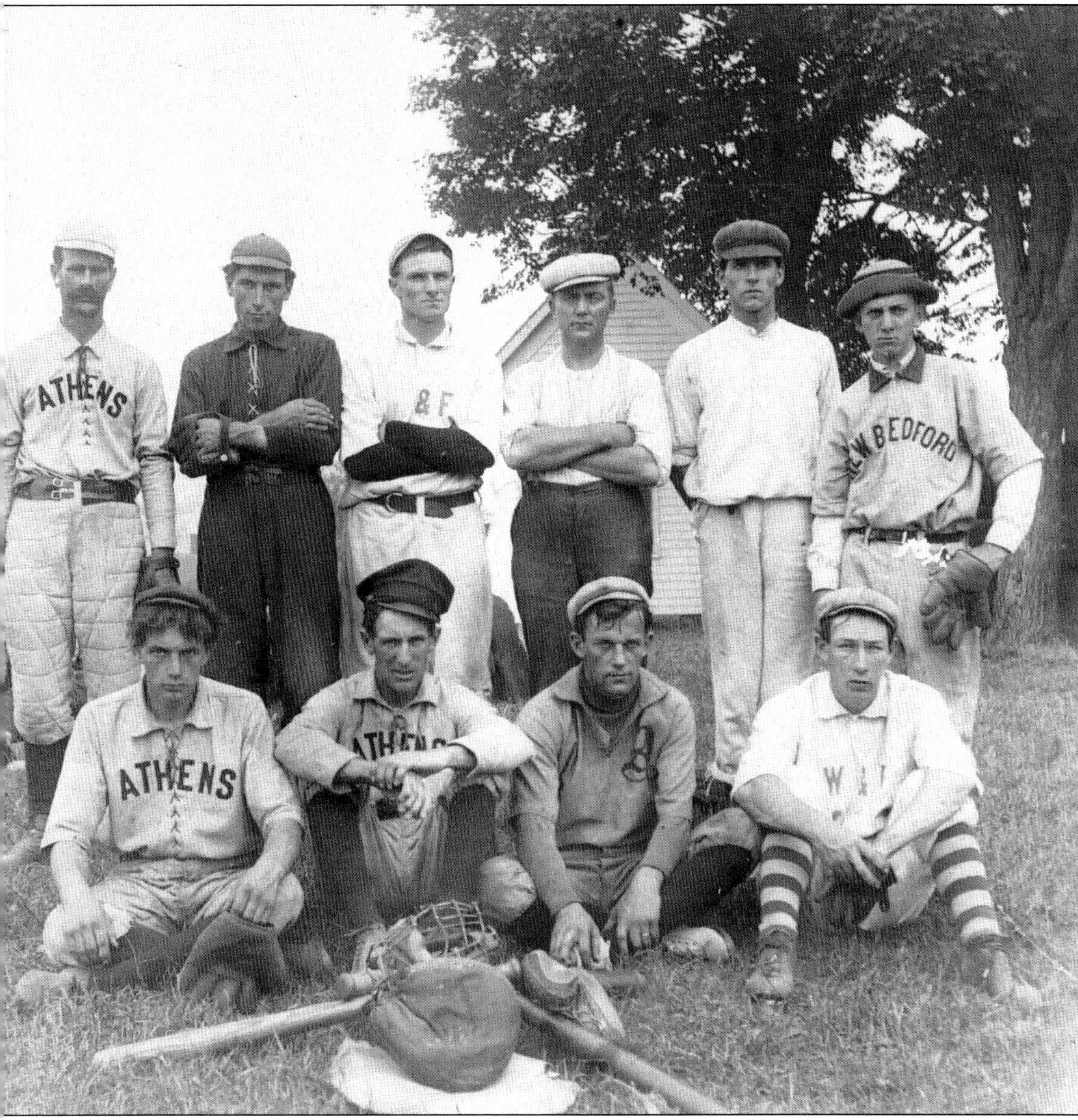

Baseball was a sport that brought communities together in the early 20th century in rural Maine. Everyone took pride in the hometown team and followed the season faithfully. The members of this Athens team were well-known local athletes in the 1920s, but today only two are identified including Myles Elliott, third from the left in the second row, and possibly Tom Fox, second from the left in the first row.

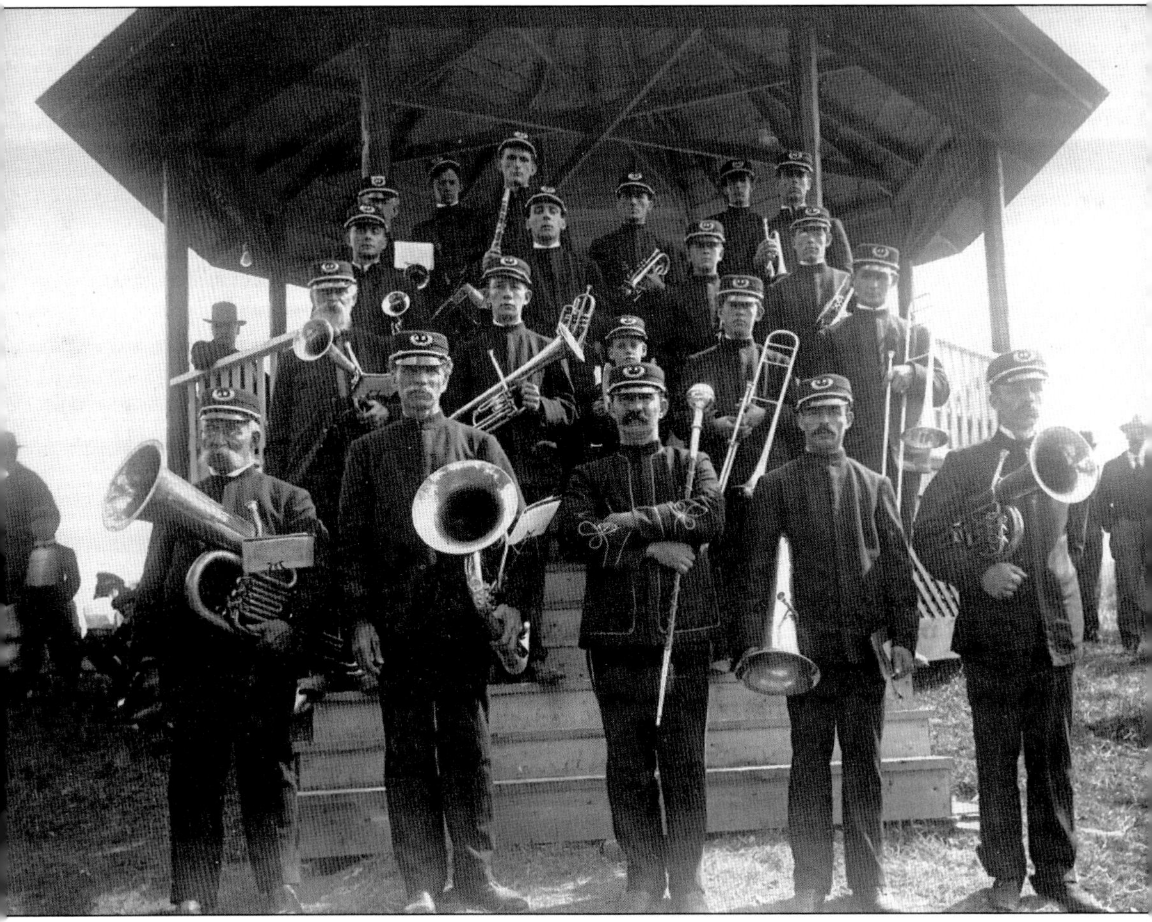

In 1904, the town of Athens celebrated its centennial. The celebration included a fair and exhibition, a parade, and likely concerts by the community band in the center of town at the bandstand. This is where the band chose to pose for their official picture marking the event.

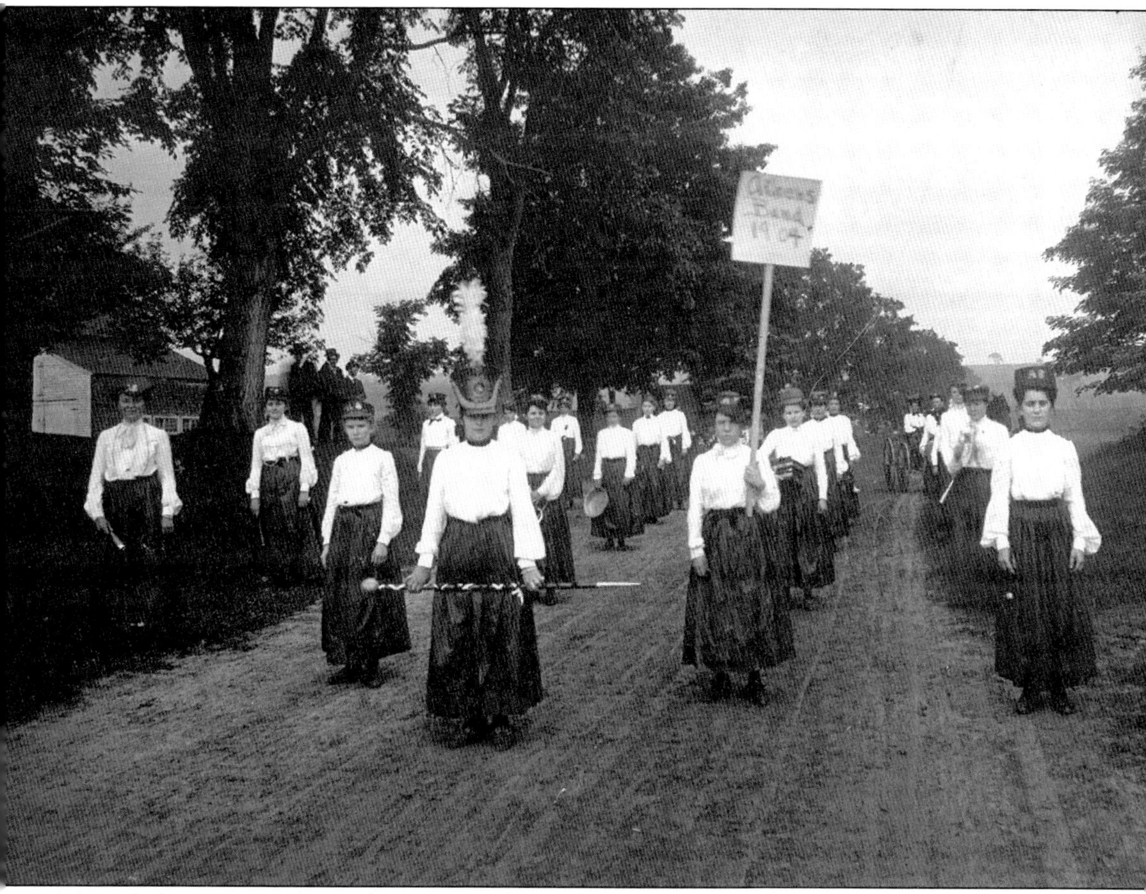

Athens ladies were not be outdone during the centennial, forming the Athens Ladies Coronet Band of 1904. Among its members were drum major Marion Holman, Bertha Cook, Marguerite Fox, Josephine Hight, Hilda Dore, Rose Scribner, Maola Walker, Florice York, Marie Bunker, and Rosie Cooley.

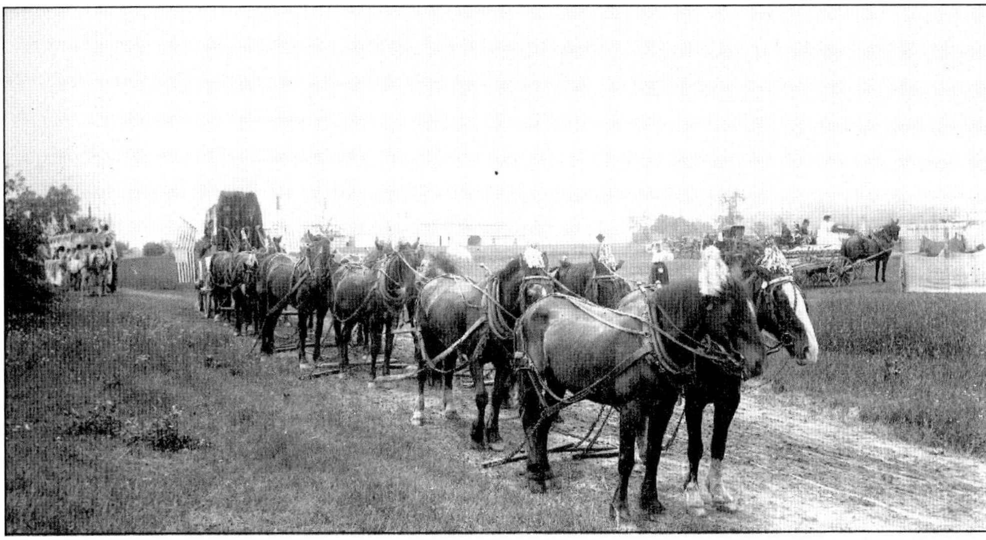

The centennial parade of 1904 included business floats and organization floats, but this one represented neighbors from Stickney Hill, drawn by 12 horses.

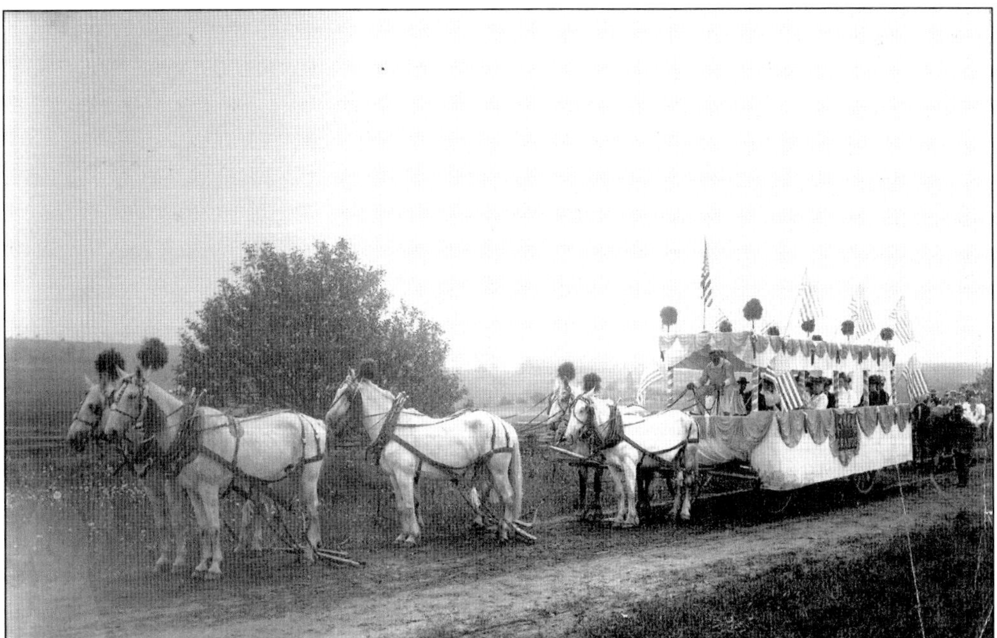

A team of white horses pulled the Athens Grange float in 1904, with several members aboard.

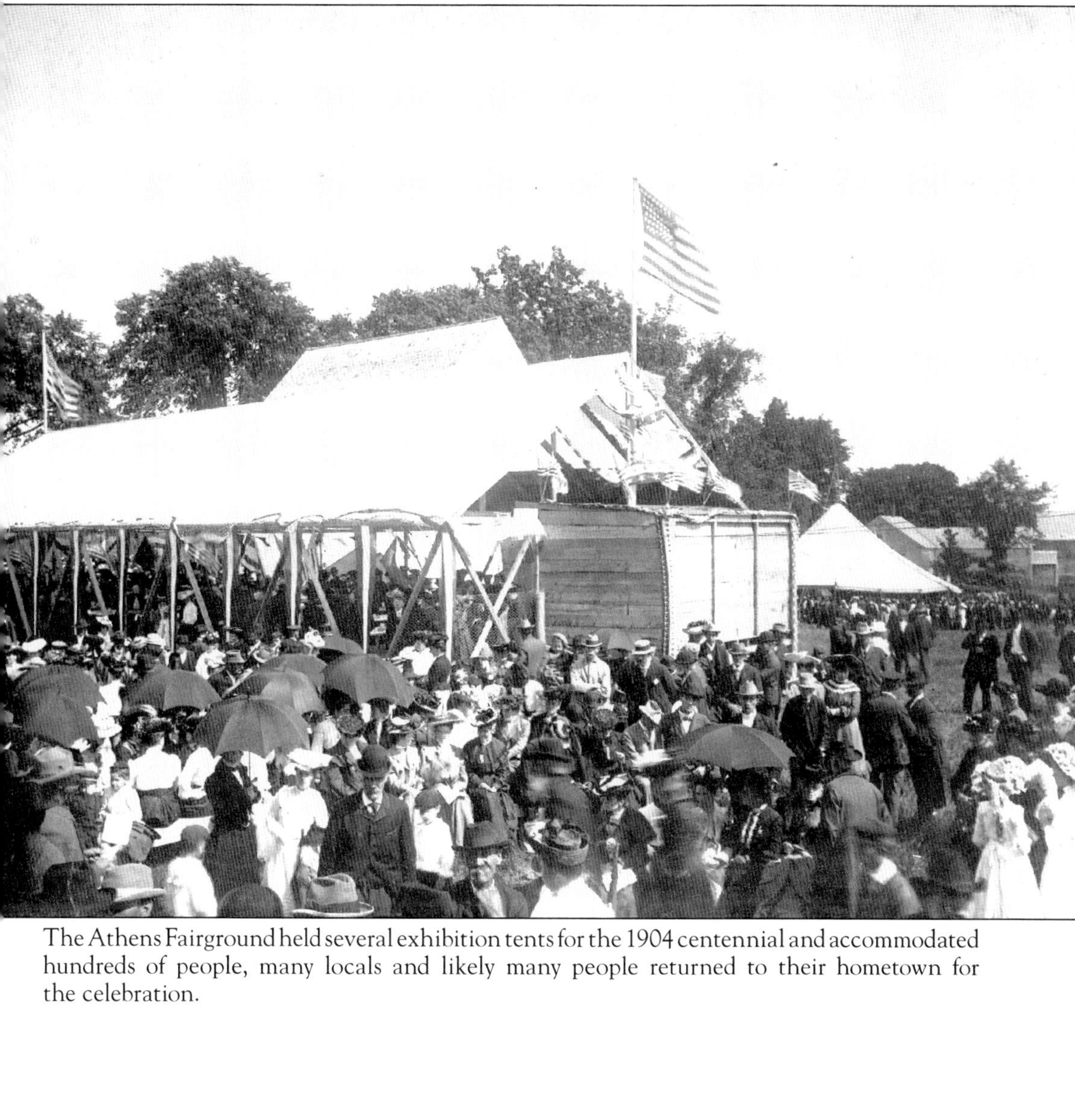

The Athens Fairground held several exhibition tents for the 1904 centennial and accommodated hundreds of people, many locals and likely many people returned to their hometown for the celebration.

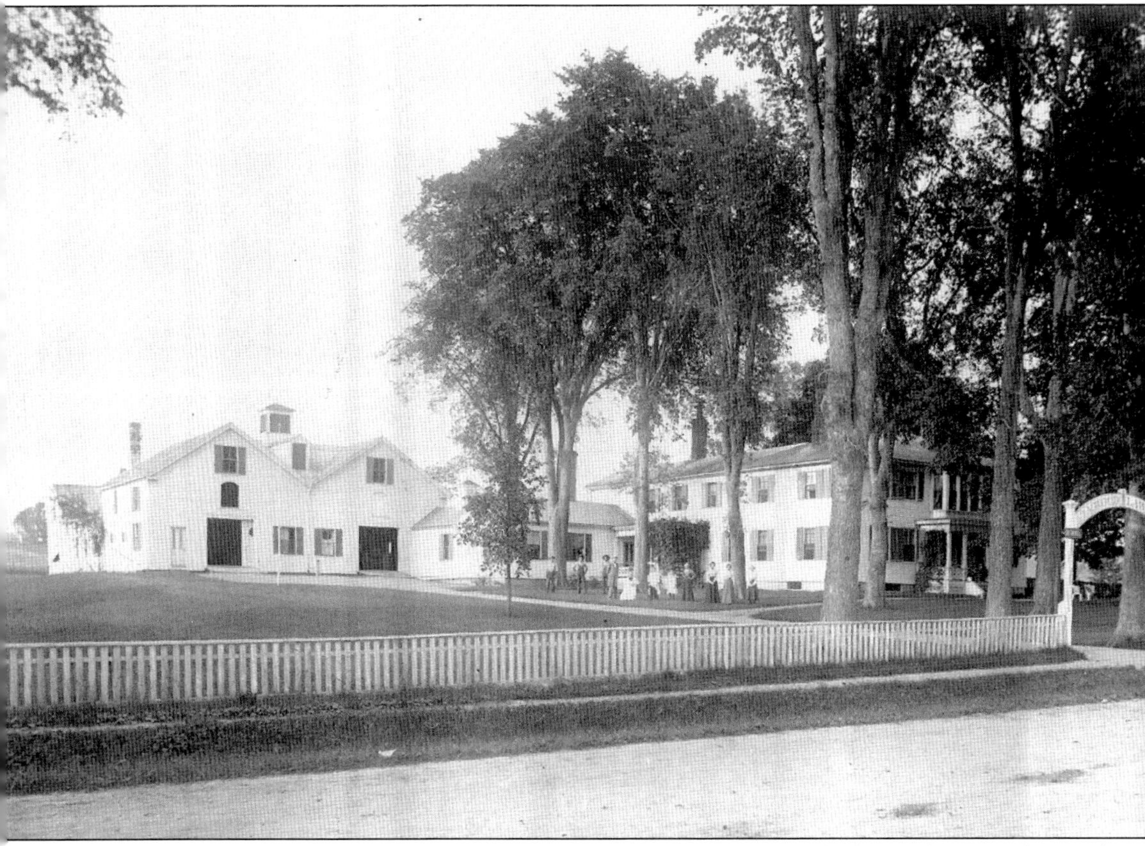

John Ware came to Athens in 1817, eventually constructing one of the largest homes, Elmwood Lawn, near the present elementary school site. Ware dealt in real estate, operated a brickyard and gristmill in the village, and controlled the community and his family with his wealth. The family cemetery plot once stood on the site of the elementary school with a large family monument prominently placed. Ware was described as a man of "excitable temperament" and somewhat eccentric. In his early years in Athens, he wanted a better route to Skowhegan than down the East Ridge Road. He granted the town $800 to build a carriage road from the village to Cass' Corner, setting the path for today's Route 150. He never married but raised two nephews to be his heirs. A story is told that after a dispute with the town, one of the nephews' sons, also named John, moved to Waterville and promptly exhumed the family members in the cemetery and moved them as well. The monument at the center of the lot was moved later to Mount Rest Cemetery. The Ware Estate became the home of Dr. Ellingwood.

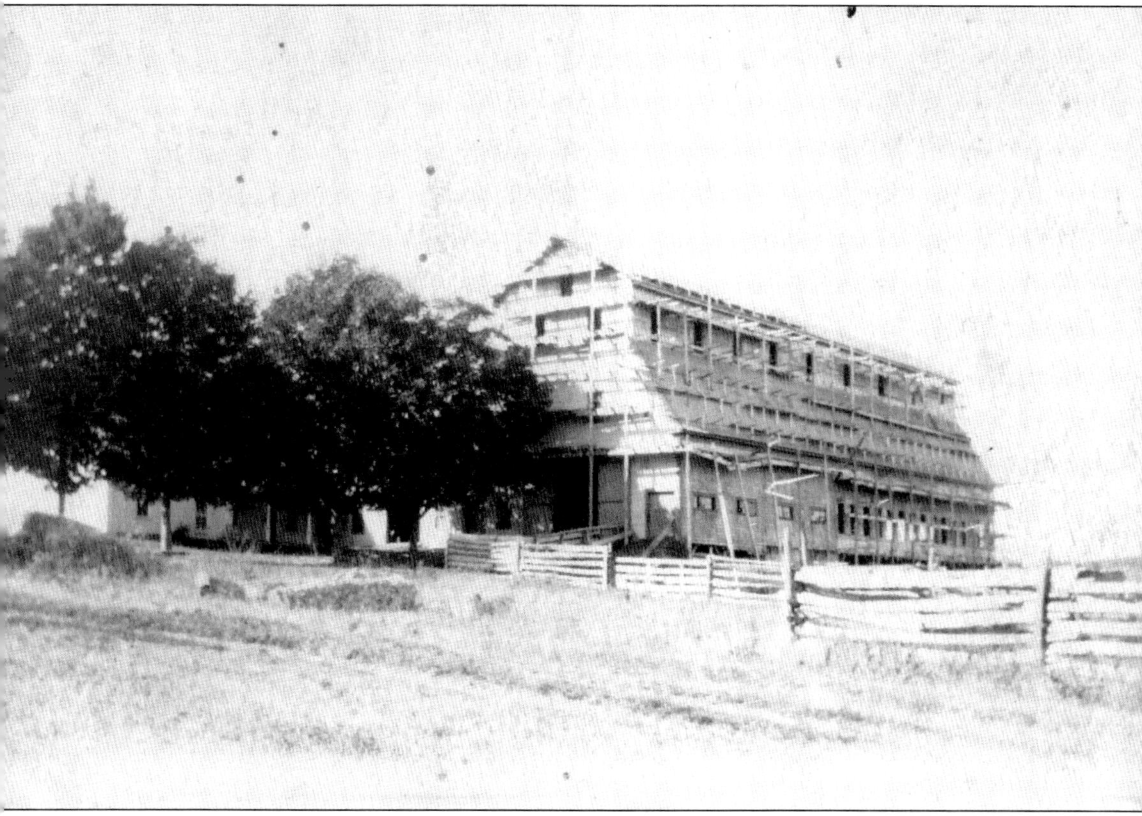

The Eaton family farm near the Solon town line boasted one of the largest barns in the area. The structure was 60 feet from the floor to the peak. It was used mostly for hay storage with plans for owner Harvey Eaton to raise longhorn cattle. The structure lasted just two or three years before it was destroyed by fire.

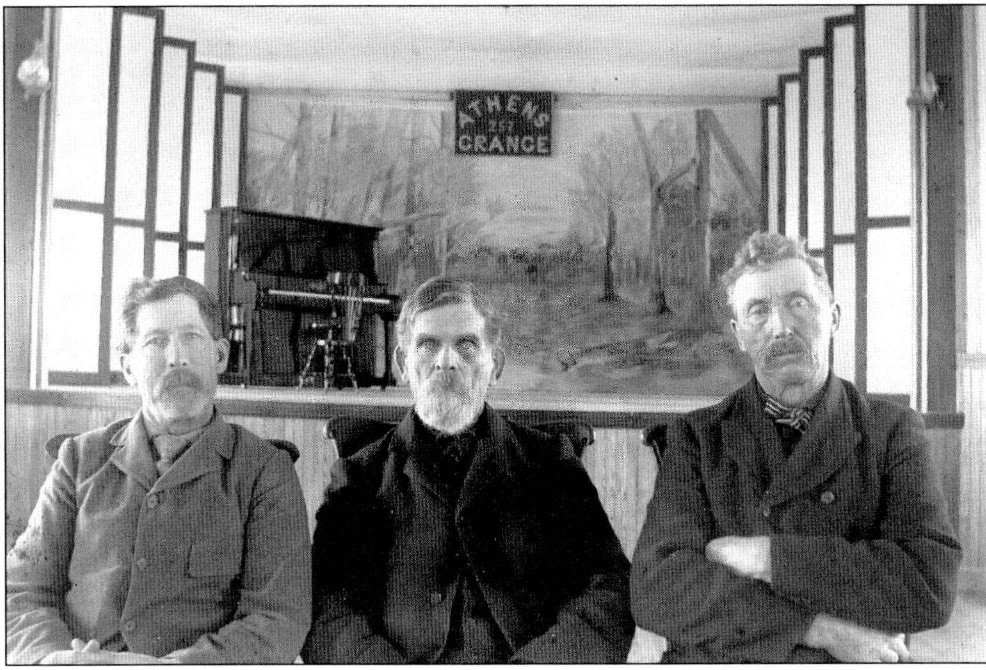

A committee of three was in charge of the Grange construction in the late 1800s including J. E. Chapman, G. H. Allen, and B. P. Barker.

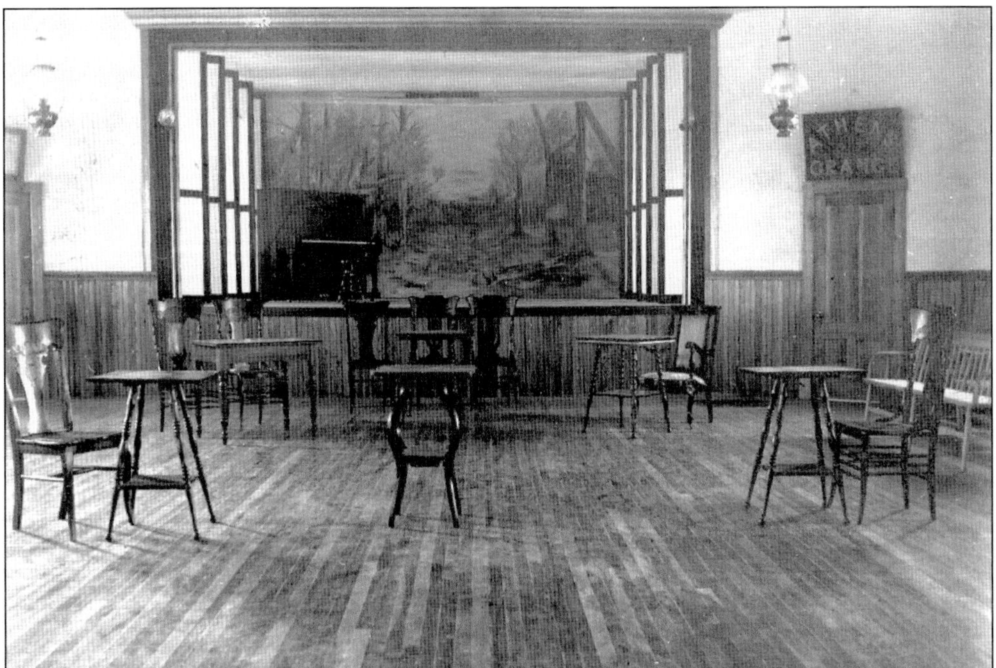

The Athens Grange Hall appears sparsely decorated in this early photograph. However, the chairs and tables are set up according to the stations of the grange ritual that honored the agricultural lifestyle of the times.

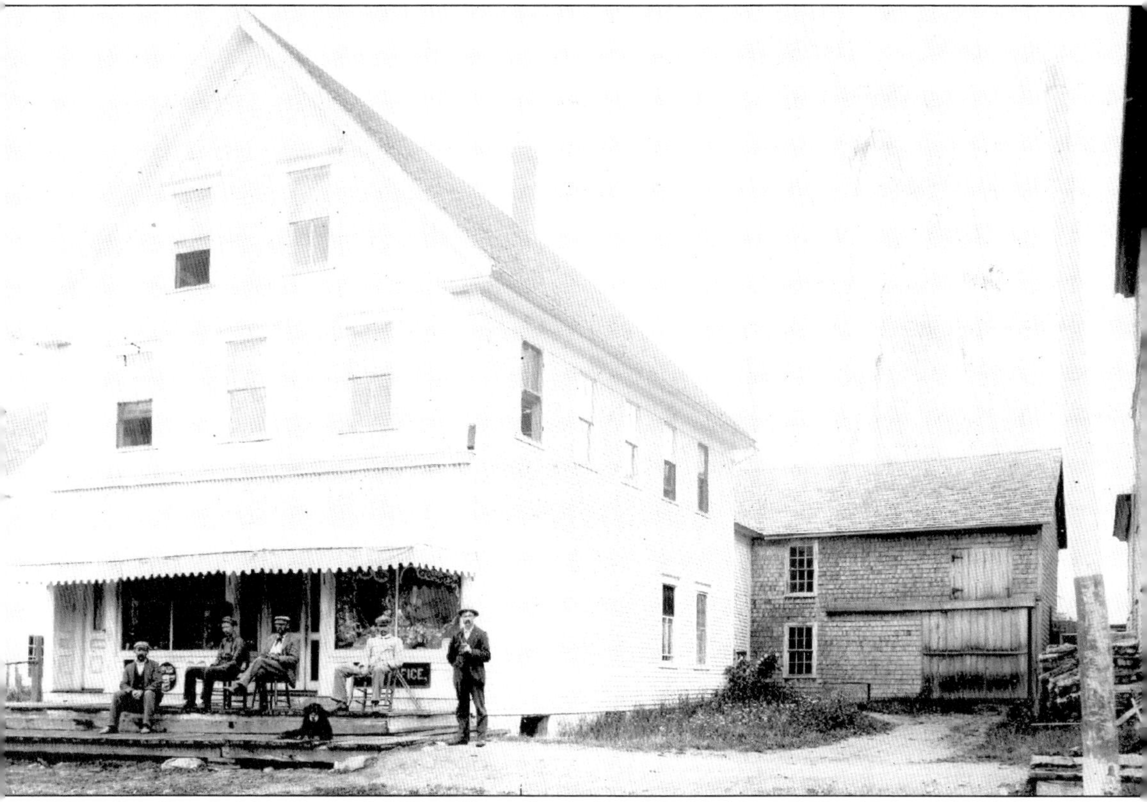

The post office and drug store of L. C. Williams burned in 1931, in the same fire that consumed the Odd Fellows hall next door. (In the other direction the Country Store structure was saved.) After the Williams building was burned, a store building from across the street was moved onto the site. It housed the Athens Post Office until the new post office was opened in January 1986.

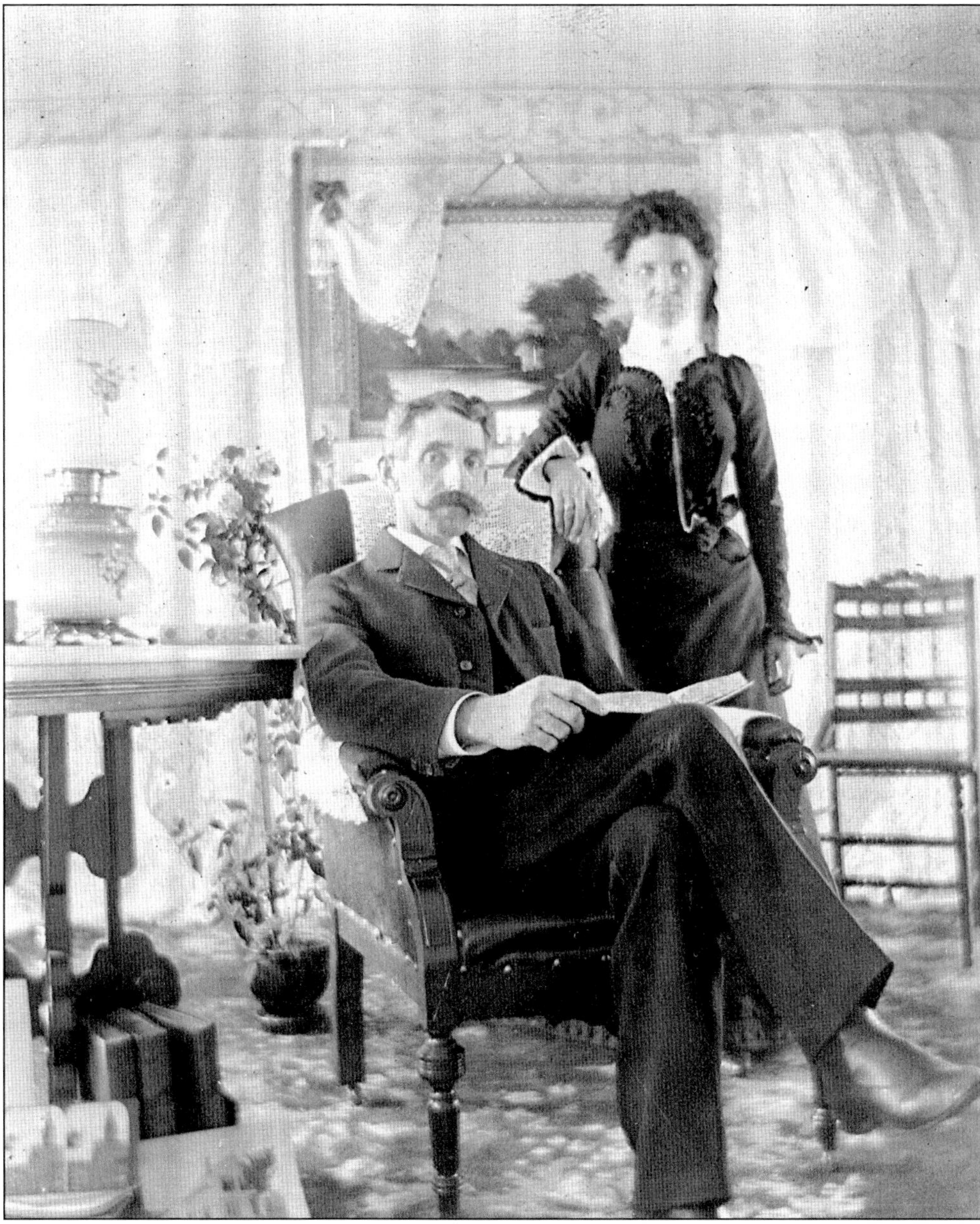

George and Jean Ayer were co-owners with M. J. Hight of Hight and Ayer General Store. Their apparently comfortable lifestyle is apparent in a formal portrait in their home.

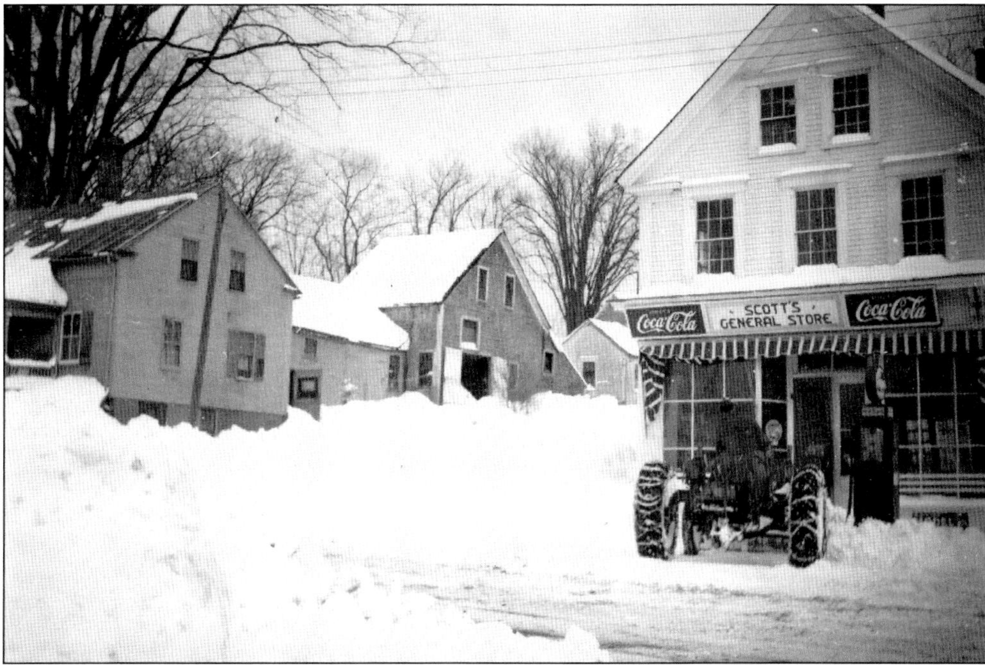

Scott's General Store of the 1940s and early 1950s is Paula's Restaurant today. The property has seen numerous owners and uses through the years.

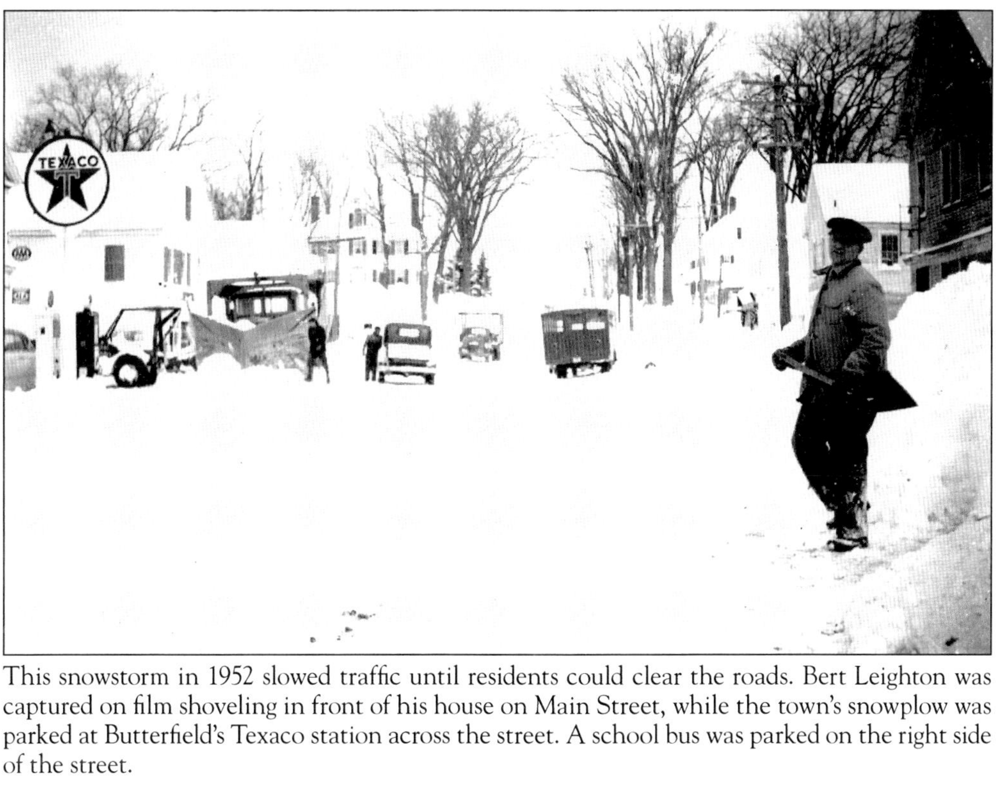

This snowstorm in 1952 slowed traffic until residents could clear the roads. Bert Leighton was captured on film shoveling in front of his house on Main Street, while the town's snowplow was parked at Butterfield's Texaco station across the street. A school bus was parked on the right side of the street.

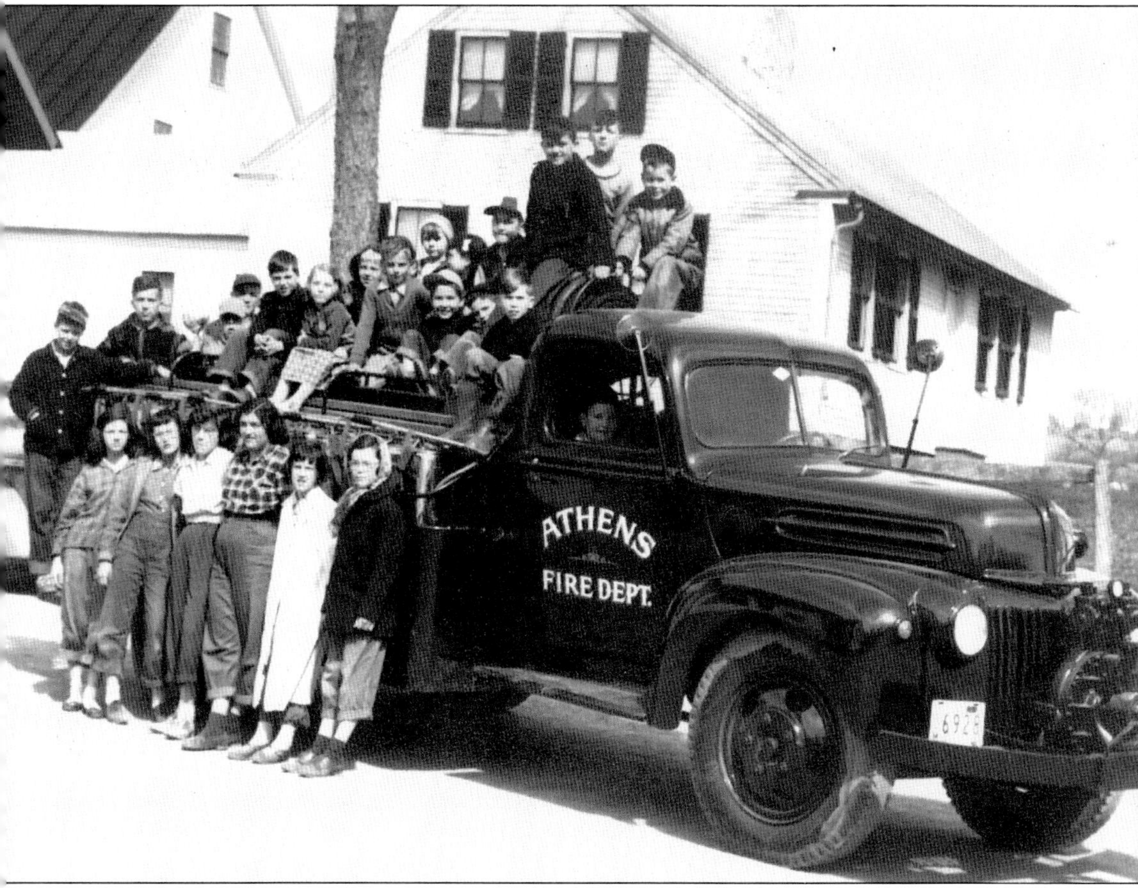

In 1947, the creation of the new fire department and the arrival of its first fire truck was an occasion for a photograph with area children. The Athens Fire Department was organized by M. J. "Joe" Stewart. The truck was parked in the front of the Washington School and the students took advantage of the opportunity to be recorded with local history.

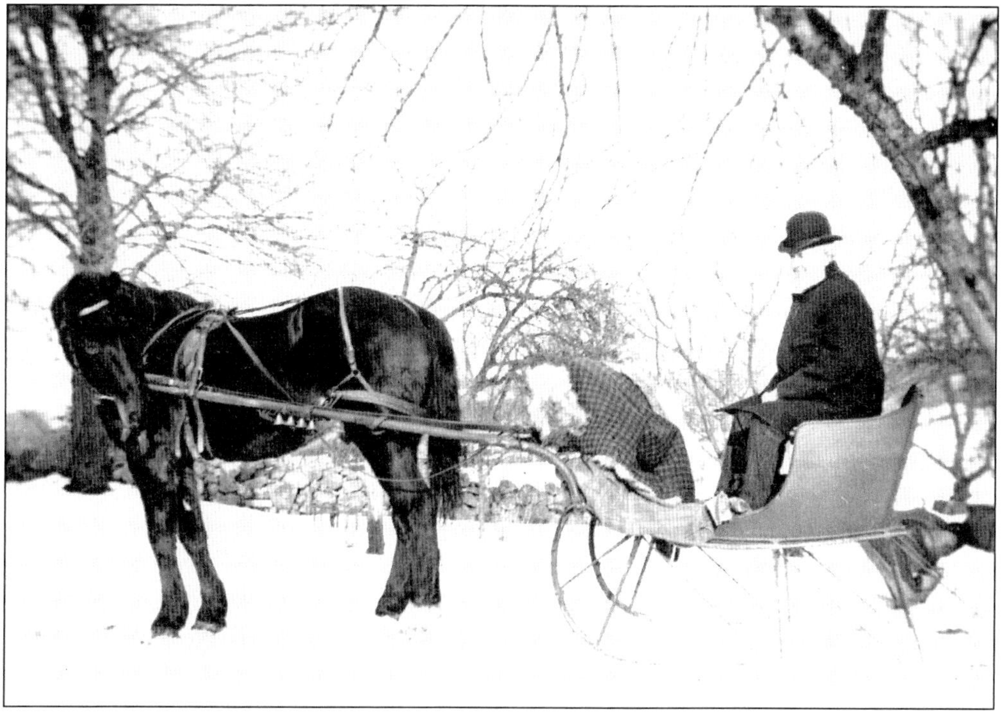

Austin Faunce was caught on film while out with his horse and carriage.

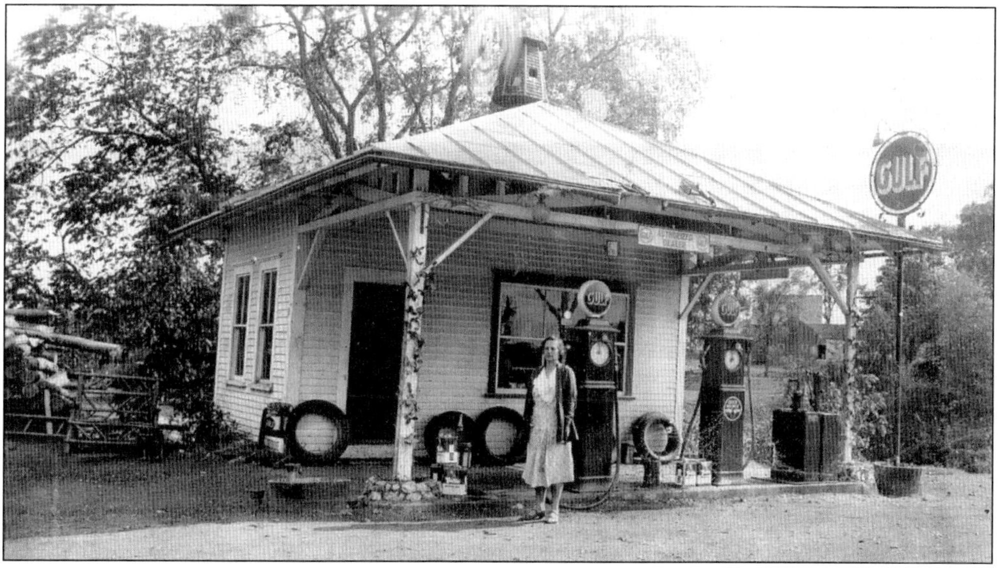

Boston's Gulf Station operated in the center of town for many years. Nina Buzzell Boston walked to work every day from her home on Route 150 until the tiny station closed in 1992. Nina posed for this photograph in 1938. The station was destroyed by fire in 1940, and was rebuilt to operate many more years. Today it houses Victory Gardens. Local residents recall Nina never had a telephone, radio, or television to help her occupy the time during her long days. As she got older, customers would often find her asleep in the chair. It was common to pump ones own gas and come back later to pay when she was awake. Nina pumped gas and ran the station until retiring when she was 91. In the early days of the station, gas was eight gallons for $1.

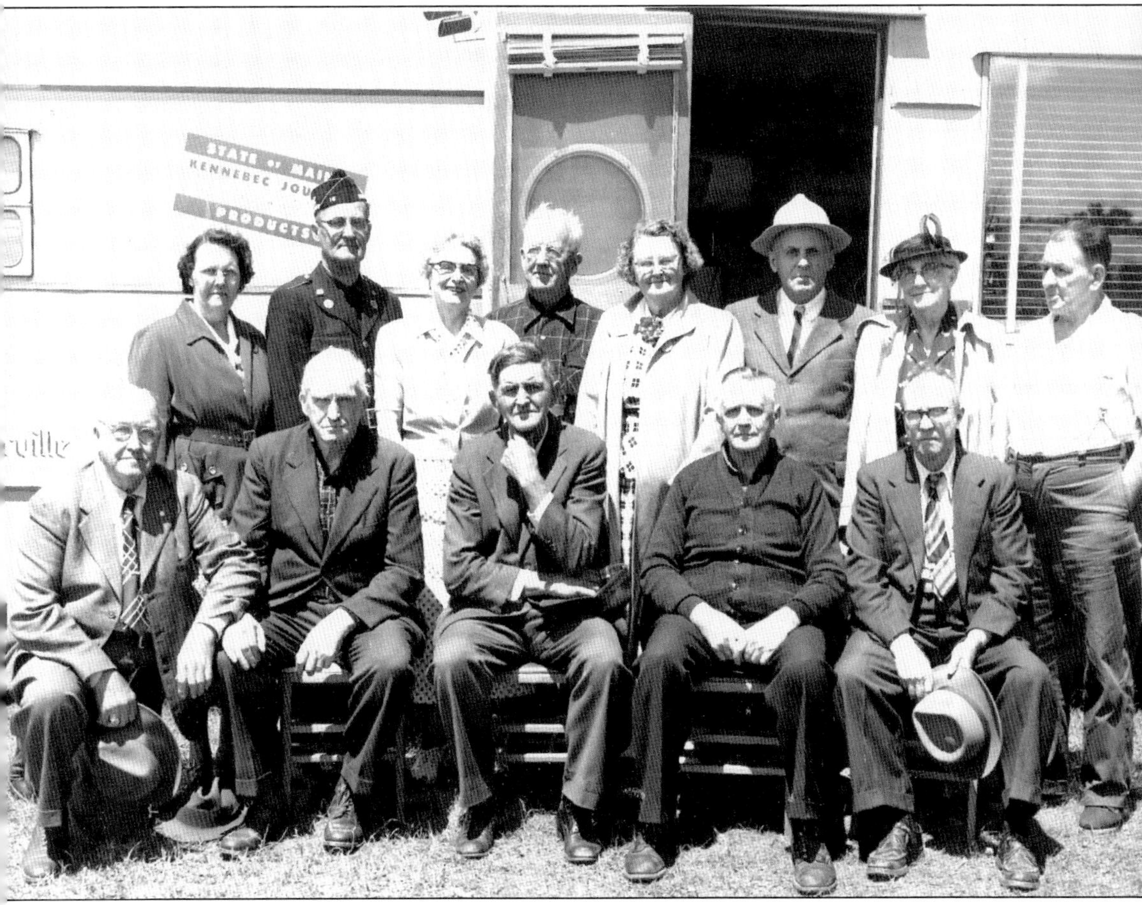

The sesquicentennial committee of 1954 included, from left to right, (first row) Newlie Hayden, unidentified, unidentified, Clyde Scribner, and Riley Hall; (second row) Gertrude L. Rowell, unidentified, Marion Turner, Henry Turner, Hazel Hanson, Oliver French, Belva French, and George Buzzell.

Six

St. Albans
The Lake and the Village

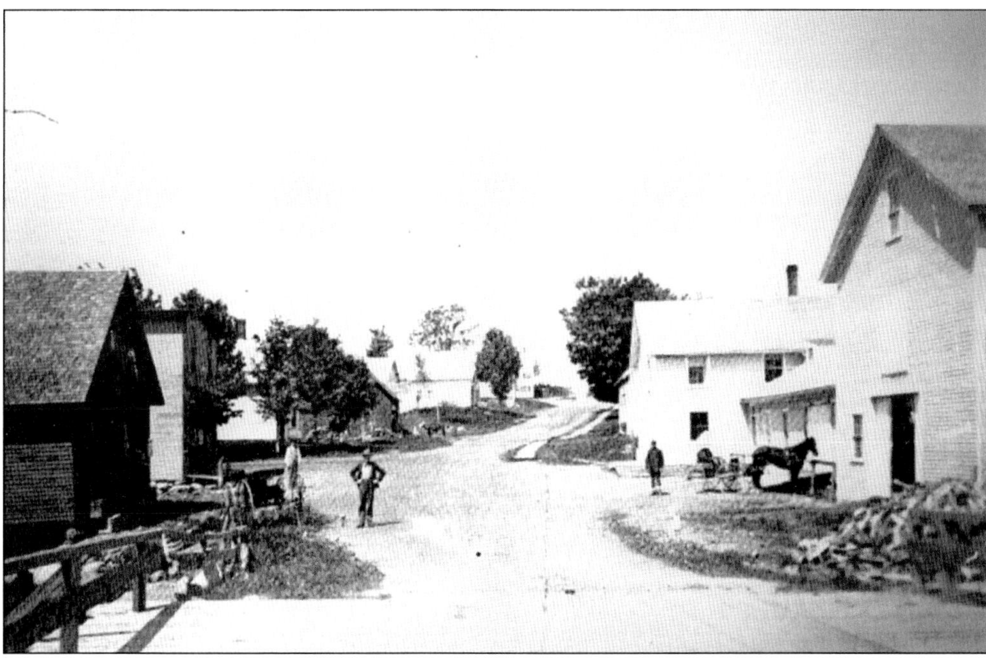

St. Albans was a growing rural community with 82 years of growth since its incorporation in 1813 when this 1895 photograph was taken from the Indian Stream bridge. The town's general store on the left is still in the same location as Indian Lake Market today. While St. Albans village is located at the outlet to Big Indian Lake, most of the eastern shoreline of Great Moose Lake is also within St. Albans's borders.

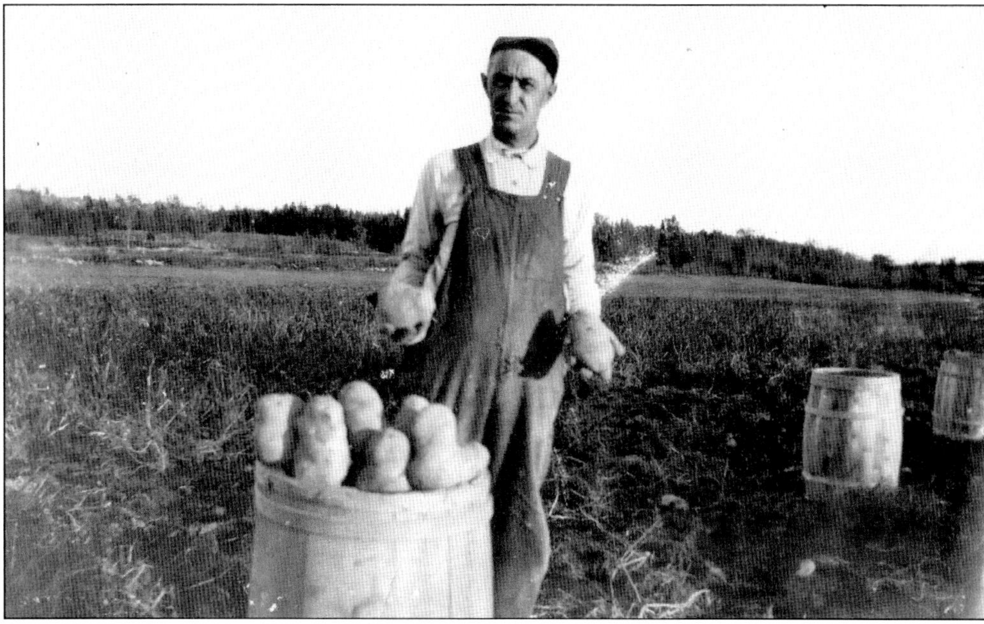

S. Wesley Seekins was a farmer and carpenter residing on the Palmyra Road for most of his life. His success with potatoes one season was occasion for a photograph. Local gardeners speculate he was growing Kennebecs that year, a variety known for large tubers.

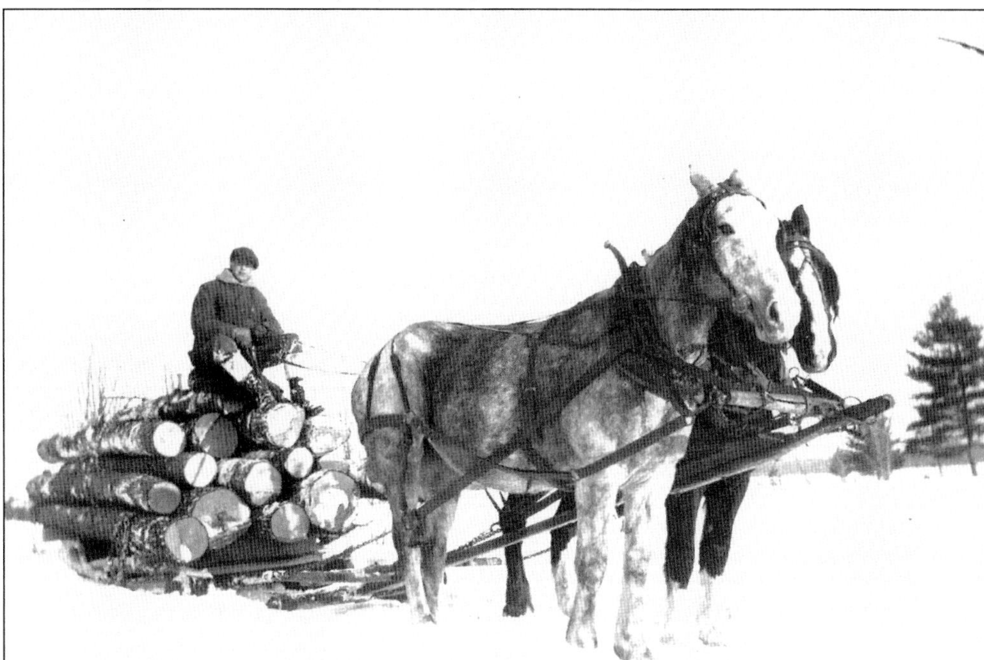

Winter weather is more amenable to the harvesting of trees in Maine when the ground is frozen. An experienced woodsman like Gilbert Neal, seen here with his team and a fresh load of logs, knew to take advantage of the season.

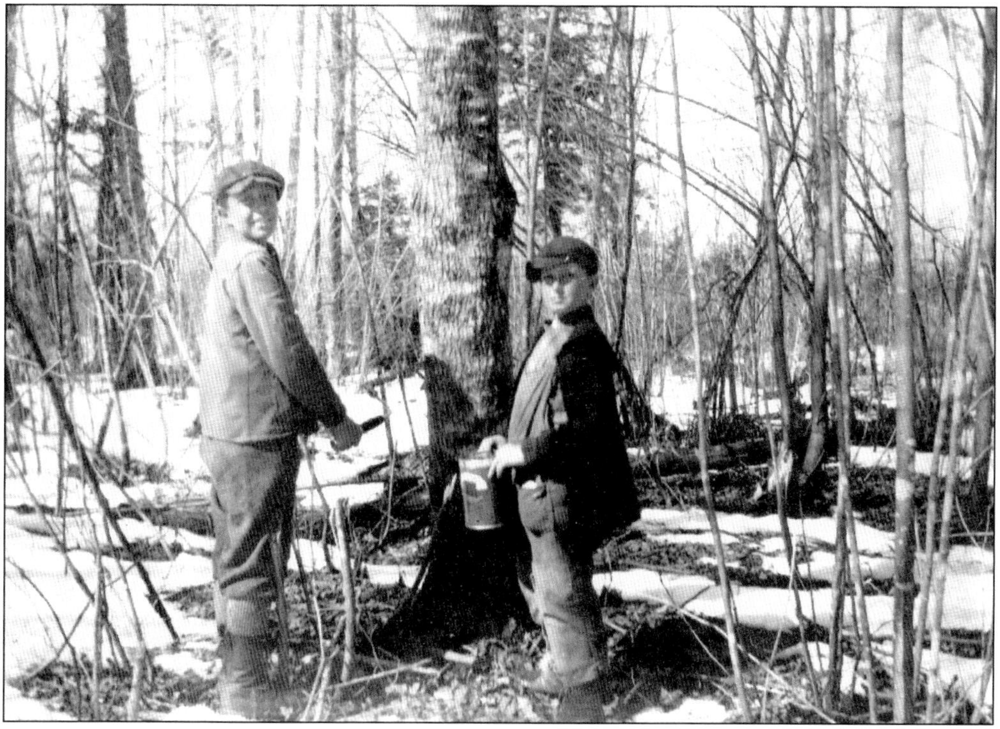

Life on a farm in 1919 included sap season for the Seekins boys on the Palmyra Road. Joe, age 13, and Harold, 10, learned early how to tap the maple trees and collect the sap. Older brother Gordon, 16, in the photograph below, was charged with boiling the sap, or is that supervising? It appears he was more interested in the latest issue of *American Boy* while Joe and Harold stoke the fire with split wood.

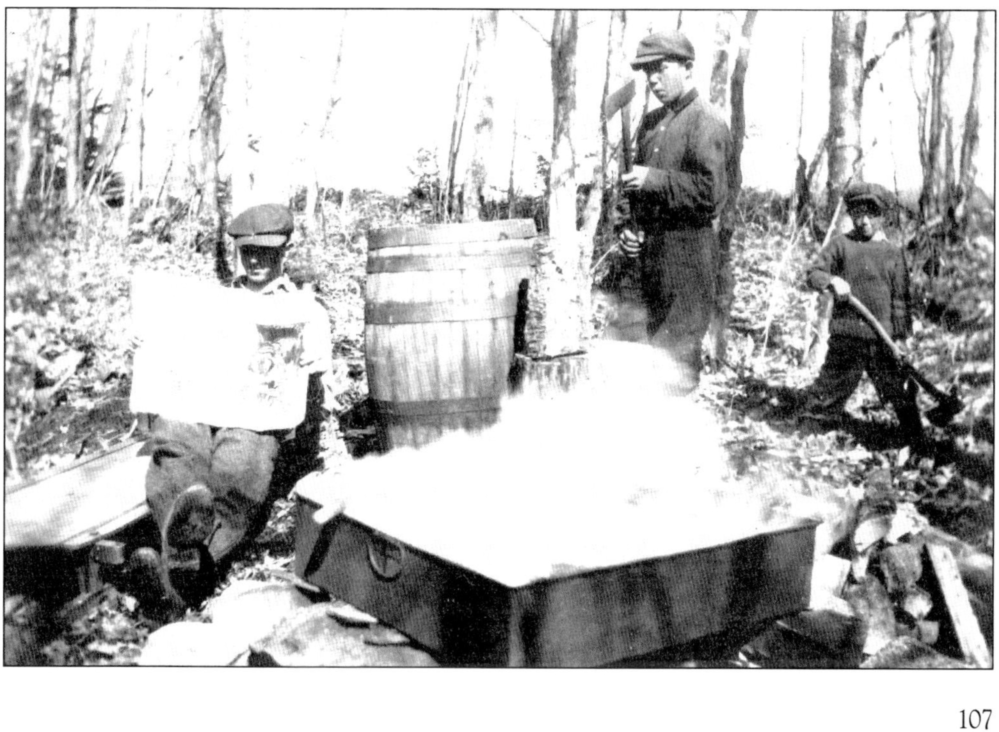

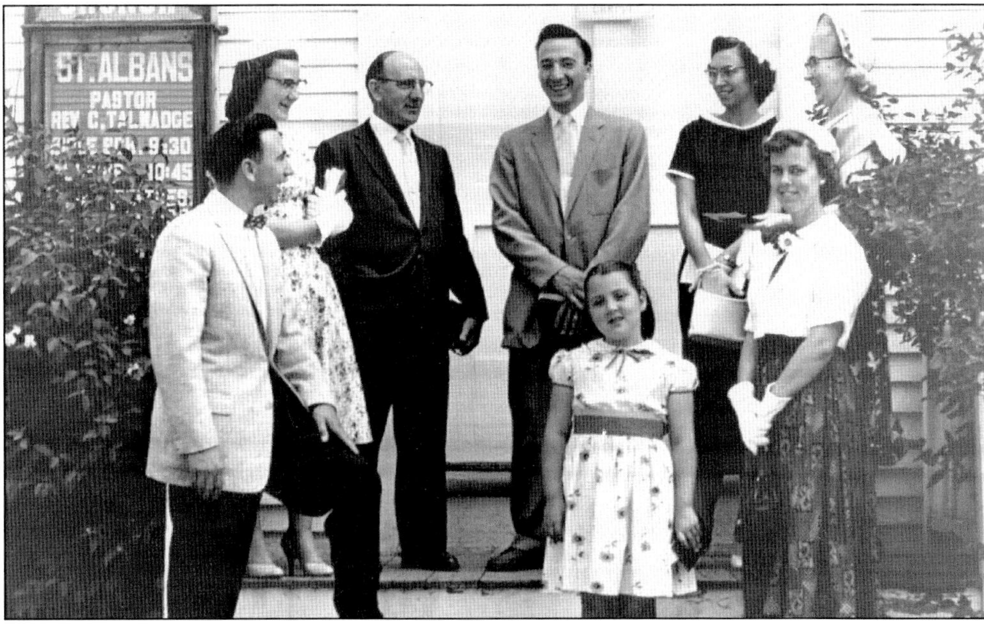

The Kenneth A. Hughes family has a long history in St. Albans. Seen here after a morning at the St. Albans Union Church, from left to right are Kenneth Hughes Jr.; Roxene Hughes Caron; Kenneth A. Hughes; Ronald Hughes and his wife, Sally; Dorothea Hughes, Kenneth Sr.'s wife; Althea Hughes, Kenneth Jr.'s wife; and Lorinda Hughes in front. Kenneth Sr., came to St. Albans as a boy when his father started Maple Shade Dairy on a farm on Palmyra Road. He served as a St. Albans selectman in 1947, 1949, and 1950, and three terms in the House of Representatives from 1957 to 1962 in the 98th, 99th and 100th Maine legislatures. He also served as a Somerset County commissioner.

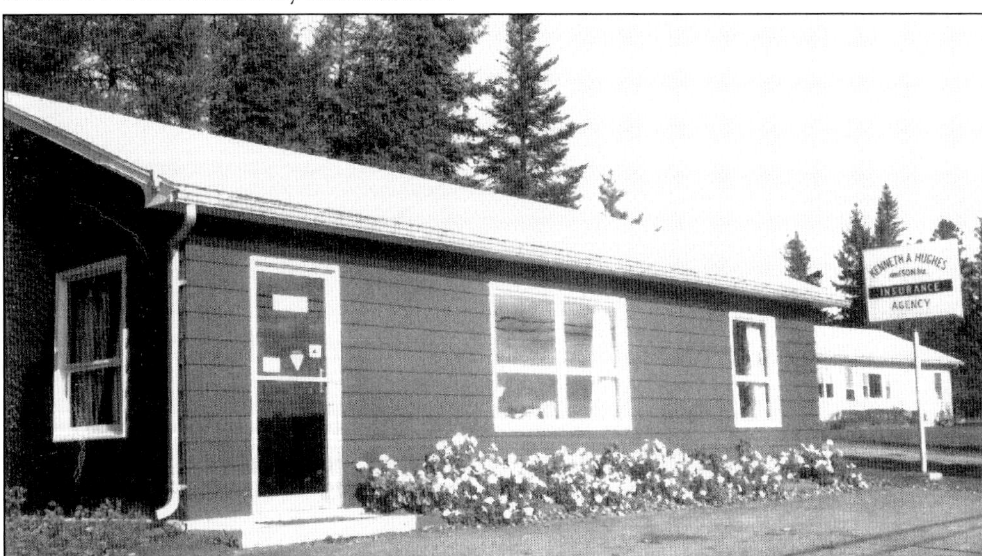

After operating the dairy farm for many years, health conditions forced Kenneth Hughes Sr. to sell the farm in 1947. He promptly started an insurance business that operated in St. Albans until 1981. In 1964, his son Ronald joined him in the business. In the 1970s, he opened a new office for his business next to his home on Hartland Road.

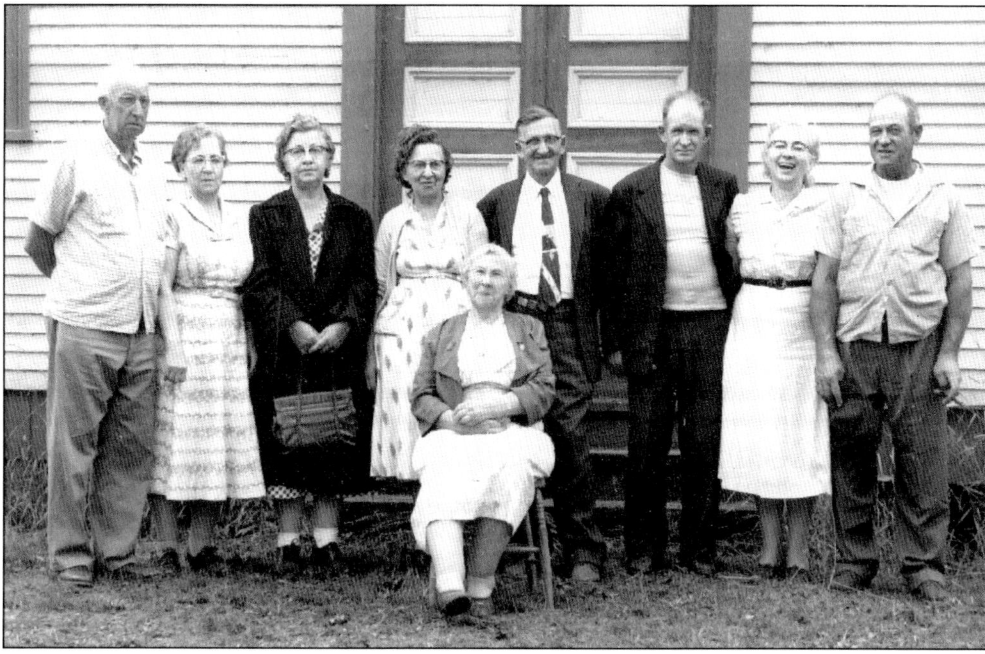

Dorothea Hughes was a member of a large local family. After a family gathering in the 1950s, she and her siblings posed with their mother, Dellie Chase (seated), outside the St. Albans Grange Hall. Included from left to right are John Giles, Relief Knowles, Gertrude Leavitt, Grace Murray, Clarence Giles, George Giles, Dorothea, and Floyd Giles.

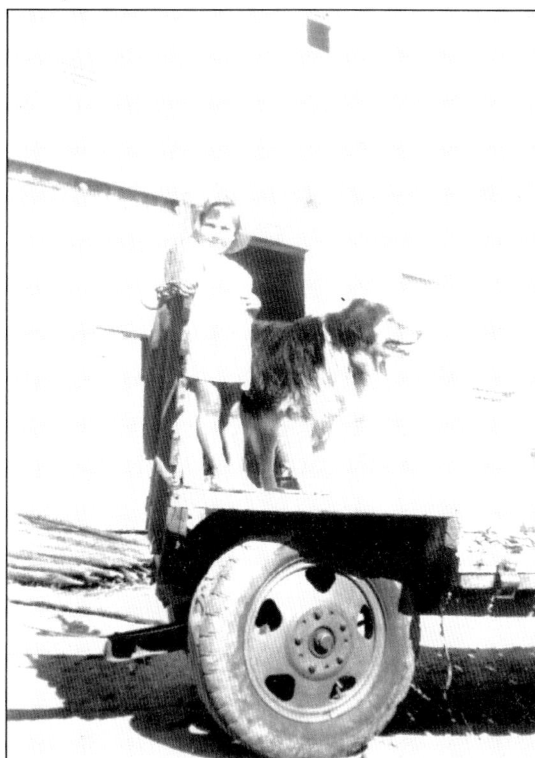

Roxene Hughes and her siblings grew up at Maple Shade, participating in the farm activities just as their father had before them. On this day, she was aboard the hay wagon with the family dog Ring.

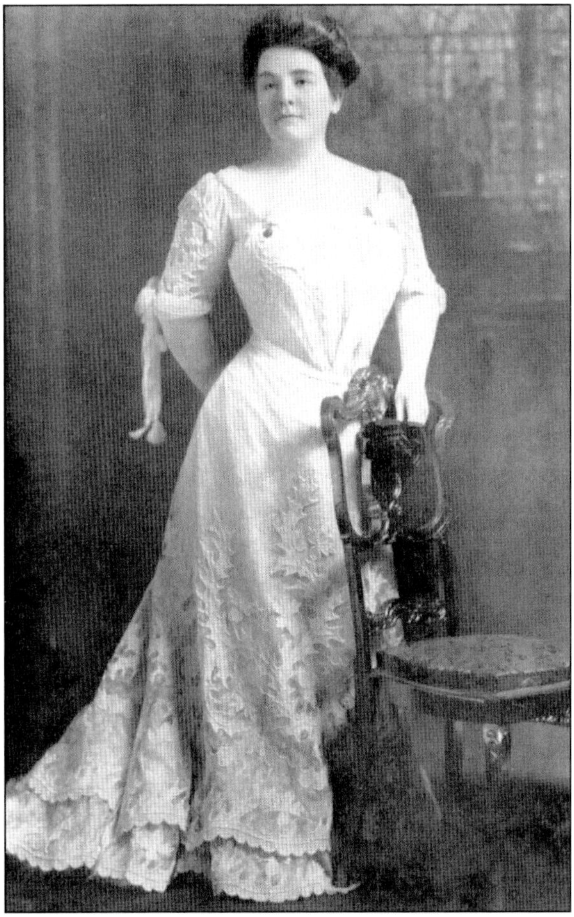

Antonia Savage Sawyer was a renowned opera singer of the late 1800s, performing around the world. One of her performances was for her hometown of Waterville for the 1902 centennial. She often visited a friend, Grace Williams, in Hartland when she was in Maine and included a visit to Williams's camp on Great Moose Lake. Around the beginning of the 20th century, she purchased Camp Illahee on the St. Albans shore and began to spend summers there. In addition to her success as an opera singer, she also was the first female opera manager, handling many successful singers of the day. One particular summer she offered weekly soirees at Camp Illahee, inviting her lakeside friends in to enjoy her singing and her tales of travels abroad and managing performers.

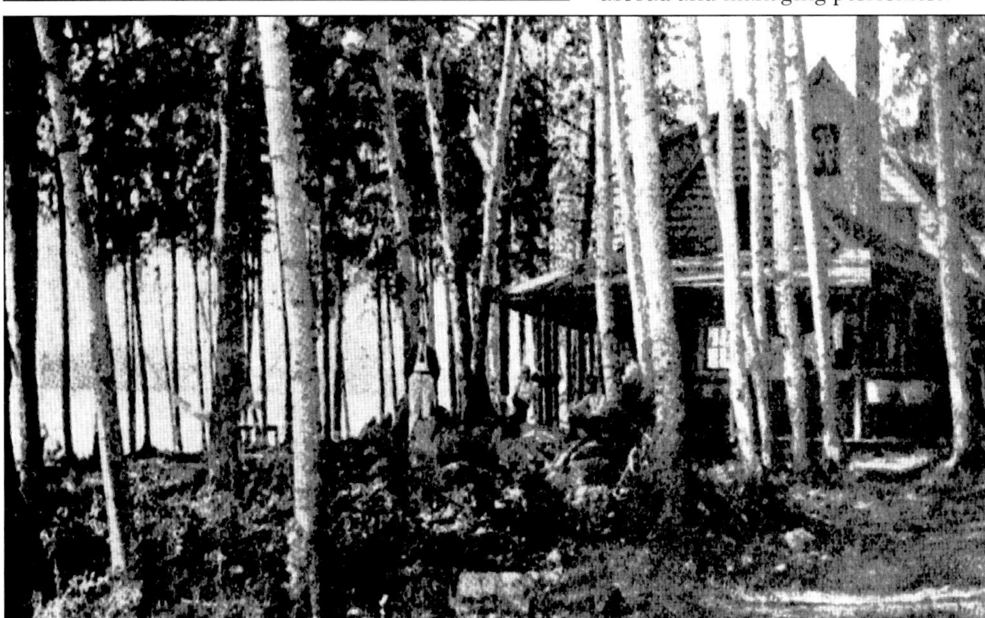

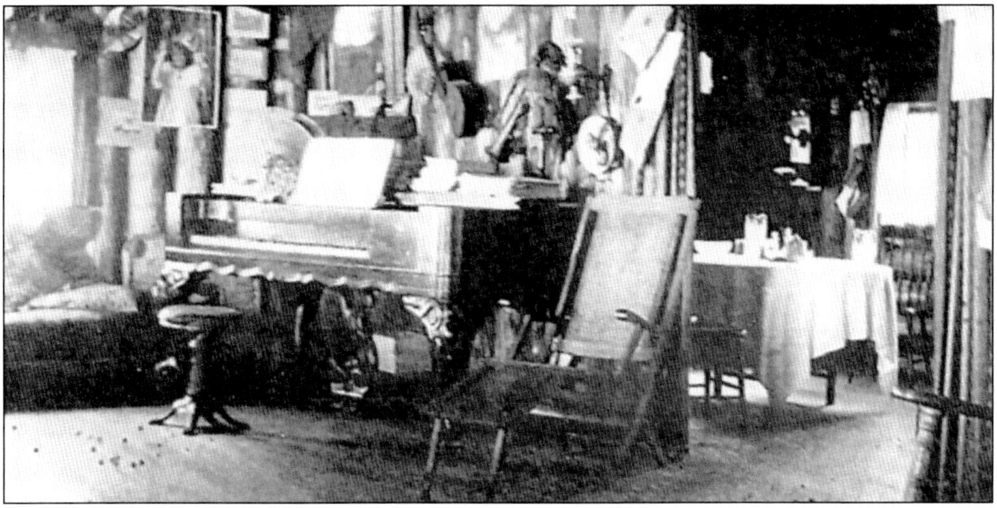

The parlor at Sawyer's Camp Illahee included a piano to accommodate her entertaining and a large fireplace to ward off the cold of Maine summer evenings. Named Stronghold for the subsequent owners, a Dr. Strong and his family of Fairfield, the property still bears the name and the lore of its time under the doctor's occupancy. Stronghold earned a reputation for fashionable, and sometimes loud, parties. The doctor's visitors were observed in the 1920s boarding motor launches at the docks in Hartland for a trip upriver and across the lake to Stronghold for afternoon and evening gatherings. Men donned formal attire and the ladies were seen in long lace dresses and carrying parasols. Rosie Strong eventually sold the property to Clancy Burton who moved his family and his furniture to camp in a boxcar along the railroad. Burton lived on the property year-round and rented cottages on the site. His descendants still own the property.

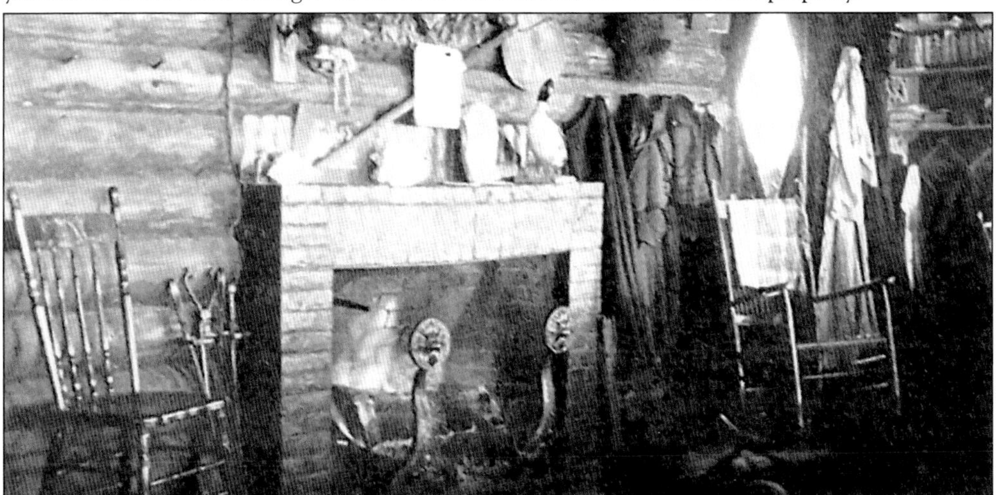

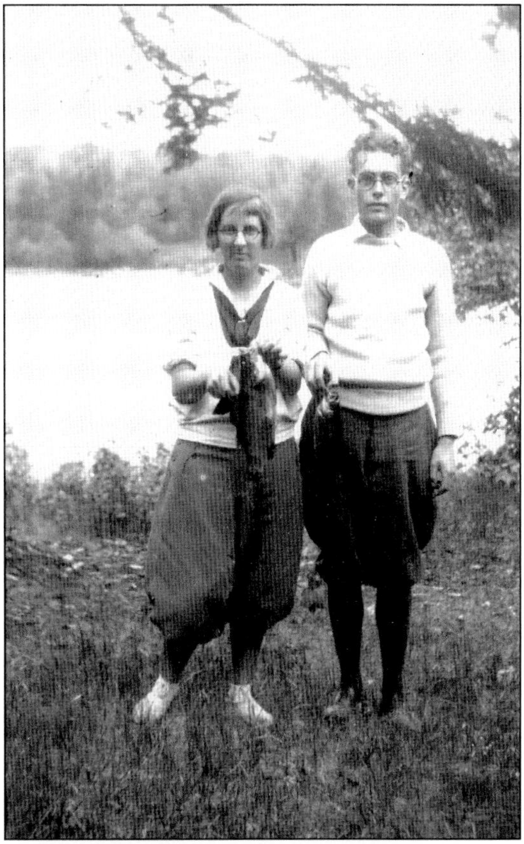

In June 1924, Edna Childs and an unidentified friend pose with their catch at Camp Hemlocks, the camp the Childs family has owned and occupied since 1903.

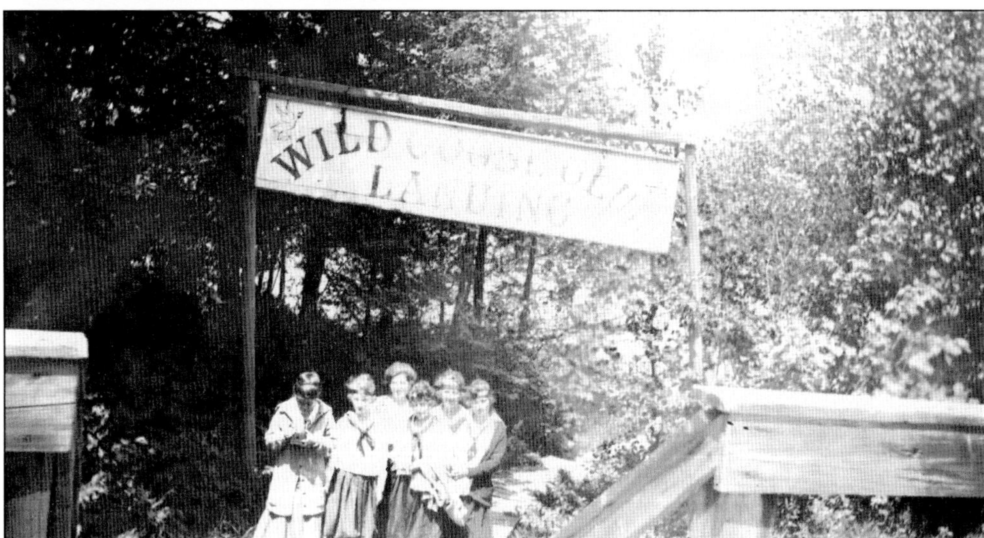

One of the benefits of having a camp on Great Moose Lake during the first half of the 20th century was the location of a primary rail line virtually at the backdoor. Edna Childs, a Pittsfield Campfire Girl in 1920, brought her troop to the family's Camp Hemlocks and hiked the rail line. In addition to a flag stop near the Childs' camp, the sporting families at Castle Harmony's Wild Goose Club also had a rail stop.

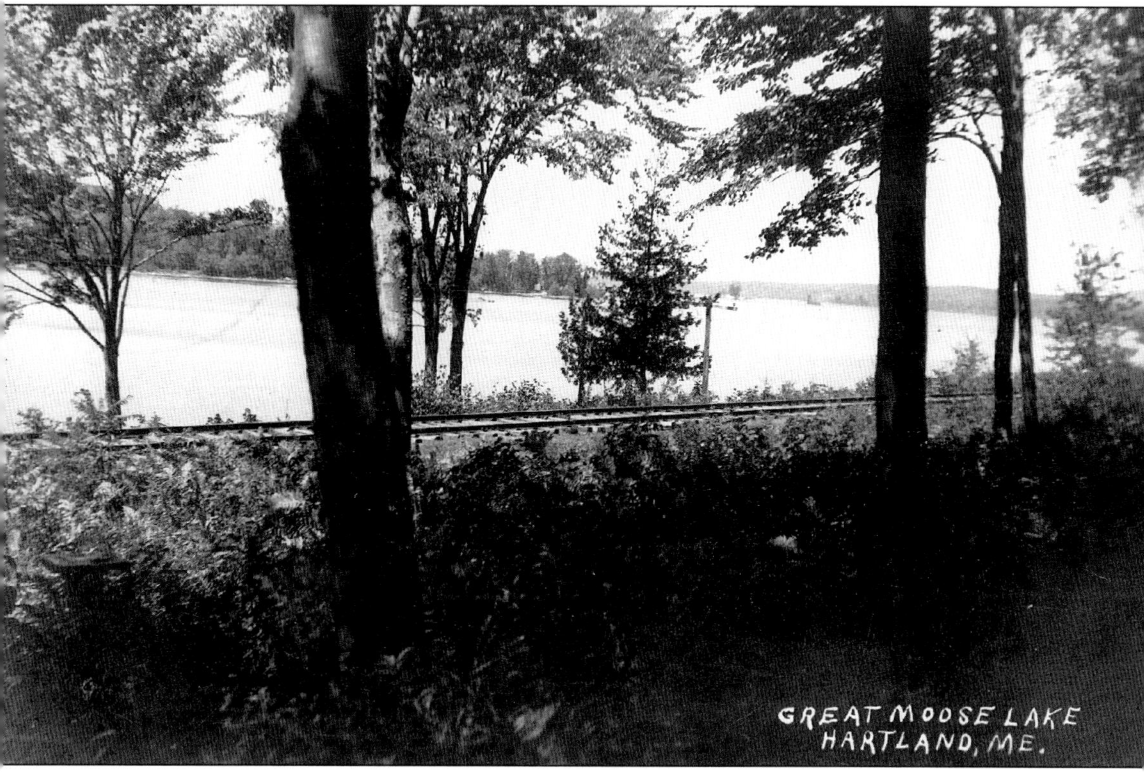

From 1911 to 1966, a spur of Maine Central Railroad bordered the St. Albans shoreline of Great Moose Lake, running between Hartland and Harmony. Campers, hunters, fisherman, vacationers, and year-round residents depended on several flag stops along the route to travel between the lake and local towns as well as connections out of New England. Little signs remain today of the long-ago railroad except a high-banked rail bed and abandoned trestle abutments.

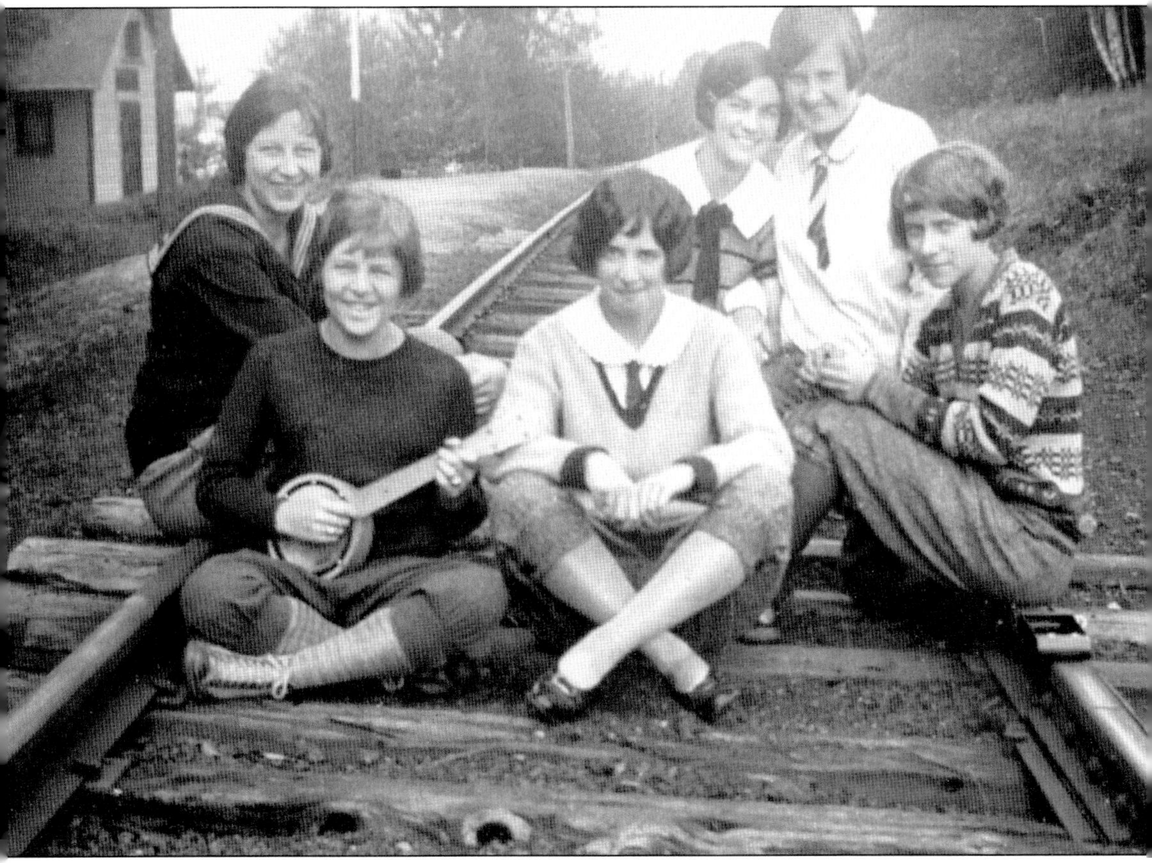

In the fall of 1925, Edna Childs Ferrucci entertained classmates at the family cottage on Great Moose Lake. All juniors at Bates College in Lewiston, the girls posed for a picture on the Maine Central Railroad tracks that followed the eastern shore. The group included, in the back, from left to right, Kay Lawton in the sailor top, Ellen Parker, and Ivy Young. The identities of the three women in the front are not known. The railroad was a vital link for summer residents along the lake as well as the communities around the lake from 1911 to 1966. Sections of the rail bed are used as trails and woods roads today.

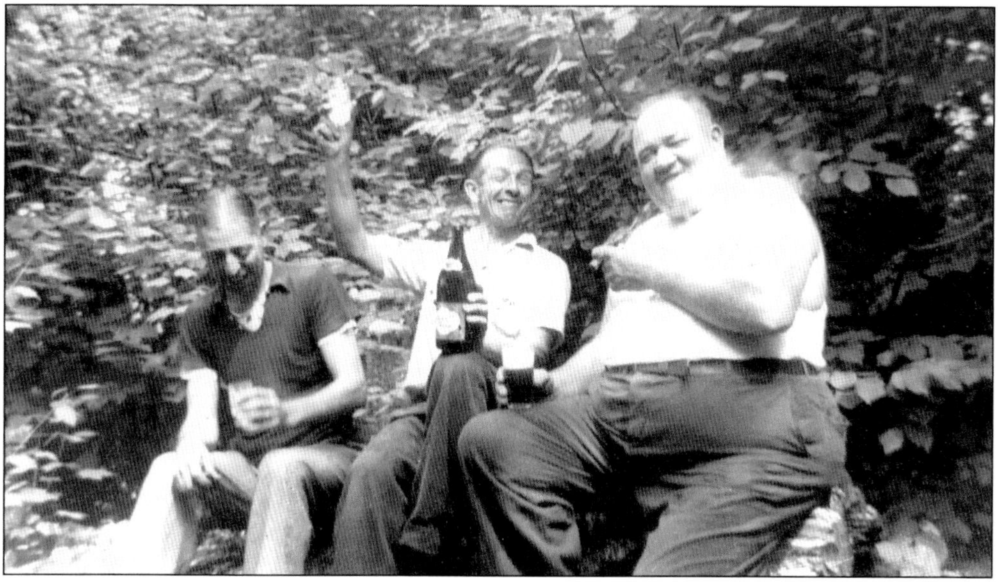

Camp owners and visitors made fast friends each summer, continuing year after year. That was the case with the Childs family and neighbor Clyde Martin (right) of Wildwood Camps, who operated a store at the lake along with his wife Claire. Martin is remembered as a jolly man whose small store supplied lakeshore dwellings with basic food supplies, gas, bait, and penny. In this photograph, Clyde joined Ralph Ferrucci (left) and Clayton Grace (center), who were regular summer residents at Camp Hemlock, next door to Wildwood Camps on the St. Albans's shore.

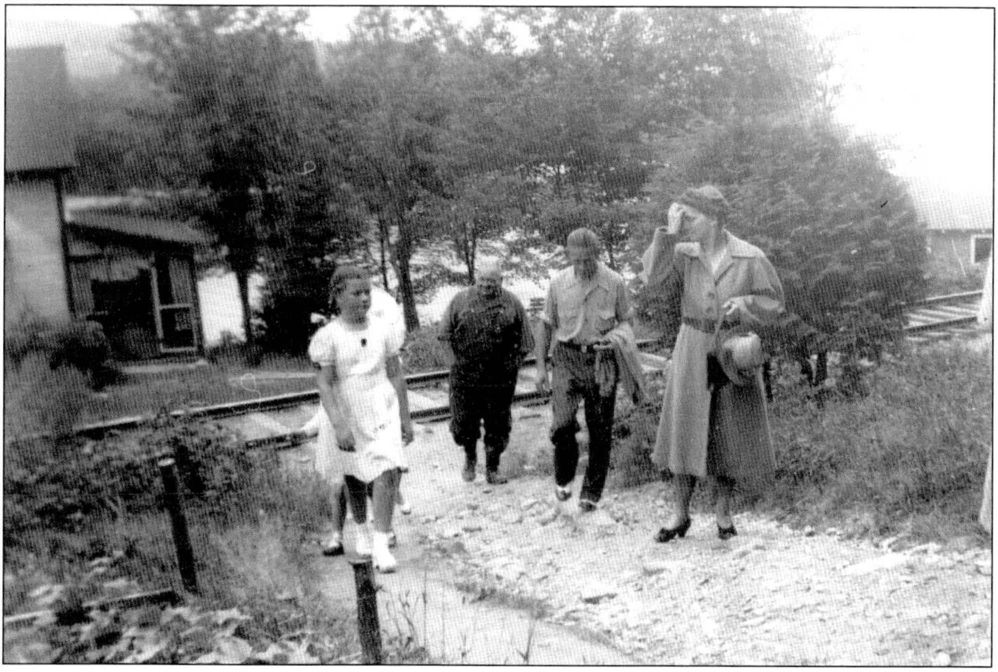

Leaving camp for the day or after vacation meant a trek across the railroad tracks to a parking area on the other side, or perhaps to catch the train. Leaving the Childs' camp on this day in 1942 were, from left to right, Ann Grace Dixon, joined by Clyde Martin, Clayton Grace, and Marion Grace.

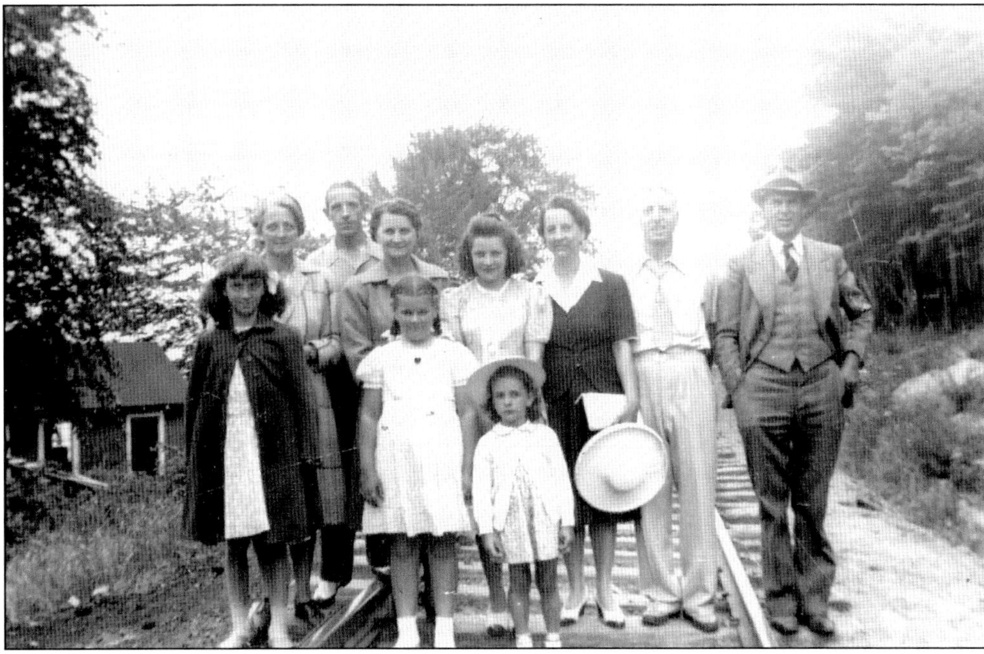

Any visit to camp by groups of relatives was occasion for a photograph with the railroad as the setting. In 1942, the Childs family and relations stopped to capture the end of another vacation. From left to right are (first row) Molly Jane Shorey, Ann Grace Dixon, and Mary Ellen Ferrucci; (second row) Helen Childs Shorey, Clayton Grace, Marion Childs Grace, Jean Grace, Edna Childs Ferrucci, Ralph Ferrucci, and Leigh Shorey Sr.

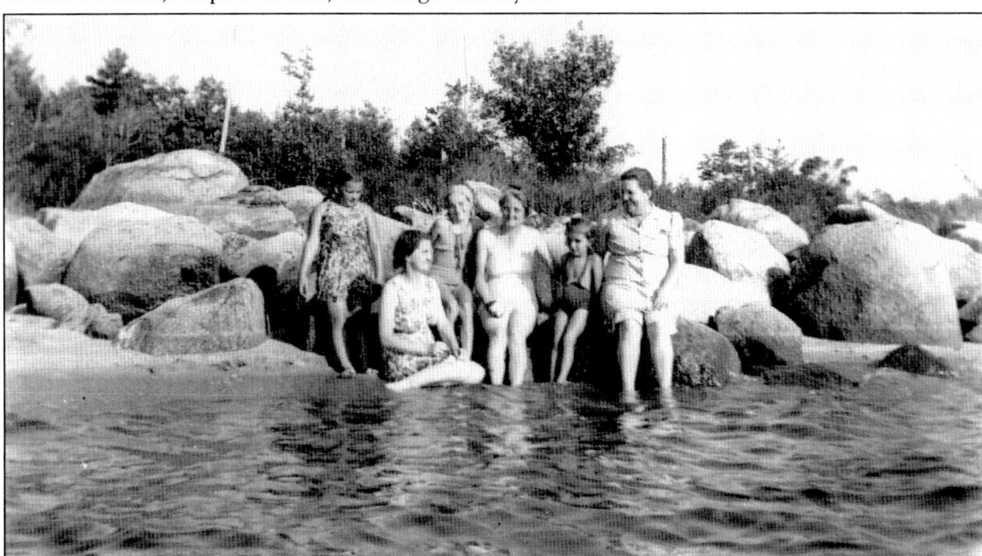

"Going to the beach" at Great Moose Lake could mean anywhere on the lake. On this occasion in the 1940s, it appears the Childs clan and friends made their way to French's Rock beach on the eastern shore. In that time period, the area was only accessible by boat, necessitating that the Childs women all knew how to handle a boat. Members of the gathering include, from left to right, Ann Grace, Marion Grace, Molly Jane Shorey, Helen Shorey, Mary Ellen Ferrucci, and Josephine Baird.

Hunting techniques of the 1920s may have been slightly different than today, but none the less successful, as this visitor with the Neal family in St. Albans demonstrates with his display of a deerskin laid across the hood of his car.

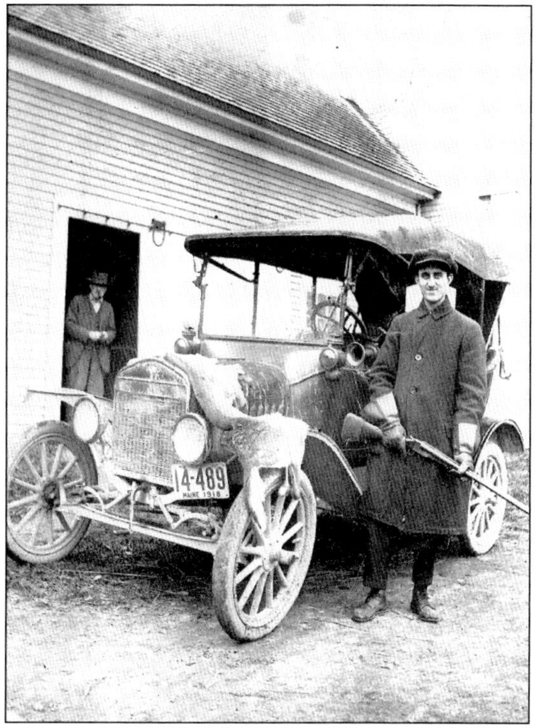

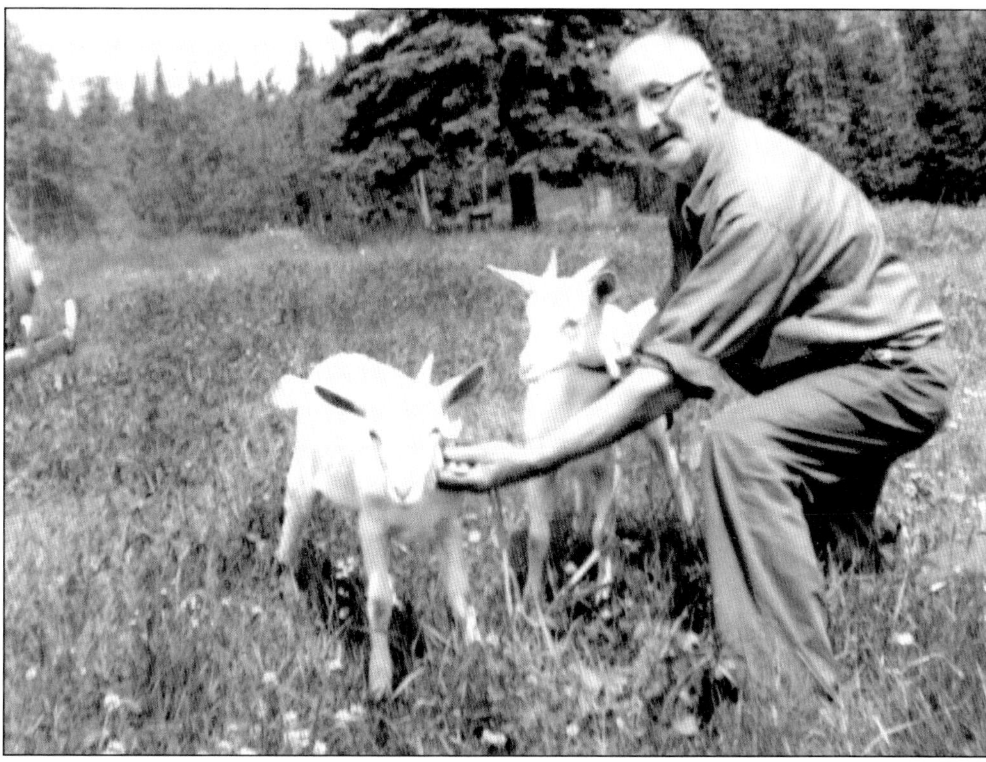

Wallace Nichols was a long time resident of St. Albans, last residing on Todd's Corner Road beginning in 1942, where he raised goats for milk. It was rare to see him without his signature hat.

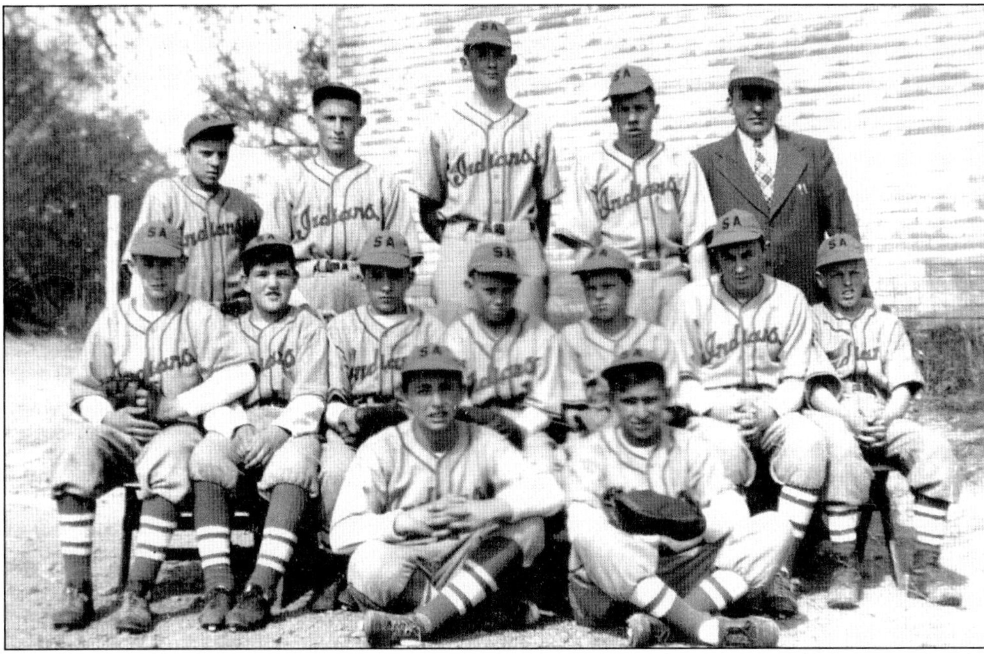

This St. Albans eighth-grade baseball team enjoyed an extraordinary year of success under the direction of coach Clifford Burton, seen in the third row, far right. The team traveled throughout the state routinely winning over competing teams including teams that added older players in hopes of beating the St. Albans group. The team includes, from left to right, (first row) Frank Nichols and Elmer Ballard; (second row) Roger Nichols, Steve McNichol, Ervin Vining, Jack Tweedie, Gordon Woodman, Gilbert Nichols, and Ronald Tasker; (third row) Roland Webber, Byron Ballard Jr., Lawrence Waldron, Keith Bubar, and the coach.

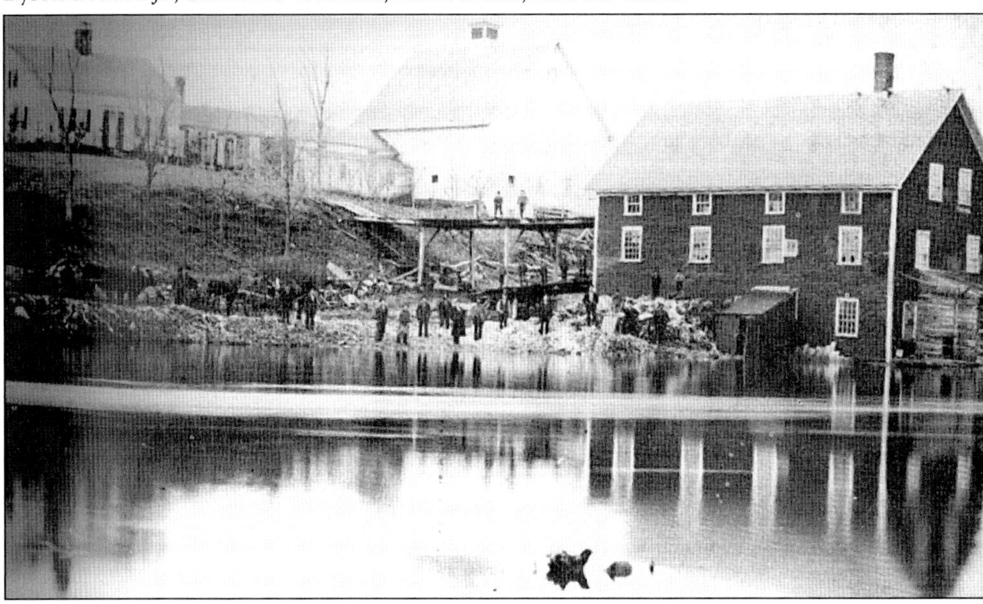

St. Albans was for many years a self-sufficient community with businesses, services and manufacturers. This included the N. B. Turner shovel handle factory on the east shore of Indian Stream in the village.

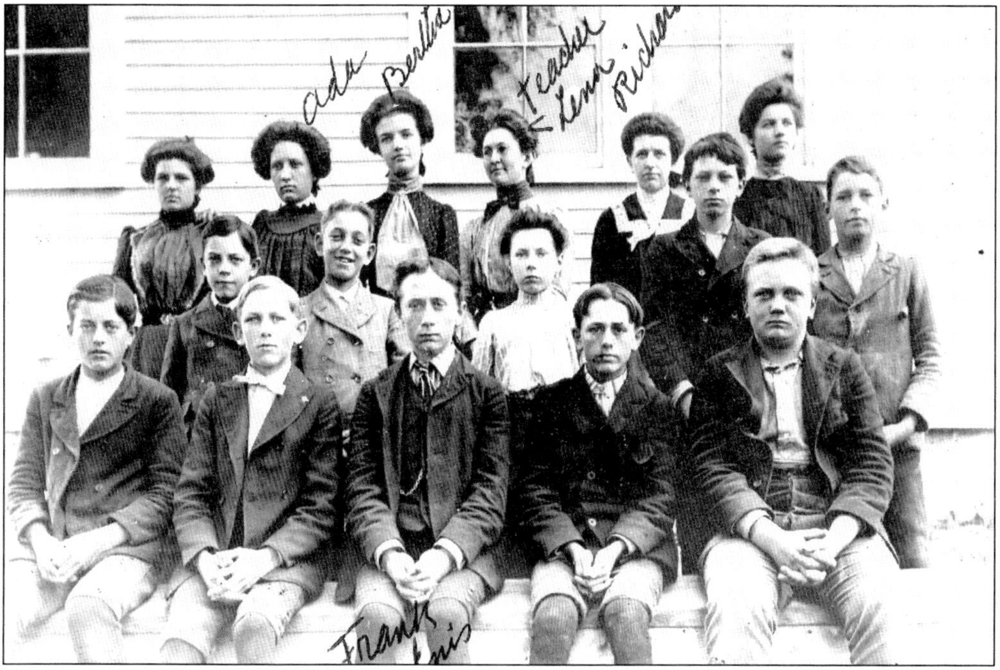

Few students can be identified in this picture from 1893 or 1894. It is known that Lena Richards, back center, was the teacher, perhaps in her early days of teaching at the St. Albans Village School. Others identified include Frank Seekins in the front row, and his siblings Ada and Bertha in the back row.

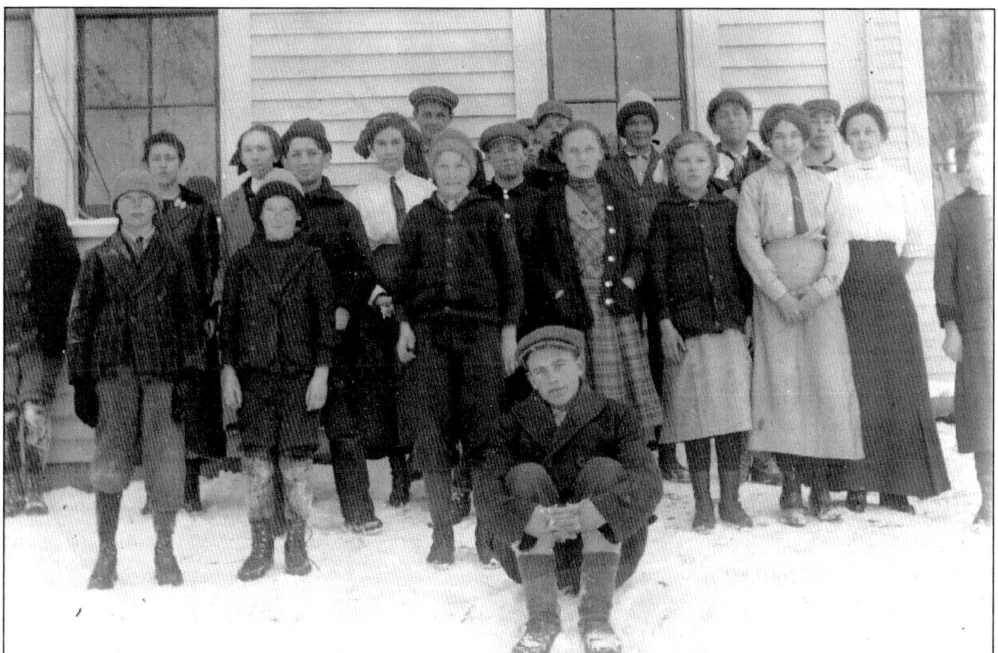

Little changed at the St. Albans Village School between 1893 and 1913, except the styles and the generation of students. The students in this group are likely children of some of those from the early time. Their identities could not be confirmed.

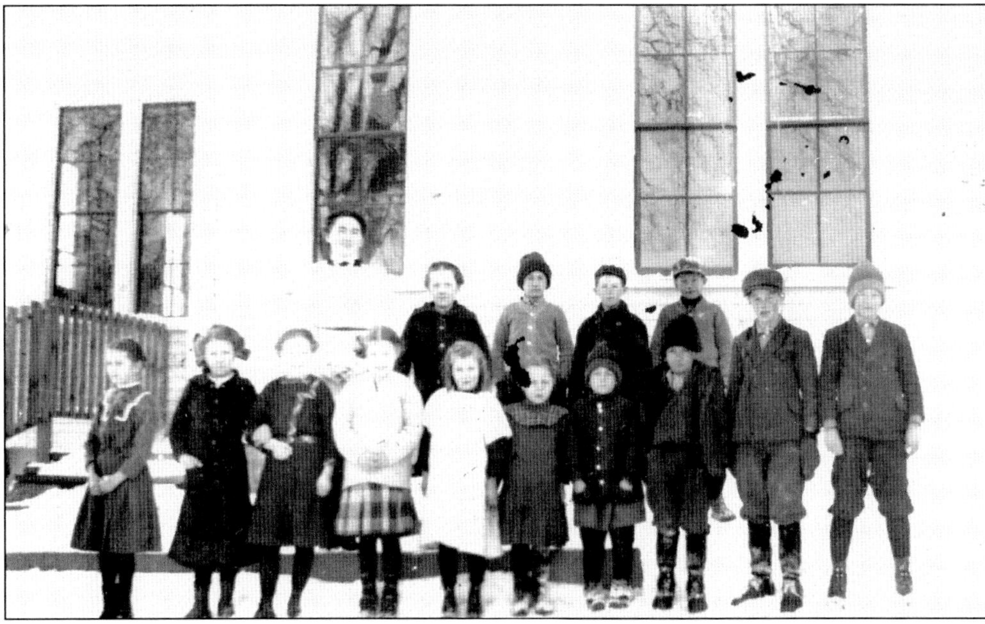

Lena Richards was still teaching at the St. Albans Village School in 1913, and is pictured here with this primary school group. Richards reportedly continued to teach to serve another generation of St. Albans children.

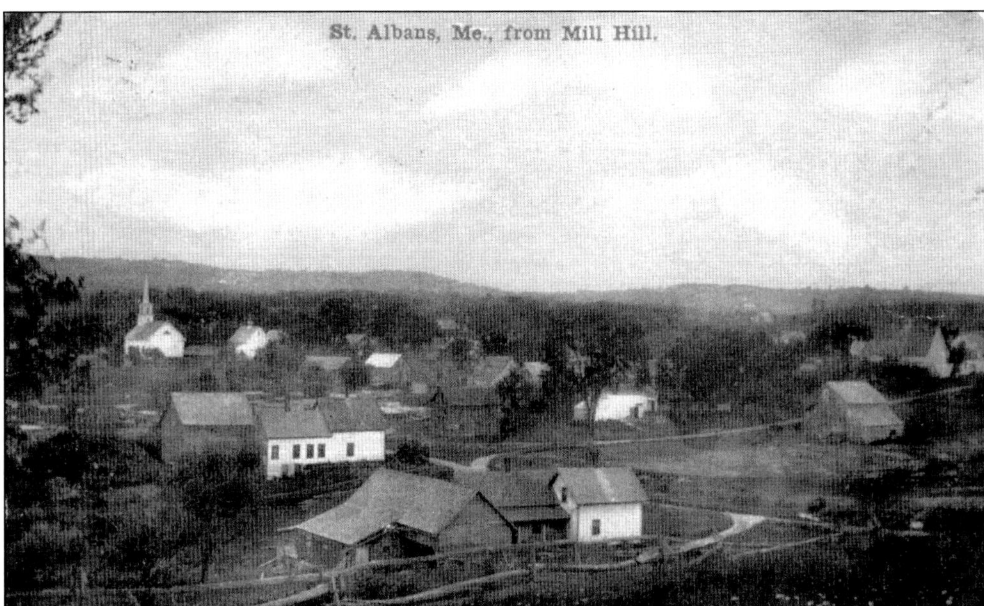

St. Albans, seen here before 1900, as seen from Mill Hill and Palmyra Road, includes the steeple of the Union Church that still dominates the skyline today.

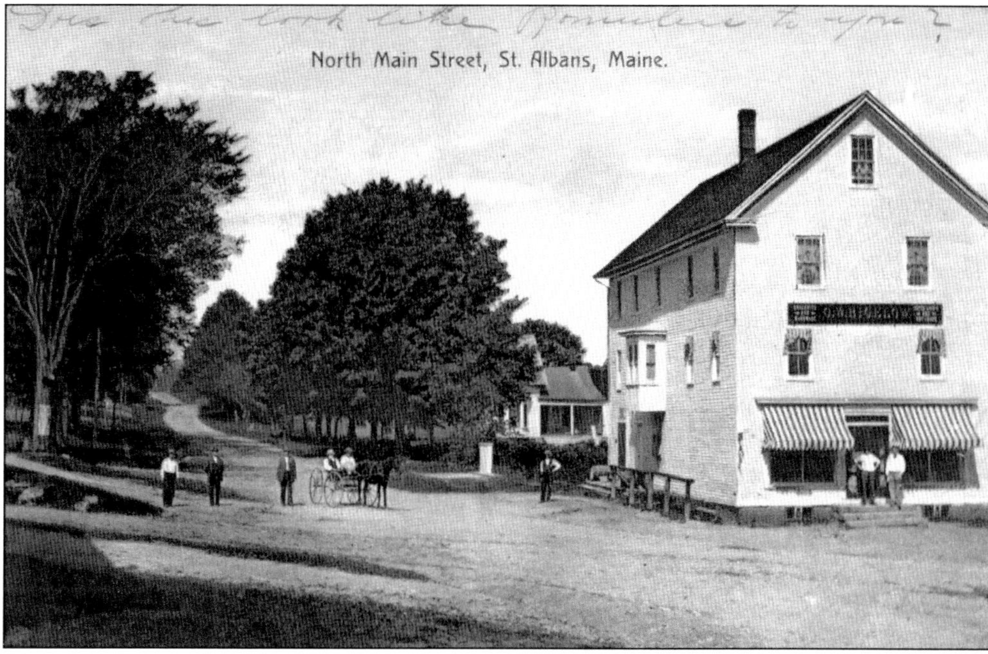

The intersection of North Main Street and Commercial Street has held one constant for more than 100 years, the general store on the corner. In its earliest operation, the O. W. Bigelow store offered groceries and hardware.

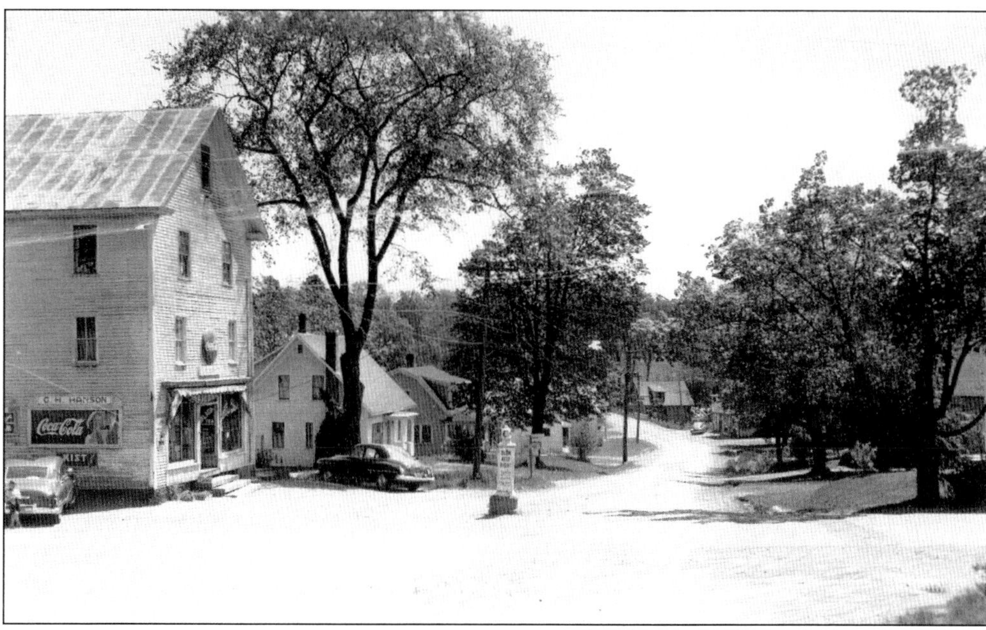

By the 1950s, the general store bore the name of G. H. Hanson, still offering the necessary staples of a general store. Coca-Cola signs had also appeared as a promotion for the popular soft drink. Looking east on Commercial Street, the homes visible still stand today, but the competing general store at the bottom of the hill is not visible.

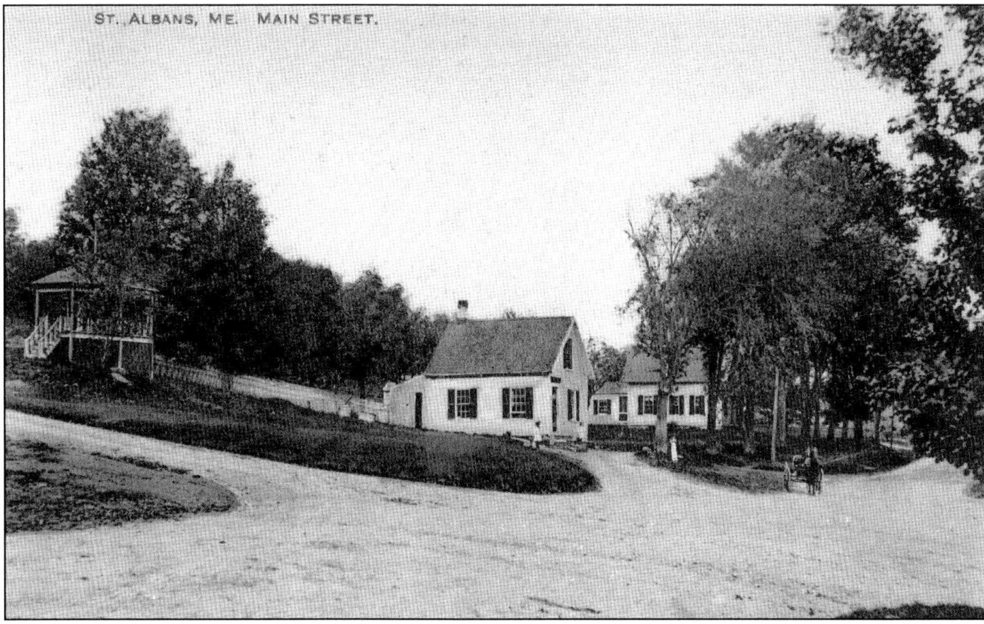

Another view at the Main Street intersection shows an early post office that later became a private home and was moved further south on the street. The house beyond the post office was the home of longtime St. Albans school teacher Lena Richards. The town also had a bandstand at this location for many years. Today the town's war memorial and a historic library building are located on this site.

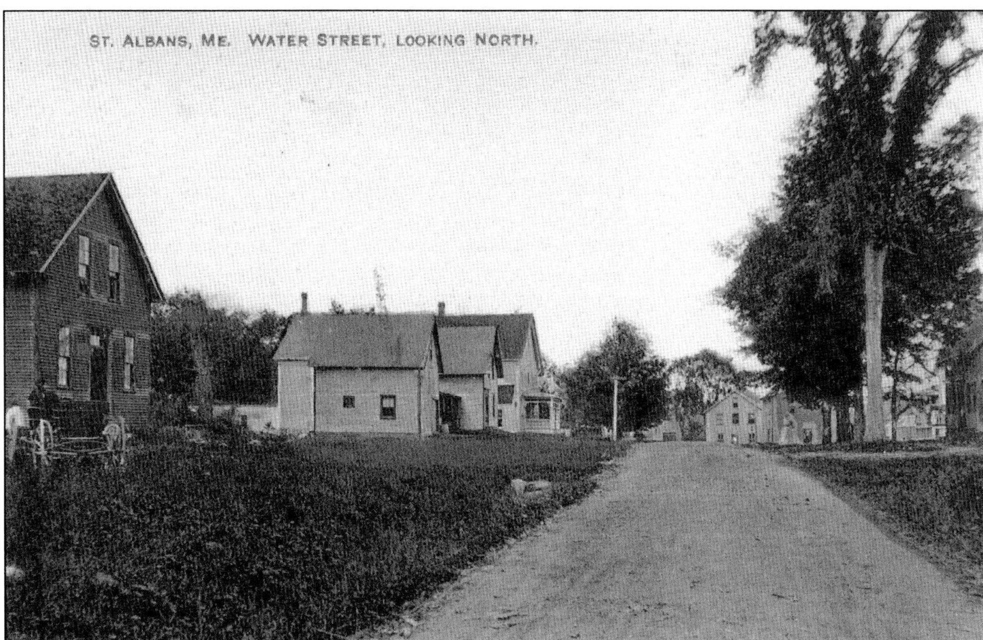

An early view of Water Street in St. Albans shows the old cider mill on the left and the original town hall further along the street. The Grange hall had not yet been built in this photograph, taken around 1900.

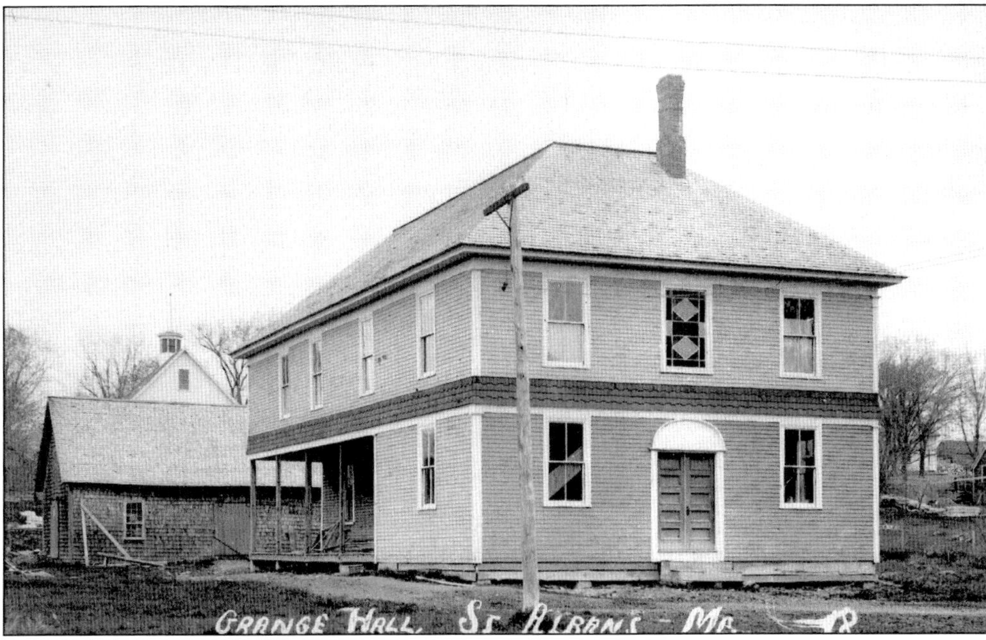

The Grange hall, shortly after its construction, shows very little change from the way it appears today on Water Street.

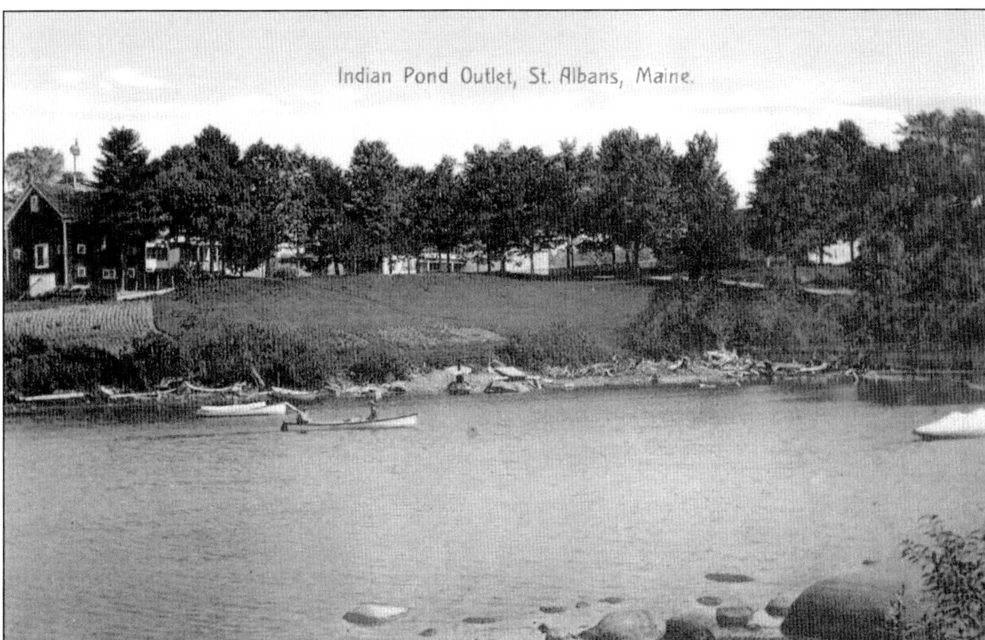

A view of Big Indian Pond near the outlet shows the eastern shore and many of the early homes that still stand today.

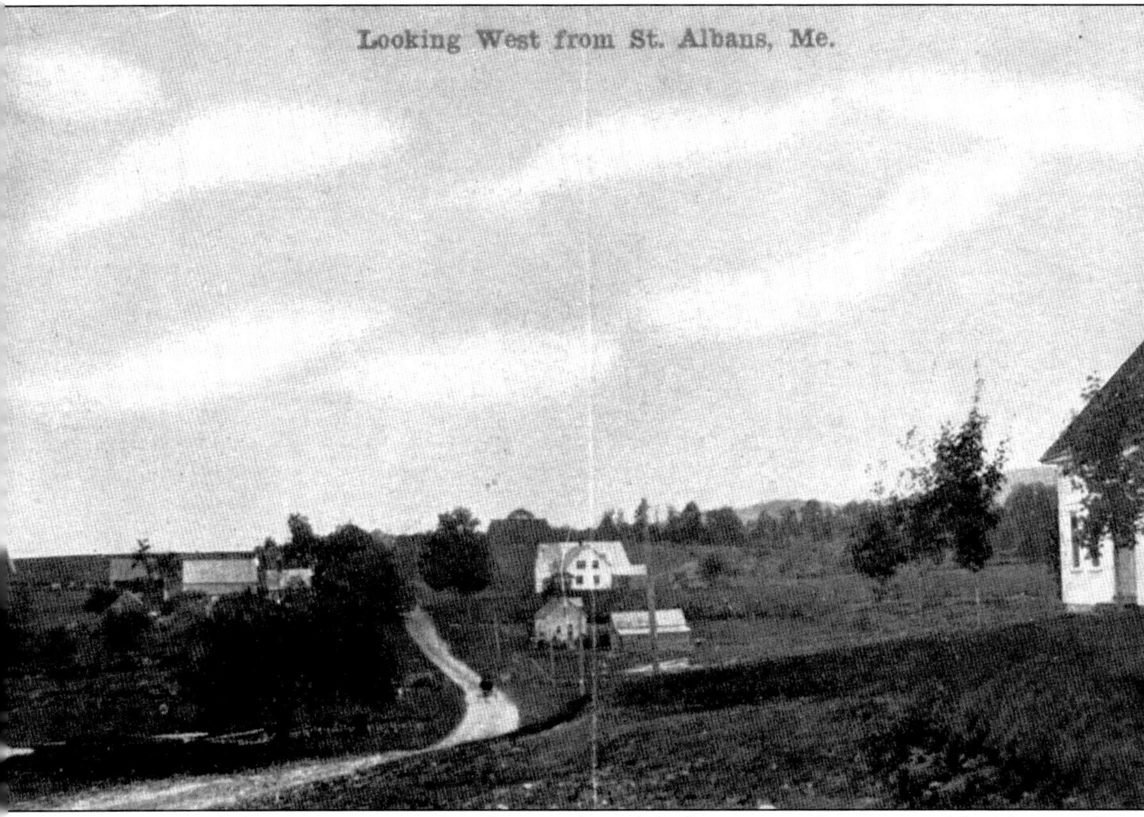

A view of the Mason Corner Road, around 1900 looking west, shows several buildings still present today including the former Merrill farm.

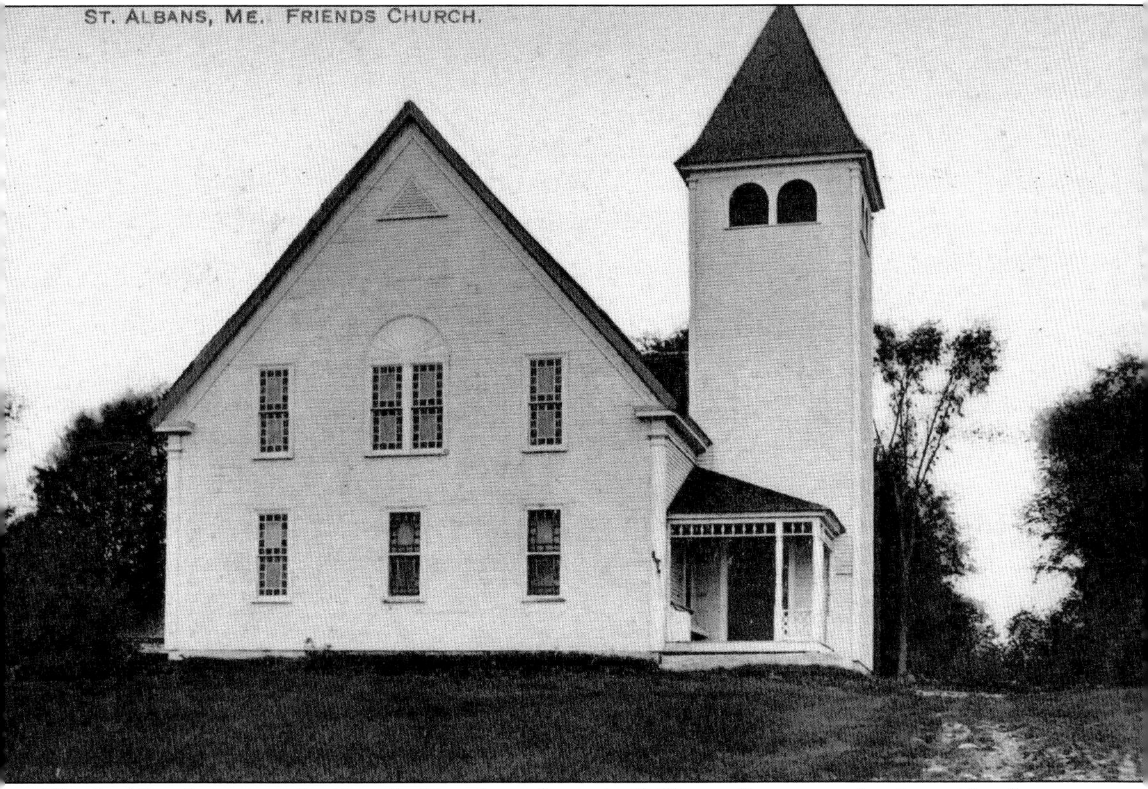

The building known as the Friends Church in the early 1900s is still in use today, but with a far different purpose. Taken over by a women's club, the steeple has been removed, but wainscoting walls still grace the interior of the building that is known as the Chatterbox Club. The old hall has been the scene of weddings, receptions, anniversaries, club meetings, and rummage sales for many years.

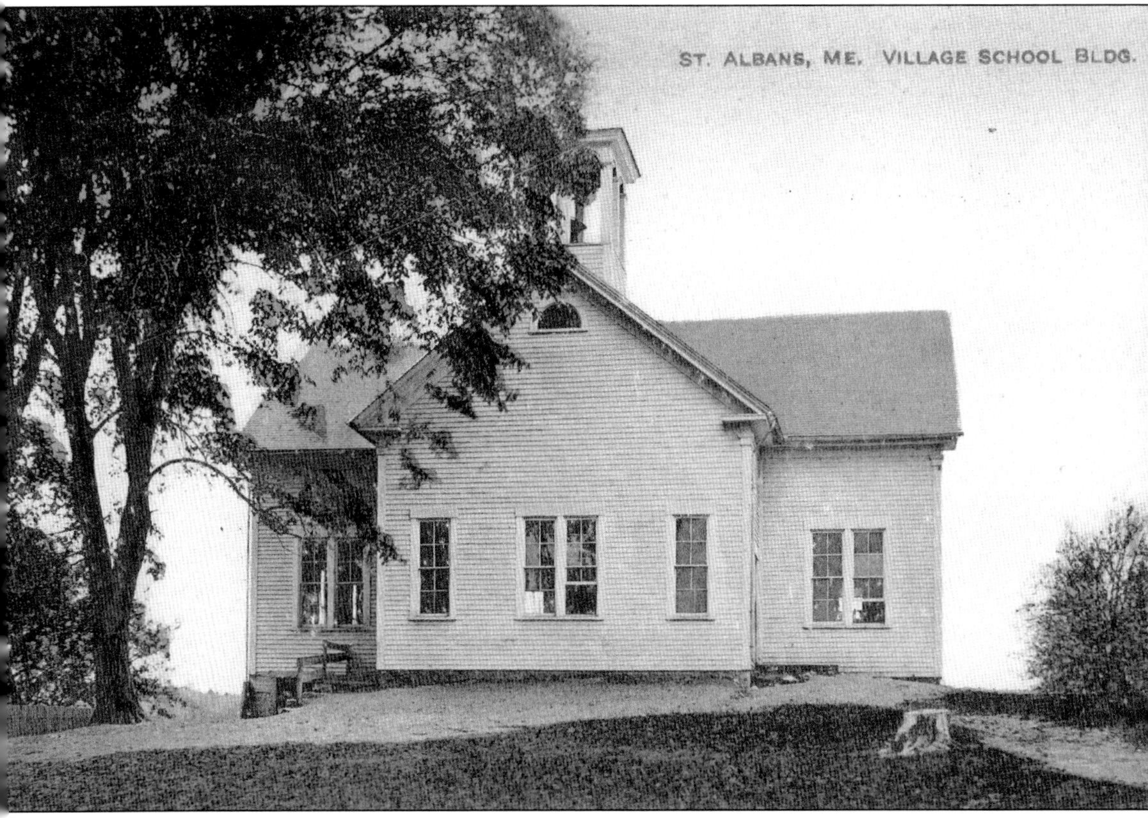

On the hill overlooking the village center, the town's second two-room schoolhouse was constructed in 1883, replacing an earlier structure from 1846 that burned. The building was moved to its hillside location in 1904 to allow for a larger and safer lot. In the 1800s and into the 1900s, the town supported as many as 17 schools in addition to the village school. By the mid-1930s only four of the outlying one-room schoolhouses remained. The village school stood until it was replaced by new construction on Hartland Road in 1981. Previous photographs in this chapter show unidentified students standing in front of this building in 1893 and 1913–1914.

BIBLIOGRAPHY

Anton, Guy. *The Story of a Small Town, Athens, Maine*. Athens Historical Society, 2004.

Herrick, Paul ed. *Harmony, Maine, Celebrating 200 Years*. Harmony Historical Society, 2003.

Knowles, Ruth M. and Gladys M. Bigelow. *History of St. Albans, Maine, 1799 to 1981*. St. Albans, ME: 1981.

Libby, F. Wayne. *Hartland, Maine, 1820 to 1970*. Sesquicentennial Committee, 1970.

———. *Hartland, Maine, 1820 to 1995*. Celebration Committee, 1995.

Sawyer, Antonia. *Songs at Twilight*. New York: Devin-Adair Company, 1939.

Seekins, Brenda. *Milestones and Memories, Pittsfield 1819 to 1994*. Pittsfield, ME: Anniversary Committee, 1994.

———. *Sebasticook Valley*. Charleston, SC: Arcadia Publishing, 2004.

St. Albans 175th Anniversary. St. Albans, ME: Anniversary Committee, 1988.